Law and Society
Recent Scholarship

Edited by Melvin I. Urofsky

A Series from LFB Scholarly

Media Laws across the World

A Comparative Study of their Evolution and Challenges

Junhao Hong and Tuo-Yu Su

LFB Scholarly Publishing LLC
El Paso 2016

Library of Congress Cataloging-in-Publication Data

Names: Hong, Junhao, 1948- author. | Su, Tuo-Yu, 1977- author.
Title: Media laws across the world : a comparative study of their evolution and challenges / Junhao Hong and Tuo-Yu Su.
Description: El Paso : LFB Scholarly Publishing LLC, 2016. | Series: Law and society | Includes bibliographical references and index.
Identifiers: LCCN 2016014978 (print) | LCCN 2016015261 (ebook) | ISBN 9781593328054 (hardcover: alk. paper) | ISBN 9781593328153 (ebook)
Subjects: LCSH: Freedom of the press. | Mass media--Law and legislation. | Comparative law. | Press law. | Freedom of information.
Classification: LCC K3255. H66 2016 (print) | LCC K3255 (ebook) | DDC 342.08/53--dc23
LC record available at https://lccn.loc.gov/2016014978

ISBN 978-1-59332-805-4

Manufactured in the United States of America.

Table of Contents

List of Tables

Preface

Media laws are a very important subject that deserves thorough and timely studies. Yet, research on media laws has not been adequately conducted due to the reason that there are various complicated factors influencing and contributing to the changes in media laws, especially after the new media/digital media came out. Particularly, for many years there is a serious shortage of comparative studies of media laws, though such comparative studies may reveal many meaningful and badly needed findings.

Given this background, this book attempts to examine and compare the laws regarding freedom of the press, libel, copyright, and cyber-piracy of 11 countries across three continents- America, Europe, and Asia, in an attempt to find out whether the three continents approach the law in similar ways or completely different from one another. Other factors examined include whether political, cultural, and economic factors affected how the concepts of freedom of the press and other areas of media laws were and are shaped.

The findings show that there is a great divide between the East and West in terms of how the press is perceived. In the West, where the original concept of a free press came from, the models of press freedom were based on the natural law within liberalism. From that natural law tradition, Western culture developed a belief in the importance of individual self-expression, and in the importance of criticizing authorities to keep them in check. Furthermore, modern democracy is based on the idea that all men are created equal and capable of participating in the political decision making process. These cultural influences and political motivations shaped how the United States and the rest of the West structured their constitutions to protect freedom of the press and how they developed media-related laws later.

In the East, for strong cultural, political, and economic reasons, the concept of freedom of the press took on a completely different meaning. Many of the countries in East Asia examined in this book were heavily influenced by the teachings of Confucianism, which espoused the ideas of keeping a sense of peacefulness within society and maintaining a deep respect for authority. Politically, a lot of these countries went through long periods of colonial rule and tried to establish themselves as legitimate authorities. Economically these countries were also trying to build their nations and transform into strong economic powers. All of these factors in the East led to a completely different concept of press freedom than in the West. For the Asian countries, it was believed that the press should be respectful of authority because of Confucianism teachings, but they should also assist and support the government in building their nations politically and economically rather than acting as "watchdogs" and undermining authority by criticizing them.

Ample evidence shows that cultural, political, and economic factors helped prominently shape the media laws, which include libel and copyright laws across the three continents. The authors would argue that in the past, cultural and political factors were especially instrumental in the development of media law; however, evidence gathered by the authors has led them to predict that political, and especially economic factors, will play much bigger roles in how media laws will advance in the future.

It is the purpose of this book to fill part of the gap both in media/communication studies and in law studies. It is hoped that this book will be able to somehow serve this purpose. In the meantime, we would like to thank the Baldy Center for Law & Social Policy at the State University of New York at Buffalo for its grant supports, which made part of the field/library research for this book possible. We also would like to thank Dr. Fang Wang, Ms. Maureen Dahl, and Ms. Qiwei Feng for their valuable assistances in preparing some of the data/materials used for this book.

Chapter 1 Introduction:

Media Law and the Four Theories of the Press

Today, freedom of the press is becoming incredibly important in every society (Overbeck & Belmas, 2012; Middleton & Lee, 2013; Koltay, 2015). Without the press keeping the public abreast of all the events happening in the world, people would not be informed; without the press functioning as watchdogs for the government and financial giants, many negative occurrences that could've had grave and widespread consequences would've never be uncovered and rectified. The discovery of the Watergate scandal and the collapse of Enron and the Lehman Brothers would not have been exposed without the press. This is not a new revelation, of course. For centuries, people have recognized the importance of the press and the media in the development of society. While the concept of freedom of the press first originated in the Western world, it is safe to say that this concept has been accepted worldwide for many years; however, given the diverse political, social, economic, and cultural background of the 200 nations on earth, it should not come as a shocker that the concepts of press freedom are interpreted differently all around the world.

According to Sieber and his colleagues, there are four theories of the press: "the authoritarian theory," "the libertarian theory," "the social responsibility theory," and "the Soviet-Communist Theory" (Siebert et al., 1956). The four theories can be summed up as follows:

1. The Authoritarian Theory: This theory was developed in the late Renaissance and was based on the idea that truth is the invention of a few intelligent men. Under this theory, the

government/state is regarded as the highest expression of institutionalized structure, and as such, it supersedes the individual and makes it possible for the individual to acquire and develop a stable and harmonious life. In other words, the State (and the elite that runs the state) directs the citizenry, which is not considered competent or interested enough to make critical political decisions. Mass communication in regions that adhere to this principle is expected to support the state and the government in power so that society as a whole can move forward and the state can function properly to accomplish its goals. The mass media, under authoritarianism, are educators and propagandists by which the power elite exercises social control. In general, the media are privately owned in countries that subscribe to this theory; however, the leader or his elite group may own units in the total communication system. All in all, the mass media, under authoritarianism, have only as much freedom as the national leadership/government is willing to permit.

2. The Libertarian Theory: This concept arose from the works of men like John Milton, John Locke, John Stuart Mill, and Thomas Jefferson, strongly advocating that the search for truth is one of man's natural rights. The libertarian view can be traced back to England and the American colonies of the seventeenth century. Philosophy regarding man as a rational animal with inherent natural rights is what gave rise to the libertarian press theory. One of these rights was the right to pursue truth, and potential interferers of this right, such as the government or kings and queens, should be restricted. As such, individual liberties were emphasized by the philosophers who advocated this theory, along with a basic trust in the people to make intelligent decisions if an environment of free expression existed. In a state that adheres to the libertarian theory, the press is obligated to present the truth. This would not be achievable if the press were controlled by the government. Over the years, many new ideas have been linked to this theory. One of the most notable ideas was the general acceptance of the obligation to keep the public abreast of governmental activities, or being a kind of the “fourth branch of government” to supplement the executive, legislative and

judicial branches. The idea is that an unfettered free press would result in a variety of viewpoints and information, which is crucial in a democratic society.

3. The Social Responsibility Theory: This concept is a product of mid-twentieth century America and has its roots in the libertarian theory. The main difference between these two theories is that the social responsibility theory places more importance on the press's responsibility to society than on the press's freedom. It is seen as the "next-level" of libertarianism.

   This strand of the four theories is believed to have originated in the United States. Specifically, it has been drawn largely from the Hutchins Commission Report published in 1947. This theory maintains that the importance of the press in modern society makes it absolutely essential that an obligation of social responsibility should be imposed on the media. Similar to the libertarian theory, it advocates a free press without any censorship; however, at the same time, it also supports the ideas that 1) the content of the press should be discussed in a public panel and 2) the media should accept any obligation from public interference or professional self regulations or both. Consequently, the theory lies somewhere between authoritarian theory and libertarian theory because it gives total media freedom on one hand but limits control on the other hand.

   The social responsibility theory also promotes a code of conduct for the press, improvement on the standards of journalism, and safeguarding interests of journalism and journalists. Fundamentally, it emphasizes the point that the press has a responsibility to inform and improve the public in the best way possible. For instance, one principle this theory advocates is equal radio and television time for political candidates and the obligations of the newspaper in a one-paper town to assist the public in gaining knowledge of all the candidates and thus can form an informed opinion as to who to vote.

4. The Soviet-Communist Theory: This is essentially an expanded (or altered) version of the old Authoritarian theory. The communist theory of the press arose with the theory of communism itself, from the mind of Karl Marx, who drew

> heavily from the ideas of fellow German, George W. F. Hegel. The mass media in a communist society, according to Marx, were to expand the socialist system. Advocating for social policy, instead of the search for truth, was therefore the main reason for the presence of a communist media system. Consequently, mass media are considered the instruments of government and integral parts of the state. Virtually, the media are owned and operated by the State and directed by the Communist Party or its agencies. Nonetheless, it might be surprising to hear that criticism is actually allowed in the media, such as criticism of failure to achieve goals; however, criticism of basic ideology is strictly verboten. Communist theory, similar to authoritarianism, is based on the idea that the masses are too fickle, ignorant, and unconcerned with the government to be entrusted with the responsibilities of the government; therefore, the media is not concerned with giving the public too much information about official activities or government leaders. Instead, mass media's main responsibility is to do what is best for the state and party, which is determined by the leaders of the government, and they should not put out any information that will damage the reputation of the state.

The West generally associates press freedom with the characteristics of Sieber's so-called libertarian theory of the press, or the CHAOS-competition, heterogeneity, autonomy, openness and selfishness-paradigm. This classification helps to explain the West's eagerness to embrace the concept of freedom of the press, with a heavy emphasis on the media's freedom to do their jobs without interference from the government. Naturally, not every country subscribes to the same concept of free press. As Siebert and his colleagues pointed out, there are many other nations that endorse the other three theories. Consequently, some Eastern countries do not share the same concepts of 1) free press and 2) the kind of role the press should play in the dynamics between the media and the government a lot of the western countries believe in. They followed their own paths in shaping up ~~of~~ their media landscapes, which for the most part is discussed and analyzed by Siebert. Hence, even though there have been criticisms as to how these four theories of the press are outdated now or they failed to take the eastern philosophy into consideration these theories are still true and remain as guideposts for media scholars to look to when analyzing the world media system. Therefore, they are a major connecting thread of this book and discussed throughout. When the media laws of the nations included in this book are analyzed, the four theories are a major factor in explaining the reasons why certain nation subscribes to the libertarian theory while others subscribes to authoritarian theory.

As mentioned by Siebert, Peterson, and Schramm in their seminal book, a well-known and commonly cited rationale for granting the press and the media this special protection is the notion that the press is a "market place of ideas" that should be free from government interference. Stein (1966) described a free press as one that acts as a market place where ideas, opinions, and theories are conveyed to citizens for their acceptance or rejection without a government censor standing over the shoulders of editors and journalists telling them what they can or cannot do. Asante (1997) believes the definition of press freedom should be freedom from governmental restraint, frequency of autonomy, and an ability to serve as the Fourth Estate, which checks the three official branches of the government. In short, many scholars believe that in order to protect the media and allow journalists to do their jobs properly, it is extremely important that the media be operated independently from government control. Even the United Nations have weighed in on this subject by declaring, "It is the mass media that make the exercise of freedom of expression a reality."[1]Accordingly, media as a whole should be granted special protection for its role of imparting information of public concern to the masses; however, it should be noted that this rationale is more prevalent in the Western world.

Naturally, not every country and culture has the same idea about freedom of the press or how to implement it. As mentioned above, the emphasis on the press' role as a watchdog for the government is more common in the west, while other parts of the world place an emphasis on the development of their country first. Emphasizing that freedom of the press is not a fixed and isolated value that manifests itself in the same way in every society and at all times, and that its function must vary within the social context, Hocking stated in the famous Hutchins

---

[1] See more details on the United Nations Human Rights Committee General Comment 25, issued 12 July 1996.

Commission on freedom of the press that the concept of the free press could not and did not mean the same in every society.[2] It seems that this astute observation/contention agrees with the contemporary debate on relating press freedom to Asian values and other social values outside of Western society.

While the main focus of the four press theories is governmental control over the media, there are newer threats to press freedom in our contemporary society. Aside from government interference, one potential major threat to freedom of the press is the increasingly prevalent concentration of media ownership. For example, in the United States, there are essentially six major conglomerates that control all of the important media companies:

1. NBC/Universal, with an annual revenue around 160 billion, owns all the NBC stations, CNBC, MSNBC, numerous cable channels including USA networks, Bravo, E!, the Weather Channel, and the movie studio Universal Pictures. As of 2013, the biggest cable operator in the US Comcast owns 51% of the company, while another corporate giant, General Electric (GE) owns the other 49%.
2. The Walt Disney Company, with an annual revenues around $ 37 billion, owns ABC, cable channels such as ESPN, the Disney Channel, A&E, and Lifetime, movie production companies like Walt Disney Pictures, Touchstone Pictures, and Pixar Animation Studios, which has yet to produce an unsuccessful animated feature.
3. News Corporation, with an annual revenue of 30 billion dollars, owns FOX TV network, cable channels including F/X, Fox New Network, Fox Business Network, National Geographic, two major newspapers-Wall Street Journal and the New York Post, and movie production companies including Twenty Century Fox and Fox Searchlight Pictures.
4. Time Warner, with an annual revenues of 26 billion dollars, owns cable channels such as CNN, HBO, Cartoon Network,

[2] See more details on the 1947 report of Commission on Freedom of the Press, a Free and Responsible Press: A General Report on Mass Communication: Newspapers, Radio, Motion Pictures, Magazines, and Books.

TNT, TBS, movie studio and production companies including Warner Bros. Pictures, Castle Rock Pictures, New Line Cinema, and more than 150 magazines including Tim, Sports Illustrated, Fortune, People, and Entertainment Weekly.
5. Viacom, with an annual revenue of 14 billion dollars, owns MTV, Nickelodeon, Comedy Central, Paramount Pictures, and Viacom18, which is a joint venture with the Indian media company Global Broadcast News.
6. CBS Corporation, with an annual revenue of 13 billion dollars, owns CBS, CW, Showtime, and the major book publisher Simon &Schuster. CBS is now the leading supplier of video to Google's new Video Marketplace.

This list above clearly demonstrates that a vast majority of media content Americans consume comes from a few giant media conglomerates. This is not a uniquely American phenomenon, as other countries are experiencing the same high concentration of media ownership. So why is this media concentration a threat to freedom of the press? An increasingly heavy concentration of media ownership has severely limited the variety of opinions and news sources, which could lead to an undesirable state where freedom of the press remains a right for only those who publish. With only a few honchos in charge of media companies, there is a high risk that even if they do direct the news divisions to have their personal political views reflected in the news reports and ignore (or even worse denigrate) the opposing views, those in charge of the news content would be inclined to do so to please the bosses. Consequently, all of the news reports produced by the news outlets from one of the giant conglomerates would look and sound the same without any diversity and thus deprive the public of the opportunity to receive news that reflects different points of view. One could argue that one very obvious example of this is Rupert Murdoch's New Corporation, which runs Fox New Network, the Wall Street Journal, and the New York Post. In such a scenario, freedom of the press would be restricted since the people in charge of the media could fail to incorporate the right of the citizens and public interest into the equation.[3]

[3] As will be shown in a later chapter, media ownership concentration is a problem that is plaguing many countries these days.

To keep an eye on the state of freedom of the press around the world, there are several media watchdogs/organizations that either conduct case studies on countries or rank the countries based on their efforts to maintain a free press. Among these organizations, Freedom House's Freedom of the Press Index is arguably the most famous and most comprehensive on the subject. Freedom House has classified the press and broadcasting systems in countries into "free," "partly free," and "not free" categories since 1980 (Karlecker & Cook, 2008). This survey is a comparative law study, heavily featured in this study, as it provides an important annual ranking of the press freedom in almost every country but also offers a short but detailed report on the developments of press freedom in every country surveyed.

There has been, and most likely forever will be, numerous challenges facing media law researchers. For one example, many media laws are outdated, which has become a serious problem and a big concern (*Media Laws Threaten Freedom*, 2013; Bodey, 2015). For another example, a persistent challenge for freedom of the press scholars and organizations like Freedom House that conduct research on press freedom is that we live in the age of globalization and constant change. Globalization in the information age means that there is a demand for more accurate measurements of press freedom that encompasses the world system, not just individual states. In this information age, globalization has transformed the erstwhile nation-states into global states (Karlekar & Cook, 2008). Consequently, despite endogenous press restrictions, citizens may have the capability to seek, receive, and impart information and ideas through media that are generally not under state control, such as the so-termed "new media" or "digital media" (Gunaratne, 2002). The obvious example of that is the Internet and the Internet-based social media, which may offer the answer to limited public access and financial and state controls because financial barriers of conventional media are largely non-existent on the Internet and government regulators have been relatively slow in their reactions to this new phenomenon that constantly presents new political and legal issues (See, for example, Packard, 2012 & 2013; Creech, 2013; Stewart, 2013; Lipschultz, 2014; Pearson & Polden, 2015).

Freedom of the press has become a widely embraced idea all over the world in the last few decades. That is not to say that the picture is all rosy for advocates of press freedom. To this day, the desire to control unfavorable information is unfortunately still common in governments worldwide but the degree of control differs (Gunaratne, 2002). This has become disturbingly apparent in recent years, with the constant threat of terrorism, and the governments' aggressive efforts to curtail press freedom in the name of national safety.

Fortunately, this worrisome development did not go unnoticed by the United States government. Since he was sworn into office in 2009, the president of the United States, Barack Obama, has made multiple headlines with his policies concerning tax reforms, healthcare, cap and trade, and financial bailouts. There is, however, another piece of law that garnered far less media attention. On May 18th 2010, President Obama signed a piece of legislation titled "Daniel Pearl Freedom of the Press Act," which is intended to promote a free press around the world. Under this new law, named to honor the journalist who lost his life in the Middle East during his pursuit for truth, the State Department is required to increase its scrutiny of news media restrictions and intimidation as part of its annual review of human rights worldwide (New York Times Staff, 2010).

This new law came into existence in the wake of the freedom watchdog organization, Freedom House's highly troubling finding that came out in the spring of 2010. The erosion of press freedom around the world continued in 2009, the eighth year in a row that press freedom was in decline.[4] Human rights advocates noted that this trend is particularly worrisome because press freedom often acts as a type of "bellwether" of the direction a wide range of political and social freedoms are taking.[5] These human rights advocates are very concerned because when press freedom is under attack, oftentimes, the attack unavoidably inhibits other freedoms as well (Karlekar & Cook, 2008).)

Some have argued that one of the major reasons for the erosion of press freedom is the emergence of the Internet (Sussman, 2000). In short, the decline in global press freedom owed a lot to the governments' efforts to catch up with new technologies and rein in the Internet and cyberspace. This of course is a response to the new crops of journalism and journalists on the Internet, namely, the questions of

---

[4] See Freedom House's Freedom of the Press Index 2010 for more details.

[5] See footnote 4, where it mentioned that freedom of the press has been consistently in decline in recent years.

"who can be considered as journalists in the new information age?" and "how can the government regulate the new legal issues that could arise (and have) from Internet communication?" have been the focus points of new media regulation today. For instance, in this new media age, aside from the basic press freedom law, other aspects of media laws, such as copyright and piracy, are also being adapted to handle the legal problems and issues that have sprung up along with the emergence of the Internet. It is this recent discussion on the decline of freedom of the press and the new legal issues that came with the Internet that made the topic of media law a fascinating one once again. It is this renewed interest in media law that provided a fertile ground for research on this ever-evolving topic.

Media law is a broad term. Given the amount of time an individual consumes television, newspapers, and the Internet, media is without a doubt a major part of our everyday lives and we should be keenly aware of its ever-changing development.[6] To put it in simple terms, it impacts what we can see and hear from the press depending on how much freedom of the press and expression is granted; it determines what kinds of rights one would obtain and enjoy if one were to write a book or make a movie; and with the explosion of the Internet and the increasing importance of new creative content on the net, there is another new area of uncharted territory that is just ripe for an update of new media-related laws and lawsuits.

Generally speaking, there is a certain consensus among nations in regards to certain aspects of media law. For instance, quite a few countries have the equivalent of the First Amendment right of the United States, which includes both freedom of expression and freedom of the press.[7] Copyright is granted to authors and creators across the board, and piracy is outlawed; however, the levels of protections and rights afforded are often diverse in different nations, and consequently, there could be confusions when two parties involved in a lawsuit are from different parts of the world.

---

[6] An example of the prevalent use of the media is television. According to the A.C. Nielsen Co., the average American watches more than 4 hours of TV each day (or 28 hours/week, or 2 months of nonstop TV-watching per year).

[7] The First Amendment of the United States also includes freedom of religion, freedom of association, and freedom to assemble.

So what are the reasons behind those different approaches towards media laws across the world? It can be argued that mass media systems of the world vary from country to country based on the economy, politics, religions, and cultures of each country. One seemingly obvious conclusion that can be drawn is that in societies that followed communism and totalitarianism, such as the former USSR and China, had limitations as to what the media could say about the government. Almost everything that was said against the state was censored out of fear that revolutions or civil disobedience might ensue and endanger the government's authority. On the other hand, in countries such as the USA, which has a long-standing democratic political system, there is virtually no censorship.

But is it really as simple as it seems? The premise that a country's media law is shaped by its political, cultural, and economic history is an intriguing one. This is a rich ground to explore because even if two countries have similar political systems, the degrees of freedom of the press can be drastically different (Van Belle, 2000). Additionally, given the increasing globalization which supposedly brings the world closer together and inevitably leads to more interactions among countries, it is not only desirable but also necessary to have a better understanding as to how the media legal systems work in other countries. To that end, this book conducts a comparative analysis of the media laws of different countries and seek to present a clearer picture of how the media laws have evolved over the years in those countries as well as where they are headed in the future. Specifically, this research is a systematic cross-cultural comparative analysis of the media laws in three continents-America, represented by the United States; Europe, represented by Italy, Germany, France, the United Kingdom and Sweden; and Asia, represented by China, Japan, South Korea, India, and Singapore. These countries are all chosen for specific reasons. The West, represented by the United States and the five European countries, was the first to formally accept the idea that freedom of the press is essential for society. These countries incorporated the concept of press freedom earlier than anybody else; however, even though their original concepts of press freedom might have been similar over the years, they have also developed different approaches toward achieving a free press. For example, France, one of the pioneering countries in terms of press freedom, has adopted numerous laws over the years to restrict the press, while Sweden, also one of the earliest countries to recognize the importance of press freedom, has maintained a consistently free environment for the press. In Asia, almost all of the countries examined have experienced periods of foreign rule at one point or another, and that colonial history tremendously influenced the legal systems of these countries. Additionally, as will be made clear later in the book, the cultural backgrounds of these Asian nations, which are completely different from the West, also shaped how they view the concept of freedom of the press. Just like the Western countries chosen, these Asian nations have a lot in common in terms of their cultural and historical backgrounds, but they also diverged in other aspects media law. For example, while Japan has consistently maintained a high level of press freedom and often rank as the country that has the freest press in East Asia, Singapore has one of the worst press freedom conditions for a democratic nation and does not seem to want to change any time soon. In short, the Western countries chosen have a lot in common in regards to the development of press freedom, but they are also different enough in terms of their current press freedom status. When comparing their media laws, a commonality emerges along with distinctive differences. The same could also be said about the Asian nations chosen.

It should be pointed out that although this book mainly focuses on these countries mentioned above, the list is not exclusive. From time to time, the constitutions and relevant media laws from other countries in those three regions are also analyzed if they are pertinent to the discussions or contribute to the overall knowledge of the topics. Why are the media laws in these countries the way they are? How were they adopted? How much freedom can a journalist in those countries enjoy? And how have the countries changed their media laws to adapt to the reality that the emergence of the Internet has bred a whole new group of "journalists?" This last question is especially pertinent today since this new wave of online journalism has unsurprisingly brought along a new set of legal issues that prior laws might not be equipped to handle. In short, the goal of the study is to present a detailed and illuminating picture of the past, present, and future of media law in those nations, and to demonstrate the similarities and differences, if any, among the media laws in the US, Western/Northern Europe, and Eastern/Southern Asia.

The book is comprised of 11 chapters, including the current chapter, and is broken down as follows: the analysis of the media laws in the United States, the analysis of the media laws in Western Europe, the analysis of the media laws in Eastern Asia, and finally an overall comparisons of the laws across the three continents. Differences and commonalities of the laws is pointed out and discussed, and the reasons behind the differences and commonalities is analyzed. In the following section a short description of every chapter's content provides a clearer picture as to how this book is structured.

Chapter 2 presents the research questions and methodology utilized to complete this book. This book attempts to answer questions regarding the evolutions of media law in the United States, Western/Northern Europe, and Asia in connection with their constitutions, and how those evolutions are related to the nations' political, economic, and cultural history. How have the media laws in those regions adapted to the increasingly Internet-influenced world of mass communication? Additionally, this book tries to answer the following questions: What kinds of rights and protections do media laws provide in these countries? What kinds of censorships exist in other countries compared to the vast freedom granted to journalists in the United States? Furthermore, the book also touches on several other areas of media law including libel, copyright, and cyber-piracy in a smaller capacity. Other questions such as: What kind of protection does the press in other countries enjoy when a public figure's reputation is damaged when a negative story that turns out to be untrue about that person is published? What are the different remedies the plaintiff in a copyright lawsuit can seek in different countries? Do recent cases in Europe and Asia and a strongly negative reaction to a proposed new Internet legislation indicate that the United States is lagging behind in providing protection in cyberspace are answered as well. Finally, in the last few chapters, questions regarding the pros and cons of media law in these countries and the reasons why these nations approach media laws the way they do are discussed.

Chapter 3 examines the freedom of the press in those countries. Specifically, it studies the concepts of freedom of the press in those 11 nations. Why is freedom of the press important in these countries? What kinds of protections do the constitutions give to the freedom of the press? How has freedom of the press evolved over the years in those countries? The main focus of this chapter is the protections, if any, the constitutions of these countries provide their press. This chapter also presents a short history of the development of press freedom in these countries.

Chapter 4 analyzes the actual laws that govern freedom of the press/censorship in the United States. All aspects of the laws are discussed, and the rationale behind the laws are analyzed.

Chapter 5 analyzes the actual laws that govern freedom of the press/censorship in the European countries selected for this research. All aspects of the laws are discussed, and the rationale behind the laws are analyzed.

Chapter 6 analyzes the actual laws that govern freedom of the press/ censorship in the Asian countries selected for this research. All aspects of the laws are discussed and the rationale behind the laws are analyzed.

It should be noted that for chapters 3, 4, 5, and 6, the constitutions and media laws are discussed individually and also in groups for comparison purposes. If the laws in certain countries are very similar, these countries are discussed together. On the other hand, if the laws in these countries are dissimilar then they are discussed individually.

Chapter 7 analyzes the libel laws in all 11 countries. What kind of protection does the press in other countries enjoy when a public figure's reputation is damaged when a negative story that turns out to be untrue about that person is published? In a libel case, who has the burden of proof? Which side is more likely to prevail in a lawsuit-the plaintiffs or the defendants? What needs to be proven in order to win a libel case in the United States? In the United Kingdom? Are the libel laws in these countries very similar or are they drastically different? The recent controversy surrounding Lance Armstrong and the libel lawsuits he filed and won in the UK is useful in answering these questions. In short, this chapter examines the different levels of protection of reputation that can be exercised by private individuals and public figures, including politicians, famous athletes, and celebrities.

Chapter 8 analyzes the actual laws that govern copyright in all 11 nations. The laws are compared and discussed, and the rationale behind copyright laws are also analyzed. How much protection an intellectual property holder can obtain in the United States? How about Europe? What are some of the criticisms of prevailing copyright? Why some of the countries are slow and reluctant to embrace the concept of copyright protections?

Chapter 9 focuses on cyber-piracy. The advent of technology, and the proliferation of Internet use, in particular, made it that much easier to illegally download a song or a movie, and that much harder for the copyright owners to track down the copyright infringers because there are too many, and the methods deployed to download illegally have gotten more and more clever. In recent years, there have been a slew of cases concerning cyber-piracy, including cases in Sweden, France, and Taiwan. This chapter analyzes these cases and the actual statutes to determine where the laws of cyber-piracy are going. In other words, what are the challenges to the existent media laws by the new media? And consequently, what are the media laws in this new information age? In the United States, the public uproar over the proposed legislations to regulate copyright infringement, Stop Online Piracy Act (SOPA) and Protect Intellectual Property Act (PIPA) in early 2012 and the subsequent block out of some very popular websites, including Wikipedia has stalled the development of new regulations of cyber-piracy. Exactly what are the opponents of these proposed laws objecting to? The main focus of SOPA and PIPA is analyzed and the controversy generated by them is discussed.

Chapter 10 analyzes the findings of the previous chapters and present a detailed comparison of the freedom of the press laws, and to a lesser extent, other areas of media laws such as cyber piracy and copyright, in those three continents. Does one region have a better media law system over the others? If so, what does a better media law system represent?

Chapter 11 presents conclusions as well as predictions for the future and suggestions for further research in this very rich area.

Chapter 2

The Importance of Press Freedom and Comparative Media Law Research

WHY RESEARCH ON FREEDOM OF THE PRESS IS IMPORTANT?

Freedom of the press has been widely accepted around the world and even the United Nations has made it a point to legitimize the importance of press freedom. Specifically, under Article 19 of the United Nations' Universal Declaration of Human Rights, "everyone should have the right to freedom of opinion and expression, and the right includes the freedom to hold opinions without interference and to seek, receive, and import information and ideas through any media regardless of frontiers."[8]

Recognizing the importance of press freedom, researchers have been conducting studies on this subject and the laws regulating it for years. Law scholars have recognized that a good starting point to examine the state of freedom of the press in every country is to look at the constitutions. Specifically, do the constitutions explicitly offer protections for freedom of the press? A prominent German scholar conducted a survey in 1994 analyzing the contents of the constitutions of roughly 160 nations with the goal of finding out whether freedom of expression and press is guaranteed in each constitution. According to

[8] The entire content of the Declaration of Human Rights can be found at the official United Nations website at http://www.un.org/en/documents/udhr/index.shtml.

Behmer's findings, 143 nations guaranteed at least one form of freedom of communication, whether it be freedom of expression, freedom of the press, or freedom of speech. Out of these 143 countries, only 58 of them had explicit freedom of press protection in their constitution (Behmer, 2007). This study was merely intended to get a "yes" or "no" answer without finding out the "why," but it was impressive based on the size of the project alone. However, as this book demonstrates, just because freedom of the press is not specifically mentioned in a country's constitution does not mean that the protection does not exist in that country. Conversely, even if freedom of the press is explicitly mentioned in a nation's constitution, the protection is not necessarily guaranteed. A prime example of this is Sweden, which is consistently ranked at or near the top of the Freedom House Press Freedom index. It might be surprising to some to know that for a country that enjoys more press freedom than almost every other country, the constitutional protection for press freedom is structured differently than other countries. In later chapters, we will discuss this discrepancy that sometimes occurs and attempt to explain the reasons behind the absence or presence of a freedom of the press clause in a country's constitution.

The countries that have a freedom of the press protection clauses in their constitutions do not all follow the same approach. Oftentimes, the provisions in these constitutions that relate to the protection of press freedom contain some type of limitation clauses as well. Some scholars further pointed out that it is not uncommon for arbitrariness to occur in matters concerning press freedom despite the constitutionally guaranteed protections (Behmer, 2009). That is why when analyzing freedom of the press across various countries, it is not enough to simply examine the laws and statutes. Other factors include the countries' economic, cultural, and political backgrounds, need to be taken into consideration when comparing different nations' press freedom statuses. This is essential and something scholars conducting comparative media law studies have to keep in mind, considering that even the idea and the importance of press freedom could be interpreted and treated drastically differently between the East and West.

Freedom of the press is considered an essential element in a democratic government and a highly regarded commodity in the western world (Cornwell, 2000). Western scholars have commented that journalists need to be independent from not only the government but also from strong economic interests to provide diverse, complete, and correct information to the citizens and make it possible for universal participation in public discourse (Czepek, 2009). In other words, press freedom is generally understood to mean freedom from governmental control so that the news reporters can freely do their job.

The presence or absence of governmental interference is certainly a factor to consider when evaluating press freedom; however, it should not be the only one. The biggest problem with associating press freedom solely with the absence of governmental control is that freedom from government control alone does not guarantee a free flow of information. Other factors also play an essential part in shaping the state of press freedom in every country. Scholars such as Behmer stated that the narrow emphasis on governmental control in the majority of freedom of the press research often lead to an absence of true, scientific consistency in the results (2009).

When examining media systems and media freedom in academic research, social, cultural, traditional, and religious issues are often neglected (Czepek, 2009). However, those issues play such an important role in the development of press freedom all over the world that to ignore them would render the resulting research not only less than persuasive but also incomplete. For example, in the United Kingdom, where class is still a sensitive issue and there is a clear difference between the types of newspapers each class reads, the media industry has a segregated the newspaper market. Specifically, there are generally two types of newspapers in the United Kingdom: 1) the infamous tabloids such as *News of the World*, and 2) the more traditional/highly regarded newspapers such as *the London Times*, which gear towards affluent/highly-educated readers (Negrine, 1994).

Historical events also played a part in shaping the media system and forming the concept of press freedom. Several historical developments, such as World War II, have been deemed to have a significant impact on the growth or decline of press freedom in the last 60 years or so. For example, Germany's press freedom took a serious turn during and especially after the defeat of Hitler's Nazi rule. Specifically, after the end of World War II, several established/traditional publishers in Germany, which supported Hitler during his reign, did not receive printing licenses from the Allied Forces. As a consequence, this allowed newer players to assert their place in the new media landscape in post-war Germany (Dahrendorf,

1979). Italy, who allied with Germany for the war, also had a significant media reform in the aftermath of a dictatorial regime post World War II (Sedler, 2011).

Another factor to discuss is the social and cultural backgrounds of the countries examined. When considering the social and cultural influence on the media in Europe, one of the unique factors that should be included is the existence of large ethnic minorities. Their influence is most prominent in Germany and the United Kingdom because of the minorities' traditional and religious backgrounds, which sometimes poses a threat to the media (Czepek, 2009).

Many noted media scholars have emphasized the connection between the media and political systems of various countries (Hallin & Mancini, 2004). It is often emphasized that the media takes on the characteristics of the political and social systems in which they operate. Most models of the press have been founded on the relation between politics and the media in a country (Siebert et al., 1958) .

Over in Asia, press freedom is not viewed the same way as it is in the Western world. Not surprisingly, democracy and press freedom usually go hand in hand in Asia; however, some have cautioned that it cannot be assumed these two notions work in the same way as the North American and Western European democracies (Doronila, 2000). In discussing the media laws and philosophies behind them, Western scholarship on press systems tends to disregard the cultures, philosophies, and traditions that distinguish Asian mass media. In short, the field's influential *The Four Theories of the Press*, and its supporters keep this western emphasis when examining the relationship between mass media and government, and that some scholars have vigorously argued that it might not be enough to fully explain the developments of press freedom in other parts of the world.

Today in Asia, just like the western world, press freedom can be measured by the degrees in which journalists can be critical of the ruling government and their society without interference from the government; however, that is not always the case. Culturally speaking, the concept of an adversarial press was not a natural one to a lot of Asian nations; therefore, this played a critical role in the shaping press freedom and media laws in East Asia. One can argue that these values lead to a more restricted sense of press freedom in Asia because they generally call for a high degree of deference to the authorities and keeping the peace instead of rocking the boat. These characteristics are not very compatible with the idea of press freedom promulgated by the West (Nerone, 1995). These "Asian values" and their impact on shaping media law in the countries that subscribe to them are discussed in a later chapter.

An interesting finding regarding press freedom in East Asia is that the analyses of the Asian financial crisis in 1997 have shown that the countries that were hit hardest by the crisis were the ones that had the least transparency regarding their policies. Conversely, the countries least affected were the most open. Here, transparency includes granting the press freedom to do their jobs effectively (Doronila, 2000).

The fact that East Asian countries were slower than the West to develop into democracies also altered the evolution of press freedom in that region. In East Asia, the model for the formerly authoritarian regime in countries/regions such as South Korea, Taiwan, and Indonesia, before their democratic transformations was an attempt to combine free market economics with closed and isolated political systems, including a tight control over the media, as Doronila pointed out (2000). Our research shows that it was not until after these countries established their economic prowess that press freedom became a more visible research topic.

Censorship is another way to gauge the degree of press freedom. In many parts of Asia, censorship or self-censorship is still an issue that hinders journalists' ability to do their jobs. Self-censorship is often a concern in journalism and it usually occurs when media companies rely heavily on funding from the government or other powerful conglomerates (Sedler, 2011). This also occurs when the government asserts an inordinate amount of control over the media, as in communist regions such as China and North Korea (Tong, 2009). Another unique example of strong governmental control over the media is a country that has a media environment not quite communist-soviet style oppressive but also far from the western idea of a free press-Singapore. The government has a strong control over the media. Another thing worth noting is the fact that this country has a government-run communications network, which brings the Internet to every home. Why is this significant? While this might seem like a benign and even welcome measure at first glance, the flip side is the fact that the government can (and does) check up on the citizens' online activities, including journalists' activities. Ironically, despite strong governmental control, the media industry has truly flourished in

Singapore; yet, the growth only occurred in form, not in media content. By using a combination of legislation and ownership concentration, the government keeps a tight leash on the media (Williams, 2000). In short, the recent development of Singapore was a mixture of free market capitalism and political controls, and the media are certainly under control. The decision to follow this path came straight top. The most powerful political figure in Singapore, former prime minister, Lee Kuan Yew, made it clear that he believed that in order for the country to grow economically, the government would have to curtail certain personal freedoms, including press freedom, to achieve social stability (Wong, 2001). The unique development of the media in Singapore is discussed more thoroughly in a later chapter.

China, like Singapore, also keeps tight control over its media and flow of information; however, there are signs that this may change. Given the integration that has taken place in ~~of~~ this once-closed economy into a global economy, it has become necessary for the country to be more open and transparent. Another recent change is that reports on government corruption is now occasionally allowed and even encouraged. The Chinese government, as controlling as it is, is increasingly allowing state-run media to report on governmental corruption; however, the Communist Party still has the final say as to what information can be relayed to the public. This is most evident in the fact that only mid-level government officials have been tried and sentenced. Journalists who refuse to toe the party line can still be put in jail (Sedler, 2011).

When combining all of the suggested factors to examine press freedom, there are four different aspects to consider:

1. Structural conditions- legal, political, economic, historical, and cultural conditions.
2. Individual journalistic freedom including harassment, censorship, and self-censorship.
3. Content diversity.
4. Possibilities for participation (Czepek, 2009).

In summary, all the above factors could make an impact on the development of press freedom. As Stevenson pointed out, in authoritarian systems such as the former German Democratic Republic, press freedom was regarded as freedom from economic constraint as well as the possibility of taking part in the development of socialism (1994). In the so-called third world countries, many of which were previously colonies, media and the press in general are utilized as tools to facilitate nation-building after years of foreign rules. Stevenson noted that in these countries, media's main job was aiding nation-building and social and economic development (1994). He also pointed out that press freedom and the idea of pluralism were unimportant and even considered detrimental by some.

The differences among media law systems around the world seem like an interesting research topic; yet, some scholars have noticed the paucity of comparative media research. Even in countries that supposedly have strong and vibrant media research track records such as the United States and the United Kingdom, this area of academic research has not been progressing and receiving the attention it deserves (Czepek, 2009). A major problem or concern with this type of cross-national comparisons is "how do you design the research in a way that will allow it to be conducted in a fair and meaningful fashion when there are many different country-specific factors that need to be taken into consideration?" The formidable challenge of figuring out an acceptable answer to this question is what makes this type of research exciting but difficult as well.

However, there are signs that comparative media research has been on the rise in recent years. Livingstone remarked that funding bodies and policy imperatives increasingly favor comparative research, perhaps influenced by the rapid rate of globalization and the increasing occurrence of cross-national comparative media projects (2003). Today, the two most high-profile and well-known comparative media research projects are "Freedom of the Press: A Global Survey of Media Independence" by Freedom House in the United States and "World Press Freedom Index" by Reporters Without Borders in France.

The Freedom of the Press project from Freedom House started back in 1980 in Washington D.C., and their survey result on press freedom is shrewdly published every year on May 3rd (Karlekar & Cook, 2008)). Prior to 2004, Freedom House only published written reports on press freedom around the world. In 2004, Freedom House began to rank the countries included in the survey making it easier to compare them. It should be pointed out, however, that this project has received several criticisms over the years including its ranking methodologies and their perceived pro-American bias. The fact that

Freedom House received the majority of their funding from the United States Federal Government certainly fueled the latter criticism. Another criticism is that the project does not consider the possibilities of access to the media and the quality of coverage in the media (Behmer, 2009) . At the same time, this survey is also the most respected press freedom project. As discussed in the following section of the book, the Freedom House press freedom index is fairly complex. This part examines the political, economic, and legal situations of every country in the survey to determine how they impact press freedom.

Another well-known measurement of freedom of the press is Reporters Without Borders (RSF)'s "World Press Freedom Index," which is a relatively new press freedom-watch project. Originated in France, it has been published every year since 2002.[9] Compared with the Freedom House project, this survey has a much tighter and narrower focus, which is whether the reporters in every country examined are facing serious threat of danger to their personal safety or prison time.[10] While conducting their research, the question RSF focused on is "how many journalists were murdered, jailed, tortured, or threatened?" in each country. Just like the Freedom House Index, a ranking chart is also published and despite the two organizations' different emphasis, the results of the two rankings are quite similar. For example, the Scandinavian countries are usually top-ranked on both charts.[11]

There are other media studies that are on a much smaller scale, such as the Konrad Adenauer Foundation's Media and Democracy Report. Smaller projects like these may be narrow in scope, but scholars have pointed out that when only a few countries are included in a study, or only case studies on certain states are carried out, these may "turn out to be much more precise" (Behmer, 2009) . On the flip side, it would be much more difficult, if not altogether impossible, to have truly meaningful international comparisons.

---

[9] See a comprehensive chart at Wikipedia's Press Freedom Index, http://en.wikipedia.org/wiki/Press_Freedom_Index.

[10] See a comprehensive report on the website of Reporter Without Borders for Press Freedom, retrieved from http://en.rsf.org/

[11] A comparison of the two charts show a great deal of similarities, especially the nations ranked at the top and the bottom of the charts.

By simply glancing at these press freedom charts, one could easily see that most of the highly-ranked countries are in Western/Northern Europe. In Europe, it would seem like freedom of the press, which is generally defined as an "absence of state intervention" in the way the media operates, is taken for granted. This is perhaps due to the fact that all of the EU members today have either incorporated the concept of press freedom into their constitutions, or their judicial systems clearly demonstrate the existence of press protection (Czepek et al., 2009). It is worth noting, however, that aside from the EU mandate to have a free press, factors such as economic influences, historic, cultural, and social conditions also have a substantial impact on media independence and on the media's ability to fulfill their societal functions. In fact, despite the almost uniform pledge to safeguard freedom of the press by the European countries, the media systems here vary widely in regards to the above-mentioned factors (Sedler, 2011). Consequently, some countries in Europe have a strong tradition of press freedom, while others are rated much lower on the press freedom index, such as Italy.

In fact, in recent years, like many other areas in the world, there has been wide-spread concern about the state of press freedom in Europe. For example, in Italy, which is one of the lowest-ranked European countries in the Freedom House Press Freedom Index, the re-election of the flamboyant and perennially controversial media mogul Silvio Berlusconi as prime minister further exacerbated the problem of monopolization in the media industry (Greenslade, 2010). In Germany, there were alarming reports about police monitoring journalists' emails (Stark, 2010). In light of this worrisome trend, Czepek, Hellwig and Nowak argued that economic concentration and the dominance of commercial objectives in media systems, increasing government control due to anti-terrorism efforts, and new digital technology all pose new challenges to the European media, their autonomy, and their capabilities in providing a platform for free and pluralistic exchange (2009).

Some of the case studies also made the same conclusion. They indicate that media freedom in Europe, and to a certain extent, the United States, may increasingly be impeded by economic factors, such as increasing financial dependency on mass markets. Additionally, concentration of ownership increases dependency on a few of the powerful media conglomerates. Czepek and colleagues also noted that security policies, especially with regard to the prevention of terrorism, have a growing impact on media freedom (Czepek et al., 2009). Asian countries are also not immune to the increasing economic pressure, which affects the media industry as well (Teo, 2005). With the Internet becoming such a prevalent form of media and the many issues that come with it, we also see some countries react to this phenomenon by enacting stricter laws that might potentially hinder the future of press freedom (Gunaratne, 2002).

Overall, media scholars have made some progress in media law research, pointing out several important factors that should be included when discussing freedom of the press. The goal of this book is to build upon these studies and expand the scope of the existent studies to hopefully present an expanded and updated picture on this subject.

QUESTIONS RESEARCHED

As previously mentioned, this book focuses on the evolutions of media law in the selected 11 countries. In particular, the focus of this study is placed on how and to what extent those evolutions are related to the nations' political, economic and cultural history. Specifically, this book attempts to answer the following questions:

1. What are the concepts of freedom of the press in these 11 countries? How is press freedom protected under the constitutions in those countries? In short, what is the relationship between the constitutions and the press freedom in those countries?
2. Media laws, like any other type of law, have gone through several transformations over the years. What is the history and the development of press freedom in these 11 countries?
3. Analysis of the actual laws. What kinds of rights and protections do the media laws provide in these countries?
   3.1. Does the First Amendment right give the Americans more freedom of the press than any other countries? Do the countries that have explicit constitutional protections for freedom of the press in reality really have a freer media environment than those that do not? Do American journalists enjoy more freedom in terms of having access to official documents and protecting their confidential sources?

3.2. Does the United States libel law give the defendants in a libel suit an advantage over the plaintiffs compared with libel laws in other countries? Why do some countries provide the plaintiffs with the right of reply? Generally, in a libel case, who has the burden of proof and why is that the case?

3.3. Does the United States give the authors/creators stronger or weaker copyright protection compared with other nations? What are the different defenses the defendants in a copyright lawsuit can utilize in different countries?

3.4. What are the governments in these countries doing to combat cyber-piracy, the most prevalent and persistent problem confronting the authors/creators today? Do recent cases in Europe and Asia indicate that the United States is lagging behind in providing protection in cyberspace? What happened with the proposed bills, SOPA and PIPA, which were designed to combat cyber-piracy in the United States?

4. Following question 3, this book provides comparisons and analyses of the media laws in these 11 countries. This is where the history, political, and cultural influences come in.

THE IMPORTANCE FOR COMPARATIVE MEDIA LAW RESEARCH

This book mainly deals with comparative law research. Comparisons are an integral part of most sciences. Some might even argue that no research or study can be conducted in isolation without at least some type of comparison involved. This is, claimed some scholars, especially evident for law study or media research. More importantly, as a natural consequence of globalization, it is absolutely essential to understand how the consistently revamped media systems across the world are functioning, which also brings with it the re-construction of relationships among the nations (Verhulst & Price, 2008). Comparative law study offers many benefits to scholars, as it can inform the readers about foreign laws, oftentimes for the purpose of facilitating an international transaction or resolving a conflict of laws problem (Reitz, 1998).

Comparative law study advocates have pointed out that comparisons can lead to new and exciting insights and a deeper understanding of the main issues at hand in different countries (Verhulst & Price, 2008). They can also identify the differences in knowledge and polices and could point to possible directions that could be followed by ways that are previously unknown to people. Additionally, comparisons may also help sharpen the focus of analysis of the subject matter under review by offering different and perhaps better perspectives (Reitz, 1998).

Comparative media law research can give scholars a better understanding of how one country borrows or imitates the legal systems and judicial practices from another country. In this age of the Internet, globalization, and advanced technology, it is also helpful to learn through international comparative law study how nations should handle the increasingly complex problem with the intellectual property on the web and exactly which countries have the most effective legal system to regulate new information technology.

Despite the importance of comparative media study, scholars have lamented that there has not been sufficient effort in the academia of this field. This is to say that comparative law research is, surprisingly, still in the early stages of flourishing (Verhulst & Price, 2008) . Some speculate that this might result from the combination of language barriers and the lack of knowledge and understanding of other cultures; however, the number of comparative media law research projects is on the rise as of late (Reitz, 1998).

As Lahav pointed out, comparative law research is a methodology that aims to offer comparative solutions and a better international understanding (1985). Specifically, there are usually four functions that comparative law research serves, and for this book, the main function of a comparative law study is to add value to the historical and cultural study of media law. As some scholars pointed out, studies of the place of law in society, the nature of law itself, and its relationship with news communications technologies become illuminated when comparative law and historical research are combined (Reitz, 1998) .

Owing to the rapid globalization and the universal emphasis on the creation of free markets, some have predicted that we would witness a high degree of uniformity and similarity in media law all around the world, especially statutes relating to communications infrastructure and economic regulations (Choudhry, 1999). However, the heavy and persistent influence of cultures and traditions ascertained that not all media laws are alike. This hypothesis is the central theme of this study.

The best way to test this hypothesis is to conduct a comparative law research. Comparative law research can lead to the realization that sources and conceptions of free speech and free press often vary from country to country. For example, some of the essential western legal concepts such as the rule of law and individual rights are not fully recognized, or not at all, by nations that place a bigger value on the notion of "keeping the peace" and "conciliation." On the other hand, with the increasing globalization and the ongoing effort to revamp media laws to keep up with the challenges brought on by the new information technology, it should not come as a surprise that there is a fair amount of "law imitation" among nations (Verhulst & Price, 2008).

This means that a comparative law study could only lead to two conclusions: 1) the special and unique natures of the legal systems being examined, which would allow the researchers to clearly define the unique and distinctive feature of each legal system, and 2) a finding of commonalities among the nations in regards to the specific legal subject, which could crystallize perhaps the best and thus universal approach to the particular legal issue in question. It is, however, very important to keep in mind a simple principle: One cannot simplistically assume that two countries have completely different views on a certain area of law just because two countries on paper do not have the exact same laws regarding that subject. For example, if country A has an explicit statute regulating libel in its constitution, and country B does not, it does not mean that country B cannot achieve the same goal of regulating defamation in other ways (Reitz, 1998). In other words, statutes alone do not present the full picture. When judging and evaluating a certain law, one also has to look at how these laws are enforced because oftentimes, even though a provision may seem strict on the surface, it is not usually enforced, or vice versa (Verhulst & Price, 2008). Additionally, other types of legal opinions and documents, such as court opinions or scholarly writings, may indicate that what one thinks of as law based solely on the statutes is not necessarily how the actual law works (Reitz, 1998).

Another aspect of comparative media study is to potentially answer the question of whether there should be a more uniform and harmonized legal system across the board to minimize the problem of "whose law should I follow?" which inevitably results when two parties from different nations are involved in a media-related dispute (Verhulst& Price, 2008).

At the very least, as scholars such as Behmer pointed out, comparative research on press freedom can make a sizeable and important contribution to the as-of-now diversified understanding and interpretation of freedom of the press (2009). That understanding, we believe, is and will be essential in today's increasingly globalized world. Another positive aspect of comparative law study is that it has the potential to lead to even more fascinating analyses by challenging the researchers to explain the reasons behind the similarities and differences among the legal systems or to analyze their significance for the cultures of the countries examined (Reitz, 1998).

As mentioned above, there are many benefits that can come from conducting a comparative media law research. The authors recognize these benefits and will attempt to contribute to this area of study.

THE COMPARATIVE LAW RESEARCH METHOD AND THE FREEDOM HOUSE MODEL

This research uses the comparative law approach. As other scholars pointed out, there are a few main reasons for comparative law studies, but ultimately, the search for the uniformity and dissimilarity among the laws and the attempt to find an explanation is the main focus of comparative law study (Ogus, 1999).

To answer our research questions, the authors will first look at the constitutions of these 11 countries to see if they explicitly provide freedom of the press/expression. If so, to what extent are those rights and protections granted? The most well-known constitutional law regarding freedom of expression and the press is probably the First Amendment of the United States Constitution, but what about others? After a quick search, it seems that most of the other 10 nations have similar provisions in their constitutions as well, but the scopes and rationale behind them can be very different. The authors will explore and analyze these differences. In order to illustrate the differences, charts detailing the differences will be provided when necessary. Other factors other than the statutes themselves will be featured in the analyses.

Part of this research is modeled after the methodology employed by Freedom House for its annual freedom of the press report. In short, the legal, political, and economic environments of these countries are examined by answering questions such as, "Do the constitutions or other basic laws contain provisions designed to protect freedom of the press and of expression, and are they enforced?" "Is freedom of information legislation in place, and are journalists able to make use of it?" Is there official censorship?" "Is private media ownership highly concentrated, and does it influence diversity of content?"

After reviewing the relationships between the constitutions and media law and the history behind the enactments of media law, the authors will look at the numerous media law statutes and case laws. We will examine the laws and policies or regulations regarding the media, including the electronic media, in those 11 nations. This includes the Digital Millennium Copyright Act (DMCA and Sonny Bono Copyright Term Extension Act of 1998. The Berne Convention and the resulting WIPO copyright treaties are also discussed, and how different countries adopted WIPO are mentioned. Other statutes that are examined include Germany's Copyright Act, the United Kingdom's Official Secret Act, and many other related pieces of media law legislations throughout the years worldwide. These laws are carefully looked through, and we identify the pros and cons of these laws and conduct a thorough and comprehensive comparison analysis of these laws in those 11 nations, which is the main focus of this book.

Additionally, to supplement the law comparisons, landmark and recent cases involving freedom of the press, copyright, and piracy in different countries are analyzed in order to help determine and predict which direction media law is going in those countries. For example, a relatively recent 2009 case in Sweden where the founders of the popular file-sharing site, the Pirate Bay, were arrested and tried for helping millions of Internet users illegally download copyrighted movies, music, and computer games. This case is analyzed and discussed to predict its impact on cyber-piracy in Sweden. These cases can be good indicators of present and future media law.

There are basically two kinds of comparative law study. One is called micro-comparison, which entails analyzing laws that belong to the "same legal family;" the other is called macro-comparison, which means investigating laws in various jurisdictions in an effort to obtain insight into other cultures and legal systems. Given that our aim is to analyze media laws across three continents and the different origins of these laws, this book applies both methods but emphasize the second approach-macro comparison (Verhulst & Price, 2008) .

Given the number of languages involved in a comparative law study and the unlikelihood that the scholars participating in the studies understand all these languages, it is only natural that scholars in this area of research have to rely on secondary literature written by foreign law specialists to complete the studies (Reitz, 1998) .

Chapter 3

Constitutional Protection for Freedom of the Press and Short Histories of Press Freedom in America, Europe, and Asia

In the ensuing chapter, the constitutions of every country examined in this book is discussed and a short history of the development of freedom of the press in every country is included. The United States is discussed first, then the European countries, and finally, the Asian countries.

UNITED STATES

Given that the First Amendment of the Constitution of the United States spotlights freedom of the press and how often that clause is invoked by everyone, one would expect the United States to have the most free press in the world; however, based on the Freedom House Press Freedom Index, that is not the case. According to that survey, the United States is ranked a relatively modest at number 21in the world in 2008. The latest index that came out in 2012 showed that America's ranking has gone down to 22nd. Regionally speaking, it is ranked No. 3 in "the Americas," trailing St. Lucia and St. Vincent & Grenadines.[12]

---

[12] See Freedom House Freedom of the Press Index 2012 for more details. It is available at http://www.freedomhouse.org/sites/default/

Media law is prominently featured front-and-center in the United States constitution. The famous First Amendment of the Constitution states: "Congress shall make no law respecting an establishment of religion, or prohibiting the free exercise thereof; or abridging the freedom of speech, or of the press; or the right of the people peaceably to assemble, and to petition the Government for a redress of grievances." The press clause is separate from the "freedom of speech" clause and therefore should not be considered the same. If they are indeed interchangeable, then it is reasonable to assume that the founding fathers of the country would not have included both of them separately. Freedom of the press, in other words, had its own origins separate from other rights included in the First Amendment (Watkins, 1994). It should be noted that although the language of the press clause was absolute -"Congress shall make no law." Once the Supreme Court started to discuss issues that sprang from this clause, it ruled that the First Amendment did not guarantee unqualified immunity for all expressions (Lively, 1992). It is also interesting to know that the lauded First Amendment was actually the Third Amendment in its first incarnation, and it was not until amendments one and two were proposed and rejected by the states that the "freedom of the press" amendment became the first (Anderson, 2009).

Freedom of the press was viewed not merely as a desirable civil liberty, but as a matter essential to the structure of the new government. That means that freedom of the press in the United States is much more than a legal concept. It is almost part of a religion. The press clause was born out of the people's desire to change, since there was no guarantee of press freedom during the colonial rule, and the demand for this protection was expressed at the same time as the demand for independence. In colonial America, the press was quite robust and un-intimidated by the authorities despite a fairly repressive regime, and the government's efforts to control the press always failed (Anderson, 2009). This strong press tradition helps to explain why there is highly effective press protection to this day.

The revolutionary backdrop from which the press clause was created, the concerns of those who demanded protection, and the language in which its role was expressed, all suggest that the framers of

---

files/Global%20and%20Regional%20Press%20Freedom%20Rankings.pdf.

the Constitution viewed the press clause as a structural provision of the statute, and that the primary purpose of the constitutional guarantee of a free press was to create a fourth institution outside the government as an extra check on the official branches (Anderson, 2009). This reverence for a free press in the United States is closely related to the English tradition of John Milton and John Stuart Mill, but the Americans also believed that the writings of Thomas Jefferson and James Madison were unique American contributions to freedom of the press (Soifer, 1985).

The freedom of each citizen to communicate and to choose among various opinions is at the center of basic individualism, which Americans value greatly. This might explain why the Americans place such an importance on freedom of the press and why judges have held that freedom of the press enjoys a favored position among constitutional rights (Soifer, 1985).

Even though the First Amendment was arguably the most famous constitutional provision, there is no definitive source for the basic theory supporting legal protection for freedom of the press. The theory about the First Amendment and the rights it protects, which has proven most influential has been Alexander Meiklejohn's notion that expressions relating to the democratic process is the Amendment's real and primary concern (Lively, 1992) . Scholars have also argued that the writings of Thomas I. Emerson revealed the most useful explanations as to why freedom of the press enjoys such a lauded reputation in the United States. Emerson and other scholars offered the following justifications for having freedom of the press:

1. Individual self-fulfillment: This concept is usually attributed to John Stuart Mill. His argument supports individual liberty and is directly responsible for the dominant American belief in individualism. In fact, this desire for individualism can be found in many provisions of the constitution, not just the First Amendment (Emerson, 1970).
2. Search for truth: Many justices and scholars in the United States have argued that the best test for truth is the power of the thought to be accepted in the competition of the market.[13]

[13] See the decision of Abrams v. United States, 250 U.S., 616 (1919) (Holmes, J., dissenting).

This is the famous "marketplace of ideas" concept, which advocates that truth will always conquer falsehood in a free and open market where numerous ideas compete for acceptance (Watkins, 1994) .

3. Self-government: This justification stemmed from James Madison's belief that a popular government must have popular information, and that people who want to be their own governors must "arm themselves with the power which knowledge can give them" (Watkins, 1994).
4. Safety Valve: This is the idea that freedom of expression/press is a method used to mediate between societal stability and the need to allow change (Watkins, 1994).

There is still debate in recent years as to whether the press should enjoy special constitutional protection (Anderson, 2002). Those in favor of added protection for the press point to the important role the press plays in a democracy, since it provides a check on government activities and abuses, as well as a source of information for the public (Watkins, 1994). Those opposed to special press privileges believed that granting the press special protection would lead to the problem of defining "who is a journalist," or who should be the beneficiaries of the privileges (Anderson, 2002). Additionally, even though the discussion of freedom of the press often centers on the role the press plays in public affairs, the Supreme Court had ruled that press protection is not limited to political speech but also for the purpose of entertainment, which is also protected under the law (Watkins, 1994) .

There were two especially important moments in the development of freedom of the press in the United States. The first was the passage of the Alien and Sedition Act of 1798, which was orchestrated by president John Quincy Adams to silence newspaper criticism of public officials (Foerstel, 1998). Specifically, many believed that this Act could be attributed to Adam's conflicts with his then political opponents, Thomas Jefferson and James Madison. The Sedition Act precipitated America's first constitutional and political crisis by specifying criminal penalties for anyone who wrote anything negative about the United States government, and many newspaper editors fell victims to the new laws and suffered the consequences of being charged with the crime of seditions libel (Soifer, 1985) .

The second important moment in the history of American press freedom was the Americans' participation in World War I. In the wake of the war, there was a sense of xenophobia in the country, which led to a campaign that invoked national security interests to charge various people and publications suspected of disloyalty to the country (Soifer, 1985). After the war ended, the majority of freedom of the press-related cases decided by the Supreme Court suppressed the ability of the press to express their opinions, such as criticizing the government's foreign policies. These rulings were often justified on the basis of protecting national security (Watkins, 1994). It was not until 1931, when the Supreme Court reached a decision in the case of *Near v. Minnesota*, that the press finally received some positive news. In its decision for *Near*, the Supreme Court held for the first time that newspapers enjoy a strong constitutional presumption in favor of their freedom to publish. It is worth noting that this case remains highly important today because of the serious limitations, it has imposed on the use of prior restraint.

During World War II, censorship again reared its ugly head. In fact, censorship was essentially unchallenged during the war (Watkins, 1994). The situation got even more dire for the press later when the Cold War led to a harsh and effective crackdown on dissenters in the late 1940s and early 1950s. It was apparent from the Supreme Court's decisions during this period that the threat of communism was sufficient justification to impose a variety of limitations on freedom of expression and press. Since then, the Supreme Court has dealt with a number of cases that restricted press freedom, while in other instances giving the press more latitude to print controversial stories (Lively, 1994).

To sum up the development of freedom of the press in terms of the United States Supreme Court's interpretations of the First Amendment clause, it can be said that the Supreme Court did not decide one important First Amendment case until 1919. Before that, it could only be described as a matter of minor importance (Lively, 1994). The first important decision invalidating a state restriction on the ground that it violated the freedom of the press as guaranteed by the First Amendment was the previously mentioned 1931 case *Near v. Minnesota*, which ruled that a state could not impose a prior restraint on a newspaper. In the following decades from the 30s to the 60s, the Court often relied on the press clause to invalidate state laws that restricted freedom of the press. Gradually, however, a new phenomenon occurred in the First Amendment cases in the Supreme Court. Freedom of the press was advanced by decisions that were based on the speech clause rather than the press clause. Their rulings were more inclusive and designed to protect all speakers, not just the press (Anderson, 2002). This has to do with the Supreme Court's unwillingness to grant the press special treatment.

Since then, the media has not been too successful in the Supreme Court. The press tried numerous times to have the Court interpret the press clause in a way that meant the media should be given rights not granted to others, including the right to resist subpoenas, and the right to enter prisons and interview prisoners. Up to this point, the Court had rejected these claims and expressed its unwillingness to recognize rights that would be available only to the press, mainly because the judges were concerned about the issue of determining "who qualifies as press." Now, the Court has stopped referring to the press clause as the constitutional basis for press freedom. In fact, the Court sometimes would go out of its way to grant the press protection without actually creating special rights. For example, in response to the press's request for access to the courtrooms, the Court agreed to the request, but held that the public, not the press, had a constitutional right to attend trials, even though this admitted that the press would be the prime beneficiary of the ruling (Anderson, 2002).

As a result of the Court's increasing reluctance to cite the press clause to grant the media special protections, the rapid expansion of constitutional protection of the press during the mid-20th century had stopped. By the end of that century, press-related cases became more rare in the Court room, and in turn, the Court had essentially stopped being an agent for the expansion of freedom of the press (Bezanson, 2003).

Nevertheless, the cheerful news for the press is that there has been no decrease in press freedom because the Supreme Court has never been the only source of legal protection for the press. In fact, many important protections are embedded into other statutes. For example, the federal "Freedom of Information Act" gave the press the power to demand the government to release information. In another example, while the Court rejected the press's request to outlaw police searches in newsrooms, Congress along with several states set up laws to do just that. Although there is no constitutional right for the press not to testify in court, which has become a problem for journalists in recent years, state shield laws have popped up over the country (Anderson, 2002). In some cases, state courts and lower federal courts are more protective of the press than the Supreme Court because the United States has a strong press tradition.

As mentioned above, one press protection that can be found in state laws but not federal law or the Constitution involves demands by prosecutors for information gathered by reporters, including materials from confidential sources. Several journalists have gone to jail on contempt of court charges for refusing to hand over materials in recent years, and others were spared jail time only because the cases ended in settlements and the legal proceedings against them were dropped. This all stemmed from the famous case of *Branzburg v. Hayes*, in which the Court ruled that the First Amendment did not give a journalist the right to refuse a subpoena from a grand jury.[14] The issue discussed in the case was whether a journalist could refuse to appear and testify before state and federal grand juries, with the media basing their argument for their refusal to testify on the belief that such appearance and testimony would erode freedom of speech and freedom of the press guaranteed by the First Amendment. The Court ultimately rejected this argument. The protection of confidential sources and information for the press are discussed in a later chapter.

Another potential threat to press freedom in the US is national security concerns, especially after the tragic even on September 11, 2001. Even though the Supreme Court held in *Near v. Minnesota* that prior restraint on speech and press is unconstitutional, it also made it clear that the government is allowed to prevent certain sensitive information from being published, namely national security-related information. The Court essentially held that the balancing process utilized in First Amendment cases operates differently when matters of national security are involved. In such a case, the scale would tilt toward government restrictions on expression (Watkins, 1994) .

Arguably, the most famous case involving a conflict between national security and press freedom is the Pentagon Papers case. In this consolidated case, the government, citing national security reasons, sought to prevent several newspapers from publishing top-secret information regarding the United States' involvement in the Vietnam War. The case ultimately made it to the Supreme Court, where the

---

[14] See the rulings of Branzburg v. Hayes, 408 U.S. 665 (1972).

justices ruled in favor of the newspapers because they decided that the government did not meet the heavy burden of showing a justification for a prior restraint; however, the Justices' opinions included different degrees of support for the superiority of the First Amendment, and some Justices' opinions even seemed to indicate that there might be reasons to prevent the press from publishing sensitive national information.[15] Because of these factors, no clear verdict appears to have come out of this case. Nevertheless, the significance of the case and the wording of the Justices' opinions turned the case into a landmark case in the history of precedents for allowing exceptions to the rights protected by the First Amendment. Accordingly, this case and the language used in the opinion has been cited in numerous Supreme Court cases since. In other words, the Pentagon Papers case laid the groundwork for further expansion of the national security exception to the First Amendment (Watkins, 1994) .

The Pentagon Papers case and several subsequent similar cases revealed that the answer to the question of "who is to decide whether the disclosure of certain information would harm the nation?" is the government (Anderson, 2009). On paper, the final decision makers of whether a prior restraint should be applied in respect to national security-related information are court judges, but the judiciary gives great weight to the judgment of the legislative and executive branches. It should be noted that prior restraint, although now a viable option for the government to censor the press, is not very applied frequently. Very simply put, if the press did not alert the government about the content of their yet-to-be-published stories, then there would be no prior restraint issue to deal with (Watkins, 1994).

All those rules, at least on paper, should also apply to journalists from the new media, but, this is a rather complex issue when it comes to the Internet. Approximately 76 percent of Americans are Internet users as of 2009, placing the country among the top world leaders in Internet penetration, so obviously the Internet has become a medium for more news outlets.[16] In fact, the number of Internet sites and blogs have exploded in recent years and blogs have proven to be an important

---

[15] See the decision of New York Times Co. v. United States, 403 U.S. 713 (1971)

[16] For more details, see Freedom House Freedom of the Press Report: The United States 2010.

source of information in many instances. This again raises the questions of whether online bloggers, who are not professional journalists, should be considered legitimate press sources under the law (Anderson, 2009).

Overall, the press continues to enjoy strong protection in the United States, and press freedom has strong foundations in American law. The United States Constitution explicitly protects freedom of speech and of the press, and these rights have been further buttressed by numerous state laws and lower court decisions. The Supreme Court increasingly prefers to use the "free speech" clause to grant the public (which would include the press) more freedom instead of the "free press" clause to avoid outwardly giving the press special treatments, The Supreme Court as a whole has been very generous to the press, striking down lower courts' statutes that could potentially hinder press freedom. An example of this is the "right of reply" law that requires newspapers to print the responses from those the papers had criticized. It has also ruled that as noble as it might sound to ask the press to do their jobs properly, the press clause only grants the press freedom but does not demand responsibility from the media (Watkins, 1994) . The Supreme Court and other lower courts have also given the press broad protection from libel and defamation suits that involve commentaries on public officials and public figures, although libel remains a criminal offense in some states. The libel law is discussed in a later chapter.

United States Media and the Four Theories of the Press

Within the framework of Siebert, Peterson, and Schramm's four theories of the press, the United States followed the libertarian theory model, which branched from the writings of Milton, Locke, and Mill and advocates the general philosophy of rationalism and natural rights. Overall, the purpose of the media and press in the United States is not only to inform and entertain the public but to discover the truth and keep an eye on the government. The fact that freedom of the press is prominently featured in the US Constitution and close to an absolute right, speaks volume that when drafting the constitution, the founding fathers intended the press/media to be as free from–governmental control as possible. Accordingly, the media system and the media laws that regulate them in the United States undoubtedly reflected the libertarian theory.

As mentioned previously, another branch of the four theories originated in the United States. The social responsibility came out of the Hutchins Commission Report published in 1947. In that report, W.E. Hocking wrote about the need to have media codes and the Commission on Freedom of Press. Moreover, he emphasized that media must take on the obligation of social responsibility to make sure that the media is doing their job in an ethical manner and the public is informed enough to have genuine and productive discussions about important issues. If the media are not fulfilling these responsibilities or following the codes of conduct, then someone will make sure they do. The more recent laws concerning the regulations of the media, including the Internet, have incorporated Hocking's writings. For example, television news programs are required to give the candidates roughly the same amount of free time so that the public will be equally informed about all of them in order to make an educated decision as on who to vote for. In short, the general consensus in the United States is that instead of the libertarian model, the media should be held to a higher standard in terms of their job performance and are expected to follow certain ethical guidelines so that the public will greatly benefit when they consume media content.

EUROPE

In the following section, the constitutional protections for freedom of the press in every European country is discussed. A short history of the development of press freedom in these countries is also included. Since every country has its own unique story, every one of them is discussed individually.

France

Based on the 2008 Freedom House's freedom of the press index, France was ranked 40th, which represented one of the lowest placements in Western Europe (Karlekar & Cook, 2008)). In fact, it was ranked 20th out of 25 countries in that region. In the most recent index published in 2012, France's score has gotten even worse but it remained at 43rd.[17] For a country that was the first in the world to formally recognize freedom of the press as a fundamental right in 1789 (Eisendrath, 1982), this placement comes as a surprise.

Freedom of the press is guaranteed by the French constitution, but the constitutional recognition of press freedom in France takes a different route to achieve compared with other countries. The first official law that introduced the idea of freedom of the press in France was passed in 1881, after the Republicans came into power. This law provides for 1) an administrative arrangement specific to the written press and 2) the definition of various offences (defamation, provocation to crimes and offences, etc.) aiming to institute a balance between freedom of speech and protection of people.[18]Even though the law of 1881 regarding freedom of the press was quite advanced for its time, that statute was amended numerous times since its creation. Over the years, the amendments added more and more restrictions on the press, frequently as a response to political and social crisis. In fact, French laws actually put a lot of restrictions on the press, and one might be surprised at how many press offenses could be found in the statutes. Some examples of the offenses are incitement to crimes and offense (the notion of which was broadly interpreted), defamation (including damaging the reputation of foreign dignitaries), and offense relating to the armed forces, such as military incitement (Errera, 1985).

In the last hundred years or so, the French Constitution went through several changes. The latest version, the French Constitution of 1958, does *not* contain an express mention of freedom of the press. Nevertheless, freedom of the press is given recognition equivalent to that accorded a constitutional guarantee because of two important documents. First, the Declaration of the Rights of Man and the Citizen of 1789, which has constitutional value and was mentioned in the preamble of the 1958 Constitution. This declared that there should be unrestrained communication of thoughts and opinions. Second, the preamble of the Constitution of 1958 refers to the preamble of the Constitution of 1946, which mentioned the fundamental principals

---

[17] This is made clear when comparing the 2008 Index to the Freedom House Freedom of the Press Index of 2012.

[18] See the article on the website of France in Canada, which is about the World Press Freedom Day Debate. Retrieved from http://www.ambafrance-ca.org/spip.php?article2977.

recognized by the laws of the Republic. Freedom of the press was included in these principals (Errera, 1985). The Declaration of the Rights of Man and the Citizen is a fundamental document of the French Revolution that was highly influenced by the doctrine of natural rights. It called for the elimination of royal privileges by proclaiming an end to exemptions from taxation, freedom, and equal rights for all men, and access to public office based on talent. The monarchy's power was restricted, and all citizens were to have the right to take part in the legislative process (Flower, 2010). Freedom of speech and press were declared, and arbitrary arrests were no longer allowed.[19]

The concepts in the Declaration came from the philosophical and political principles of the Enlightenment, including individualism, the social contract concept advocated by the French philosopher Rousseau, and the separation of powers (Errera, 1985). Some of these concepts and principles were shared by the U.S. Declaration of Independence in 1776.[20] It is worth noting that Thomas Jefferson, who was the primary author of the U.S. Declaration of Independence, was at the time residing in France as a U.S. diplomat and in correspondence with members of the French National Constituent Assembly.[21] It should also be noted that the Declaration was not deeply rooted in either the practice of the West or even France at the time. The Declaration emerged in the late 18th century out of war and revolution, and it encountered resistance as democracy and individual rights were frequently regarded as synonymous with anarchy and subversion. In short, the declaration encompasses ideals and aspirations France promised to uphold in the future (Lauren, 2003).

Based on the ideas mentioned above, the French envisioned the press as both the instrument and the expression of democracy. The press not only provided the means for everyone to participate in

---

[19] See Wikipedia's article on Declaration of the Rights of Man and of the Citizen. Retrieved from http://en.wikipedia.org/wiki/Declaration_of_the_Rights_of_Man_and_of_the_Citizen. It should be noted that articles from Wikipedia should be regarded with caution.

[20] See note 16.

[21] An article on Thomas Jefferson describes his connection with France. This article can be found at http://sc94.ameslab.gov/TOUR/tjefferson.html.

political debate, but also served to protect political diversity; however, freedom of the press had been limited by various legal devices employed by the executive branch of the government. Those methods include prior restraint and censorship (Errera, 1985). Indeed, the one sentence in the clause of the declaration, "each citizen may speak, write, print cases as set forth by the law," has given the French government a lot of leeway to restrict press freedom (Eisendrath, 1982) . In other words, "set forth by the law" became the phrase that could be used to control the press, and the French government in the last one hundred years or so had indeed taken advantage of that clause to set up laws restricting the press.

One such law designed to restrict the press' freedom was set up during World War II. During this time, foreign press had already entered the French market, and the French government believed that some of the foreign publications, which propagated their own agendas had corrupted the local press environment. In response to this, a law was set up to control and restrict the foreign press. More importantly, the political developments taking place at this time led the French government to strengthen its belief that the press needed to be controlled by the state (Eisendrath, 1982).

One press freedom-related event that occurred in France illustrated not only this point but also a significant difference between the United States and France. In 1980, the French government brought criminal charges against the country's biggest newspaper, *La Monde*, for criticizing court decisions including one involving the then president Valery Giscard d'Estaing's acceptance diamonds from an African emperor. Officially, the charges were not related to the content of the story. Instead, the newspaper was held accountable for bringing "dishonor" to the judicial system. Despite the fact that the president later admitted taking the diamonds, the damage had already been done. In the history of French media, this lawsuit had a huge impact on the press because it silenced the biggest newspaper when it came to reporting on sensitive subjects. By extension, the rest of the press in France was affected as well. Comparatively, in the United States, presidents and other public officials simply lack the prosecutorial machinery to do anything remotely like this (Eisendrath, 1982).

Similar to many other countries, one of the more current problems with press freedom in France is media ownership. Most of France's 100+ newspapers are privately owned; however, many media outlets, print as well as broadcast, are owned by companies with close ties to prominent politicians and defense contractors. In addition, close associates of former President Nicolas Sarkozy own or hold prominent positions at France's leading newspapers and television stations. This close relationship between the government and the press led to an uneasy balance when it came to freedom of the press (Karlekar & Cook, 2008)). In fact, press freedom has long been an uneasy subject in France, which is understandable when many newspapers rely on government subsidies and defense contractors controling large segments of the print and broadcast media.

This close relationship between the government and the press has existed for decades, but it has gotten even cozier since Nicholas Sarkozy, a media savvy, former communications minister, became president. Since Sarkozy's election in 2007, relations between the government and the press have been closely scrutinized because of the concentration of media ownership amongst the Sarkozy's close friends and allies. It might astonish some people to know that among those French media moguls are Arnaud Lagardère, who calls Sarkozy a "brother"; Martin Bouygues, who is a godfather to Sarkozy's youngest son; and Vincent Bolloré, who lent the president his jet and yacht for a post-election vacation. In one instance, Sarkozy's wife was allowed to pick the photographs and write the captions for a magazine article about her and her husband. In one of those captions, she actually described herself as Sarkozy's "ray of sunlight." Perhaps it was these close ties with the media industry that emboldened Sarkozy to lash out when he did not get his way with the media. In 2008, Sarkozy publicly criticized a news agency for failing to report on one of his political rivals' alleged past misdeeds and being too lenient to his oppositions in general (Bennhold, 2008). Sarkozy was unsuccessful in his re-election bid in 2012, and it is still too soon to tell what kind of approach his opponent from the French Socialist Party, François Hollande would take in regards to press freedom and media regulations.

In terms of regulating the Internet and journalists online, there were no governmental restrictions regarding journalism on the Internet, which is used by approximately 80 percent of the population; [22]

[22] This number was taken from Freedom House's annual report on France, which can be found at http://www.freedomhouse.org/report/freedom-press/2012/france.

however, a 2006 antiterrorism law does allow security agencies to monitor the Internet for suspected terrorists.[23] This could potentially threaten freedom of the press in France, since journalists' online activities could be monitored, and in that process, work products and confidential sources for the journalists could be potentially exposed.

The present media landscape in France has its cultural roots in the postwar period, when the French government decided to regulate an industry that it felt had lost credit. To this day, the state is still present in the written press, the TV, the radio, and more recently on the Internet for copyright infringement, with regulations on cultural products, downloading and property rights known as Hadopi (Karlekar 2010) . The combination of the mentality of having to control the press and the close ties between the government and the press makes France, one of the first countries to endorse freedom of the press, a nation that has a surprisingly unstable and unpredictable press freedom condition.

Four Theories of the Press in France: It would seem like the Constitutional protection for the press in France was born from individualism, natural rights, and the marketplace of ideas. Accordingly, it would suggest that France subscribes to the libertarian theory; however, while that might be an accurate assumption at the time the constitution was written, the French media laws have gone through some substantial changes in the last few decades, and the regulations on the media have become increasingly stricter and the call for the media to behave more responsibly has become louder. As such, in today's France, the social responsibility theory guides the development of new media laws.

Sweden

Sweden, along with its neighboring Scandinavian countries, has been ranked at the top or near the top of the ranking in the Freedom of the Press Index. In the 2010 Index, Sweden was ranked No.1, while the latest index in 2011 showed that Sweden dropped one spot and was

---

[23] Freedom House expressed concern that this could lead to further erosion of press freedom. Given France's recent history with press freedom, this is a valid concern.

ranked No.2. In the 2012 index, Sweden has once again returned to No.1, shared with Finland and Norway.[24]

Freedom of the press is a major part of the Swedish Constitution. Consisting of four fundamental laws, the constitution includes the Freedom of the Press Act. It should be noted that the Act is a long set of laws and regulations composed of 14 chapters, unlike the freedom of the press provisions in the constitutions of other countries, which usually are condensed into one or two short sentences.[25]

In terms of freedom of the press, Sweden is universally considered to be a pioneering country. Specifically, in 1766, Sweden became the first country to introduce a constitutional law where censorship was abolished and freedom of the press guaranteed.[26]The origins of modern Swedish press law can be traced to the political environment during that period, when Sweden experienced a period of parliamentary sovereignty known as the "Era of Freedom." Prior to this period, Sweden was an absolute monarchy, and press freedom was exercised less rigorously. When the king's power was drastically reduced following a power shift, the Estates of the Kingdom took control of the country. It was the Estates that abolished the formal censorship in 1766, and the first version of press law was adopted (Kent, 2008). Even though this act was called Printing Freedom Ordinance, it was essentially functioning as fundamental law (Strömberg, 1985).

The Law on the Freedom of Printing of 1766 was also the first in the world to make most documents from the state authorities open and available for anyone who wanted to view them (Strömberg, 1985). This principle from 1766 is still an important part of the Swedish Constitution, and more significantly, it has a long and widespread influence worldwide. This is due to the fact that nowadays, just about all "Freedom of Information Acts" " in the world have grown out of an application, usually in a less powerful fashion, of this Swedish

---

[24] See the latest Freedom House Freedom of the Press Index 2012 for a complete ranking, which can be found at http://www.freedomhouse.org/sites/default/files/Global%20and%20 Regional%20Press%20Freedom%20Rankings.pdf.

[25] Seethe Constitution of Sweden, the 1949 Freedom of the Press Act.

[26] Sweden's Official website, http://www.sweden.se/eng/Home/ Society/Government-politics/Facts/Openness/, offers a concise history of the country.

"principle of public availability"[27]. The most important founding father of this part of the Swedish constitution was Anders Chydenius, who was a member of parliament in the ecclesiastical estate (Kent, 2008) .

This is not to say that censorship never materialized in Sweden. There were periods when censorship was abolished and reinstated during political instability; however, in 1809, the political climate more or less stabilized. Consequently, freedom of the press was re-born and immortalized in the 1809 constitution. There have been several incarnations of the press law since then, but the central ideas of freedom of the press promulgated in the 1809 constitution. Prohibition against prior restraints as well as the requirement that subsequent punishment be applied only through the judicial process, have long been the cornerstone of Swedish press law. After 1809, freedom of the press was further cemented by the enactment of the new Freedom of the Press Act in 1810. The Act went through a few revisions over the years, but the 1949 version became the definitive version and is still in force today. Another important development in the evolution of Swedish law occurred in 1974, when the Constitution of 1809 was replaced with a modern one. This modern provision incorporates the extant Freedom of the Press Act, thus providing more concrete protection for the press (Strömberg, 1985).

The justification for the ample protection afforded to the press is that, historically, the purpose of a free press in Sweden has been regarded as a political matter. Accordingly, the Freedom of the Press Act emphasizes that in deciding whether certain types of expressions constitute abuse of press freedom, the important principal to take into consideration is that freedom of the press constitutes the basis of a free government. This is not to say that the Act only protects political speech. The Act broadly defines the purpose of press freedom as the securing of free interchange of opinions and enlightenment of the public, thus protecting expressions of religions, science, and culture as well (Strömberg, 1985).

Sweden was not only one of the first countries to enact laws to protect freedom of the press, but it also has particularly strong legal protections for press freedom under the Freedom of the Press Act and

---

[27] See the Censorship in Sweden on Wikipedia. Retrieved on http://en.wikipedia.org/wiki/Censorship_in_Sweden#cite_note-Time-1. Once again, this reference should be treated with caution.

the Fundamental Law of Freedom of Expression. Unlike France, who was also one of the first countries to have such laws, Sweden has maintained its early pledge to have a free and open press, and the Swedish government has kept a constant eye on the advancement of new media so that it can adjust its media laws to keep up with the times. For example, in 2006, the government considered the possibility of reviewing current press legislation to address new technologies (Karlekar & Cook, 2008)). In terms of government interference, Freedom House's assessment for Sweden in recent years has been that state control of the press is relatively modest. Overall, whenever government control is exercised in Sweden, it is usually to serve two purposes. First, it is to facilitate the prosecution of any abuses of press freedom. Second, it is to prevent foreign influence over its media (Strömberg, 1985).

Four Theories of the Press and Sweden: Sweden has enacted freedom of the press legislation over the years to make sure the country has a robust and unfettered press. The main reason behind these laws is to protect the press and encourage political discussions, therefore, it is apparent that this country subscribed to the libertarian theory years ago and still does today.

Germany

Germany has consistently enjoyed a strong protection for freedom of the press. According to Freedom House's Freedom of the Press Index in 2008, Germany was ranked 16th. The latest index that came out in 2012 showed that Germany is still in the 16th place.[28]

The German constitution, or Basic Law, is very clear about the protection of press freedom. The official language of Article 5, Paragraph 1 reads:

> Every person shall have the right freely to express and disseminate his opinions in speech, writing and pictures, and to inform himself without hindrance from generally accessible sources. Freedom of the press and freedom of reporting by

[28] See Freedom House Freedom of the Press Index 2012.

> means of broadcasts and films shall be guaranteed. There shall be no censorship.[29]

Like many other countries, the history of press freedom in Germany was not always positive. Even though the press in Germany enjoys a fair amount of freedom, the history of Germany was littered with tales of censorship and suppression of mass distribution of free thought.

After Gutenberg invented the printing press around 1450, the Bishop and sovereign of the state, introduced a so-called pre-publication review for all printed materials. Since the world was dominated by religion at this time any publications that contained materials, which could be interpreted as threatening to the dominant religion and the secular leaders, were censored under the new universal censorship law. During this period, the issue of censorship mainly centered on the safeguard of true faith and political legitimacy (Kohl, 1985).

In Germany, newspapers were established after the invention of printing press and other social achievements, such as the discovery of new continents. In the 17th and 18th century, the emergence of international trade and a citizen class that was better educated furthered the culture of newspaper reading. But, during this time, censorship was also established by church and by state (Kohl, 1985). For the state, the main reason for censorship was to prevent publication of potentially offensive/inflammatory stories, which could cause discord with other countries. Another reason for censorship was to protect the reputation of the state and the inner freedom of states or cities. For the church, censorship was simply a way to make sure that only the opinion of the church was published (Czepek et al., 2009).

In the late 18th century and early 19th century, the Enlightenment created a new perspective on not only religion but also freedom of expression and freedom of the press; however, this new sentiment, which was heavily influenced by the French and the Americans, did not immediately translate into the improvement of press freedom in Germany (Czepek et al., 2009). In fact, freedom of the press went through numerous ups and downs in Germany. Some of the noteworthy

---

[29]Basic Law for the Federal Republic of Germany, Art.5.

events, in chronological order, regarding the tumultuous development of freedom of the press following the age of Enlightenment were:

1. Criminal law used to penalize heretical views.
2. The 1848 revolution, which produced the 1848 Reichs Constitution giving Every German citizen the right to free expression; however, this new-found Freedom was short-lived after the revolution collapsed.
3. After Germany became a democracy following World War I, freedom of Expression and its contribution to public discussion of cultural and political affairs constituted the basic rationale for Article 118 of the Weimar Constitution of August 8th, 1919, which was essentially fashioned after the 1848 constitution (Czepek, 2009).

Adolph Hitler was a major contributing factor in the next phase of press freedom in Germany. Soon after Hitler and the Nazi parties grabbed control of the country and went on to rule roughly from 1933-1945, freedom of the press was suspended. The Nazi party enacted a new law to control the press, which severely limited the number of people who could publish. A journalist was free to perform his duty to the public by promoting the ideas and programs of Nazi ideology, but the press was basically reduced to serving as Hitler's propaganda machines (Kohl, 1985).

After World War II came to an end, the Western allies attempted to slowly rebuild a democratic press; however, this was at their discretion granting publishing licenses to anti-fascist individuals and political parties. These efforts culminated in the enactment of the Federal Constitution, which demonstrated a strong commitment to a free and uninhibited press in Article 5, going so far as prohibiting censorship (Michalowski & Woods, 1999).

The guarantee of freedom of the press was generally believed to be a reaction to Nazi oppression of free thought. The Germans regarded freedom of the press as the basis of a free, democratic society. Specifically, the Constitutional Court in Germany had stated that since it helps the public make important political decisions by informing them about the current events, the press is a medium in the process of forming public opinion and therefore entirely indispensable in a truly democratic society (Czepek et al., 2009).

The main guardian of freedom of the press is the Federal Constitutional Court, and over the years, the Court has clarified, through its rulings, how this freedom should be applied by the law. One important decision stated that all preparatory activities, especially the collection of information, as well as the act of publishing, are protected. This means that not only the publishers and journalists could rely on the constitutional guarantee, but also bookkeepers could invoke the constitution when called upon to testify (Czepek et al., 2009).

An important exception to the fairly uninhibited freedom of the press is when a published story interferes with a person's right to privacy. When there is a conflict between these two types of freedoms, defamation and the right to privacy, the court can apply a balancing act (Czepek et al., 2009). However, the German courts have repeatedly pointed out that prominent persons who are in the public eye, such as public officials or public figures like celebrities and athletes, are entitled to much less protection from the law. In fact, in factual reporting, the press only has to follow decent journalistic standards of care, and the truth is not really required (Kohl, 1985). This is somewhat similar to the defamation law in the United States.

There is a unique feature of the media laws in Germany. Given the country's history, it should come as no surprise that a glaring exception (and unique to Germany) to the press freedom rule is the prohibition of using or publishing Nazi propaganda and Nazi symbols. This strictly implemented prohibition has been in effect in Germany since the end of World War II without question (Czepek, 2009). A simple Google search would yield some high-profile cases in which Nazi sympathizers and holocaust deniers were sentenced to prison, including Germar Rudolf, who is a chemist that published a controversial paper questioning whether or not the holocaust actually occurred.

Another type of press content that might get the journalists in trouble with the law is advocating for wars. Article 26 of the Constitution prohibits a war of aggression; therefore, it is possible that writing articles discussing the benefits of attacking a foreign country might be illegal. The reason for this law is believed to be a reaction to Hitler's aggressive attack on Germany's neighboring countries (Kohl, 1985). Content that could be interpreted as a threat to internal security, such as support for unconstitutional parties or images that display symbols of unconstitutional organizations could also cause some trouble for the press. Fortunately for the press, this statute has not been widely used to prosecute the press. If, for example, the symbol in question is used for artistic, scientific, or educational reasons, then displaying it would not land the press hot water (Michalowski & Woods, 1999) .

There has been very positive developments that benefit freedom of the press in Germany over the years. Some of the regulations in Germany were designed to enhance press freedom. For example, the print media received subsidies from the government for distributions. Another example, which the print media also qualifies for, is the reduced value added tax. Furthermore, there is a "fixed price" system for print products, including books, newspapers, and magazines. This law was designed to make sure that small publishers could still make a profit (Czepek et al., 2009).

A more recent development that boded well for press freedom in Germany was the introduction of the "Freedom of Information Act," which granted all German citizens freedom, in 2006. The bad news is that not all German states decided to adopt the law, only 9 out of the 16 states in Germany did so (Czepek et al., 2009). This law is discussed a bit later in the book.

On the other hand, the German constitution does guarantee freedom of the press–and the Germans generally subscribe to the concept of press freedom as critical to a true democracy, however, there are some worrisome trends in Germany in recent years that could potentially harm this freedom.

One disturbing worldwide trend for journalists and journalism is the gradual loss of reporters' abilities to keep the identities of their sources hidden in the wake of the governments' increasingly aggressive efforts for surveillance to combat terrorism. While in Germany, the protection of sources is guaranteed under the German constitution. Germany also enacted laws that allowed the government to intrude on its citizens' private lives. An antiterrorism law that took effect in January 2009 grants German authorities greater power to conduct covert surveillance, including remote and secret searches of computers through the Internet. It also includes provisions that threaten the rights of journalists to protect their sources, which severely hampered the journalists' abilities to do their jobs. The state sometimes uses the "accessory to the betrayal of state secrets" clause to gain access to information that really belongs to confidential sources. The courts in Germany, however, have generally been more sympathetic to the protection of confidential sources and have even blocked the passage of certain laws that they deem to be violating the spirit of press freedom by putting the confidential sources in a position of being too easily revealed (Brauck, 2007). All in all, the issue of protection of sources in Germany has become an increasing concern for press freedom advocates. The German government played its part in the worldwide tightening of security legislation that took place after 9/11. As a result, many German journalists have had reasons to fear they could no longer guarantee the anonymity of their sources, which is a vital part of ensuring press freedom.[30]

Another concern is the search of newsrooms to gather information that the journalists had worked hard to obtain. One recent incident was the Cicero case. In 2005, the Minister of the Interior authorized a raid of offices of the periodical *Cicero*. This was criticized as an attack on press freedom by some members of the German press. The raid was justified by the suspicion of leaking state secrets; however, in February 2007, the constitutional court ruled that suspicion of aiding in the leaking of state secrets was not a sufficient enough reason to warrant a search, thus, the raid was illegal (Fürstenau, 2011).

The close ties between government and management in the media industry is another concern. The constitution argues that public television and radio should be entirely independent from political influence, but the supervisory boards of public broadcasters are partially staffed with politicians. In fact, the highest positions are allocated along party lines, which means that for someone who wants a career in public media, belonging to one of the two major political parties is crucial (Czepek et al., 2009).

Another threat to press freedom is the heavy concentration of media ownership and the economic framework within which media organizations have to work. Powerful publishing houses, namely Bertelsmann, Springer, Bauer and Burda, dominate entire regions of the country, which leads to clear limitations in diversity of reporting.[31] It's worth noting that because of ~~the~~ strict rules regarding newspaper

---

[30] See Ben Knight's online article on Press Freedom Remains an Issue in Germany for more details. The article can be found at http://www.dw-world.de/dw/article/0,,5526471,00.html.

[31] See Volker Thomas's online article on this subject. Retrieved on http://www.goethe.de/wis/med/dos/jou/pfr/en5311044.htm.

company mergers in Germany, the problem of high media ownership concentration is less of a concern with print media. Specifically, as Freedom House's reports demonstrated, there are still about 350 newspaper publishing companies, however, this does not necessarily mean that there is less diversity in terms of media content (Karlekar & Woods, 2008).

With a tough economy pushing traditional news business to the brink of extinction in the age of the Internet, there is also pressure not to offend major advertising clients (Karlekar & Cook), 2008). Bowing to the economic pressure, the media often chooses not to publish negative stories about clients. This certainly has an impact on press freedom and has caused self-censorship among journalists to be more prevalent.

Another disturbing development for press freedom in Germany is the illegal monitoring of emails. In recent years, the German Secret Service (BND) was revealed to have been monitoring emails of journalists in the name of national security and fighting terrorism. A recent case made this news public. The public was informed about the illegal monitoring of the correspondence between a German Afghanistan correspondent and the Afghan trade minister Amin Farhang, who was long considered a friend of Germany (Karlekar & Cook, 2008).

Privacy rights and commercial laws can be weighed against press freedom in civil suits. While freedom of expression has been held highly by German courts, rulings of the Constitutional Court seem to favor privacy rights over press freedom. This is especially true when the Court deems the reported information in dispute to have little public value (Czepek et al., 2009).

In short, the constitution in Germany guarantees the freedom of expression and of the press, though there are exceptions for hate speech, Holocaust denial, and Nazi propaganda. Overall, Germany has enjoyed a great deal of protection for press freedom. In recent years, there were worrisome trends that could've potentially curtailed this freedom, including the decrease of confidential source protection. In terms of regulating the Internet, the Internet is open and largely unrestricted, but there is a legal ban on access to child pornography and Nazi propaganda, and the online activities of individuals under court-ordered surveillance are known to be monitored (Karlekar & Cook, 2008).)

Four Theories of the Press and Germany: Historically, Germany has gone through a lot of chaos, major changes, and tumultuous events. The major political upheavals have played a significant part in Germany's media law transformation over the years. During Hitler rule, Germany subscribed to the authoritarian theory, as media was controlled by the government. After WWII and the fall of Nazi Germany, the country once again embraced the idea of a free idea; however, there are still laws put in place to keep the press in check when the government feels necessary, mainly to make sure the media do their part in a fair and ethical manner. In present day Germany, the social responsibility theory is the prevailing ideology behind media laws.

Italy

Based on the Freedom House survey, Western Europe consistently boasted the highest level of press freedom worldwide. In 2009, 23 countries (92 percent) were rated "Free," and 2 (8 percent) were rated "Partly Free." This remained the same for 2012. This means that on the Freedom House Freedom of the Press Index, Italy was one of the only two countries from Western Europe to have been consistently categorized as only having "partly free" press. In other words, among all the Western/Northern European countries that scored extremely high on the index, Italy is a conspicuous anomaly. In the 2010 index, Italy is placed at a low72. In 2011, Italy's ranking dropped to 75.[32] In 2012, it was ranked 70th.[33] Italy did fare a little better in other press freedom indexes, though. According to the 2010 World Press Freedom Index from Reporters Without Borders, Italy, along with France, trailed behind the rest of Western Europe and was ranked 49 out of the 178 countries rated (Reporters Without Borders, 2010).

Freedom of speech and the press are constitutionally guaranteed rights and generally respected despite ongoing concerns regarding concentration of media ownership in Italy. Specifically, Article 21 of Italy's Constitution states that everyone has the right to freely express their thoughts in speech, writing, and by other communication, and that

---

[32] See the Freedom House Freedom of the Press Index 2011.

[33] See the Freedom House Freedom of the Press Index 2012.

the "press may not be controlled by authorization or submitted to censorship."[34]

The current Constitution of Italy was created by three different groups in congress: Christian Democratic, liberal and left-wing, and because all were deeply anti-fascist, there was general agreement against an authoritarian constitution; however, each group was concerned about its success in upcoming elections after the creation of the constitution, and all fought to include provisions that reflected their values. The result was that some aspects of the text refer to natural law, while others, such as workers' rights are more reminiscent of socialist and communist thought (Einaudi, 1948). Generally speaking, it seems that freedom of the press in the Constitution of Italy falls into the category of natural law like other western countries.

Italy has a unique history in regards to freedom of the press. Some have defined Italy's media system as one of the most complex media systems in Europe due to the interrelationships among political, socio-cultural, and economic factors (Czepek et al., 2009). While the concept of an adversarial press and the need for pluralism and diversity is often associated with freedom of the press the Italians did not whole-heartedly attempt to bring that concept to life. Scholars have argued that the Italian media has never played the role of an adversarial press well because they usually cave into the control of political parties or economic groups. Television stations are usually controlled by political parties, which only espoused the points of view of those parties. The structure of the newspaper industry also restricted and influenced the flow of political information reaching the public. Specifically, since WWII ended, over 75% of national newspapers have been under the control of powerful economic groups with mostly conservative political views. All this evidence seems to suggest that despite the constitutional protection for freedom of the press, the Italian media as a whole were controlled by either political parties or powerful economic forces without the will and drive to be watchdogs of society and disseminate balanced and relevant information to the masses (Marletti &Roncarolo, 2000).

The lack of diversity in the media, particularly in the television sector, has been a concern for many in Italy since the powerful media mogul Silvio Berlusconi decided to become a politician in 1993. An

[34] See Constitution of Italy, Art. 21.

astonishing fact about him that is rarely known by the rest of the world is that he actually controls six out of the eight national television channels in Italy. As Freedom House's report (2008) showed, there was evidence that all the top executives of these television stations conferred with one another to decide which news stories to put out and which negative stories to conceal about Berlusconi. This obviously threatened the press freedom in Italy. Given that Italy is a country where people get most of their news from TV, making television the most powerful form of media in the country. The extremely high concentration of TV station ownerships means that press freedom in Italy is seriously inhibited (Karlekar & Cook, 2008).)

In recent years, there have been several trends that are harming the condition of press freedom in Italy even further. There were reports of violation of the protection of journalists' sources, the continuing concentration of media ownership, displays of contempt and impatience on the part of government officials towards journalists and their work, and judicial summons for journalists (Karlekar & Cook, 2008). All these issues, it would seem, could be attributed to one man, Silvio Berlusconi, Italy, a country with a "Partly Free" ranking, saw worsening conditions for press freedom as Prime Minister Berlusconi clashed with the press over coverage of his personal life. This lead~~ing~~ to lawsuits against both local and foreign news outlets, as well as the censorship of critical content by the state-owned broadcaster, as Freedom House reported in 2008.

In June 2008, the lower house of Parliament approved a bill that would impose heavy fines or jail terms on journalists who use transcripts from wiretaps without a judge's permission. The International Press Institute noted that the bill could restrict journalists' ability to provide the public with vital information. The draft law contains provisions that limit journalists' right to report on police investigations, and includes serious punishments for breaching these restrictions. Reporters would face up to three years in prison and editors could be fined up to €465,000 (US$576,000) for making reference to preliminary police investigations, reporting on official investigation documents before hearings have begun, and publishing leaked police information. The European Federation of Journalists also criticized the draft law, stating that journalists are not supposed to reveal confidential information about their sources, whether the source is public or private, and that their sources should be protected. In other words, Berlusconi's draft law is contrary to international conventions and to the case-law of the European Court of Human Rights (Karlekar, 2009).

Tensions between the press and prime minister got even worse in 2009, as Berlusconi repeatedly tried to interfere with journalists' efforts to cover stories about the problems within his private and political life. Berlusconi's private life came under intense scrutiny during the year after his wife filed for divorce and accused him of dallying around with minors. Becoming Italy's first head of the government to take legal action against Italian and European media, Berlusconi sued several foreign newspapers for their coverage of his private life, particularly the claim that he had a sexual relationship with an 18-year-old girl (Faris, 2011). What ensued was a constant back and forth between Berlusconi and the media which brought about disturbing evidence that in a supposedly democratic country, one man can hold so much power both financially and politically that he can have certain media outlets fighting his political battles for him.

Given all these problems and the public's seemingly nonchalant attitudes towards the protection of freedom of the press, the preservation of press freedom is then heavily dependent on the legislation, and some have argued that the history of Italy's media legislation is a strong lesson in what *not* to do. Over the years, the laws regulating the media, particularly television have been progressing very slowly. In fact, even when the legislatures enact laws to control the television industry, the laws are usually more in favor of the interest of political and industrial powerhouses, rather than protective of the public's right to have a system of robust and diverse news sources (Padovani, 2009).

To sum it up, the Italian Constitution does explicitly provide protection for freedom of the press, but the Italian media has never really played the role of an adversarial press that keeps the government in check. Since Berlusconi, a media mogul who became the Prime Minister twice, took office, the problems facing the media, such as heavy concentration of media ownership, have exacerbated further. This is why Italy has one of the lowest rankings in Western Europe in both the Freedom House Index and Reporters Without Frontiers press freedom index.

Four Theories of the Press and Italy: Just like Germany, Italy has gone through quite a few dramatic historical events in the last few decades as well. These significant historical events have impacted the evolutions of the freedom of the press concept over the years. While the idea behind including the freedom of the press clause in the constitution was based on the idea of natural rights, which would indicate that Italy might be leaning towards the libertarian theory, the country has never been willing to allow the media to have a free rein; however, aside from the period during the Mussolini rule when the authoritarian model was adopted, the media in Italy is not heavily controlled by the government either. As such, scholars have maintained that based on the legislations, when it comes to regulating the media, Italy is one of the countries that subscribes to the social responsibility theory today.

United Kingdom

The United Kingdom has a vibrant, aggressive, and rigorous media environment, but it does not have one of the freest press' in Western Europe based on Freedom House's Freedom of the Press index. The United Kingdom was ranked 25th in the world in 2008 and has more or less remained in that spot. In the 2011 index, the United Kingdom was ranked 26th, a placement lower than more than half of the countries in Western Europe. In 2012, its ranking went down to 31st. [35] The country's consistently middle-of-the-pack ranking is due to two things:

1. Journalists in the UK still encounter various obstacles and intimidations when working on stories about Northern Ireland, and
2. Restrictions with regard to national security and combating terrorism (Karlekar & Cook, 2008).)

The United Kingdom is one of the very few countries examined in this book that does *not* have a constitutional guarantee for press freedom. This does not mean that there is no protection for press freedom since the principle of press freedom is manifested in many other aspects of the law. The main reason for the absence of press protection was that unlike many other nations, the UK has no single core constitutional document. In this sense, the UK does not have an

---

[35] See the latest Freedom House Freedom of the Press Index 2011.

actual written constitution, given that much of the British "constitution" is embodied in various other written documents such as statutes, court rulings/opinions, parliamentary constitutional conventions, and treaties (Turpin & Tomkins, 2007).

The concept of press freedom in the United Kingdom originated in the early1600s, and it came from three main people: John Locke, who preferred liberalism, John Milton, and John Stuart Mill. Milton believed that the individual was capable of using reason and distinguishing right from wrong and good from bad. But, in order to be able to exercise this right, the individual must have unfettered and unlimited access to other people's ideas. Milton's influential writings gave birth to the famous concept of the marketplace of ideas, the idea that when people argue against each other, the good and better arguments will win the day (Watkins, 1994) . This freedom, however, was limited and did not apply to what is called seditious libel, and laws were in place that made it a crime to criticize the authorities, as the Royals were deemed to be above public criticism. Furthermore, truth was *not* a defense to seditious libel because the goal was to outlaw and punish all types of criticisms of the government (Negrine, 1994).

According to Watkins, Mill later espoused the idea that an individual should have the right to express himself so long as he does not cause harm to other individuals, and the ideal society is one in which the greatest number of people enjoy the greatest possible amount of happiness (1994). Applying these general principles of liberty to freedom of expression, Mill claimed that if we silence an opinion, there's a possibility that we may silence the truth. The individual freedom of expression is therefore essential to the good of the community/society. He further argued that even if one opinion is false, the truth could be better understood by refuting the error. Since most opinions are neither completely true nor completely false, he believed that granting freedom of expression allowed the airing of competing views was a way to preserve partial truth in various opinions (Watkins, 1994). These liberal teachings---"there should be a marketplace of ideas" and "the best ideas would win out in the end" formed the basis for the concept of freedom of the press in the UK and a few other western countries (Supperstone, 1985).

In the UK, prior to 1855, the press was controlled by the Royals. No one was allowed to print and publish without a special licenses and all presses were subject to regulations issued by an outfit named Star

Chamber. After the Star Chamber was abolished, the Licensing Act was terminated, which left the government without formal control over the press (Supperstone, 1985).; however, that is not to say that there was no indirect control, such as the Newspaper Stamp Duties Act, which lasted until 1855. After 1885, the government played a less and less important role in the newspaper business. A major reason why this came to be was the growth of advertising. How did the growth of advertising lessen the government's influence on the media? The revenues generated by advertising meant that the newspapers no longer needed to depend on government subsidies to survive, which helped distance the press from both the government and political parties (Curren and Seaton, 2009).

The British government is often said to take on a "non-interventionist" approach when it comes to press freedom. After licensing of the press was abolished, anyone could publish newspapers, magazines, and books without state authorization. Additionally, since the media became a highly commerce-oriented business, the press in the UK has been enjoying commercial freedom. The press in the country does not depend on subsidies from the government, which means that the government does not have much influence on the content of the news or how the media business is run (Supperstone, 1985).

Today, based on Hallin and Mancini's (2004) assessment in their famed study on media and politics, the UK media system belongs to the "North-Atlantic/Liberal" model. This means that it has the following characteristics:

1. With the exception of BBC, it is market-driven.
2. A neutral commercial press characterized by internally pluralistic journalism.
3. Professionalization and non-institutionalized self-regulation (Hallin and Mancini, 2004) .

Despite the fact that Hallin and Mancini put the UK and the US under the same category, they also suggested that the UK media system works very differently from the United States media system and functions in a very different cultural and socio-political context (2004). This is perhaps most prominently demonstrated by the differences in the newspaper industy in both countries. In the UK, there is a sharp divide between tabloid newspapers such as *the Sun* and more "respected" newspapers like *the London Times*. Unlike the US tabloids, which are generally looked down upon and confined to supermarket checkout lines, the London tabloids are feared, and they sell more copies than the traditional newspapers. In addition, a clear class divide exists between readers of the tabloids and readers of the traditional newspapers. This kind of culture does not exist in the US, which suggests that there is more consciousness/awareness and uneasiness about the class divide in the United Kingdom (Humphreys, 2009).

Although the United Kingdom does not have an official censorship system, this does not mean that the government did not try more subtle ways to control media content. A prime example was the press' coverage of the sensitive issue of Northern Ireland. Back in the 1980s, when the tense situation between the British government and the Irish Republican Army (IRA) was at its peak, the British government would carefully monitor the media's coverage of this conflict and sometimes even go so far as to invoke Section 11 of the Prevention of Terrorism Act when the reports revealed certain sensitive information the government did not want the IRA to know about (Schlesinger, 1982). In the same vein, in the UK, government restrictions on the media have largely been limited to issues of national security. Statistics have shown that the UK has resorted to using "national security reasons" as an excuse to censor the media more frequently than other Western European countries, primarily due to its still sensitive relationship with Northern Ireland (Humphreys, 2009) .

A prominent hindrance to press freedom in the United Kingdom was the enactment of the Official Secrets Acts, the latest version of which was amended in 1989. This law prevents certain sensitive information from being published, and Supperstone also pointed out that another uniquely British invention was the DA Notice system, known as D Notice system before 1993. This is an official request to news editors not to publish or broadcast items on specified subjects for reasons of national security. D-Notices and DA-notices are only "requests" and not legally enforceable. Consequently, news editors can in theory choose to ignore them; however, they are generally complied with by the media (Supperstone, 1985) . This system received a lot of criticism since its inception. The major complaint was that it is a form of censorship used by the government to suppress information for political instead of national security reasons. Despite the criticism, there are still five standing DA notices today (Humphreys, 2009).

Another unfortunate development is the heavy concentration of media ownership. In 2003, the British government enacted a new communication law, the 2003 Communication Act, to regulate electronic media. The most controversial aspect of this new statute is the loosening of media ownership rules, which makes it easier for media conglomerates to own multiple media outlets. The rationale for this deregulation is mostly financially driven, with the argument that this was needed to promote economic efficiency and to establish a foundation to build up the performance of the UK media industry. Ultimately, this new statute would seem to have left very little room for the government to control the increasing occurrence of the mergers of two giant media companies (Humphreys, 2009). Fortunately, recently, the British government introduced an amendment to the Act, which is a "plurality test" provision, that could remedy the problem. Under this new provision, whenever a media merger is about to occur, the Secretary of State has the power to block the merger if he/she decides that there is not sufficient plurality of people with control of media outlets or diversity of content. Additionally, the Office of Communication (Ofcom) is now required to review ownership patterns in the UK at three-year intervals and to report on other relevant issues.[36]

The persistent tabloid-obsessed media culture could prove to be the downfall of press freedom in the UK as well. The UK has a very vibrant and influential tabloid industry, which commands just as much attention from the public and the government as their more respected counterparts. This is mainly due to the British mentality that people in the public eye are fair game for entrapment and muckraking, which is what the tabloids specialize in. Unlike the U.S. press, which is protected by the First Amendment, even though true restrictions of the media are few and far between, the British media is periodically forced to combat threats that restrict their freedoms by legislation (Mayer, 2011). This has caused the journalists to be more pugnacious, especially since the British legal system placed the burden of proof in

---

[36] See more on how it works on the Office of Communication official website. Retrieved from http://stakeholders.ofcom.org.uk/market-data-research/media-ownership-research/rulesreview/

libel cases on the media defendant rather than the plaintiff.[37] With newspapers under constant pressure to provide incontrovertible documentary evidence to back up their stories, intrusion of privacy seems a safer bet than risking defamation suits, and the temptation is to resort to surveillance, phone hacking, or email hacking. This sordid practice finally came out in the open in July 2011, when the No. 1 UK tabloid *News of the World*, owned by the Murdoch Family, was forced to shut down amid allegations that the paper had a long-standing practice of criminally invading people's privacy to get juicy and salacious stories (Mayer, 2011). This scandal could potentially lead to the government taking a firmer stand on stricter regulations on the media.

In its latest annual report, Freedom House concluded that with a history of aggressive reporting and an editorially independent public broadcaster, the United Kingdom has maintained its open media environment in the last few years. The law provides for freedom of the press, and the government generally respects this right in practice; however, several laws that weaken press freedom remain in place. Under legislation enacted in the 1980s, journalists considered to have information vital to a police investigation could be forced to present this evidence at trial (Karlekar & Cook, 2008)). Nevertheless, in a landmark ruling in June 2009, a court in Belfast, Northern Ireland, dismissed a police application to force journalist Suzanne Breen to hand over materials she had received from a member of a paramilitary group, the Real IRA, who had taken credit for the murder of two British soldiers in March of that year. The International Federation of Journalists hailed the court's decision as a highly significant victory in the journalists' fight for the protection of sources (Karlekar, 2010).

To summarize, the three British philosophers, John Locke, John Milton, and John Stuart Mill, were the pioneers for freedom of the press, but due to the fragmented nature of the Constitution of the United Kingdom, press freedom was not actually included in it. Instead, laws that protect this freedom were spread out in various other statutes, court opinions, and treatises. For the most part, press freedom conditions in the UK are satisfactory, although several laws were set up in recent years that could prove to be hurdles for journalists who would like to publish information that is considered to be sensitive to national

---

[37] The libel law in the UK will be discussed in a later chapter.

security. Additionally, with the recent *News of the World* scandal, the unlawful practices of some of the tabloids in the UK may force the government to enact new laws that restrict press freedom.

Four Theories of the Press and the United Kingdom: Both the authoritarian theory and the libertarian theory claim their roots in the United Kingdom. During the 16th and 17th century, the UK took an authoritarian approach to regulate the media under the rule of the monarchs, with licensing requirements and censorship in play. After 1688, the three philosophers had introduced the ideas of individualism and natural rights, which are major components of the libertarian theory; however, censorship in one form or another and media regulations has always existed in the United Kingdom, so one can argue that true libertarianism was never achieved in the country. These days, most scholars categorize the UK as embracing the social responsibility theory when it comes to media law.

ASIA

In the following section, the constitutional protections for freedom of the press in every Asian country, plus Hong Kong and Taiwan is discussed. A short history of the development of press freedom in these countries is included. Since every country has its own unique story, every one of them is discussed individually.

India

According to Freedom House's most recent Freedom of the Press index, among the Asian countries discussed in this book, India is ranked 80th. This is not an especially high placement but it is by far the freest in South Asia.[38] The ranking has not changed that much in the last few years, generally holding steady in the range of 70 and 80.

To understand the reasons behind the constitutional protection for freedom of the press in India, it is essential to looks at India's colonial past. India's turbulent political history played an influential part in how the country developed, including the growth of the media. Mass media laws in India have a long history and are deeply rooted in the country's colonial experience under British rule. The earliest regulatory measures

---

[38] See the 2012 Freedom House Freedom of the Press Index.

can be traced back to 1799 when Lord Wellesley promulgated the *Press Regulations*, which imposed pre-censorship on the fledging newspaper publishing industry. Decades later, in 1835, the *Press Act* was enacted, which undid most of the repressive features of earlier legislations on the subject (Kalhan, 2006) .

Then, as in many countries before it, the licensing requirement for the print press was created. In June 1857, the government passed the 'Gagging Act', which among various other things, introduced compulsory licensing for the owning or running of printing presses. This new law empowered the government to prohibit the publication or circulation of any newspaper, book, or other printed material and banned the publication or dissemination of statements or news stories which had a tendency to cause dismay or anger towards the government (Kalhan, 2006). Like other Asian countries that have a similar past, it was clear that the Indian government wanted to keep a tight leash on the press out of fear that unflattering reports on the government and government officials would weaken their authority.

After the enactments of a few other media-related laws such as *Press and Registration of Books Ac*t and the *Vernacular Press Act of 1878*, and following its independence from the United Kingdom, India was finally ready to officially recognize the importance of freedom of the press (Srinivasan, 1998). For the press freedom advocates in India, the most significant day in the history of media regulations was the 26th of January 1950, which was the day on which the official Indian Constitution came into force (Kalhan, 2006). Years of British occupation and the repressive colonial experience, which allowed the Indians very little freedom to speak their minds, made them realize the crucial significance of the concept of freedom of the press. As Kalhan argued, the fact that British citizens could enjoy press freedom while they had no such right under British rule only further served to cement the importance of press freedom in their minds (2006). Such freedom was therefore incorporated into the constitution and was intended to empower the press to disseminate knowledge to the masses (Kalhan, 2006). The Constituent Assembly then decided to safeguard freedom of the press as a fundamental right. Although the Indian Constitution does not mention the liberty of the press or even the word "press," it is evident that the freedom of the press is included in the freedom of speech and expression under Article 19(1)(a), which reads, "all citizens shall have the right to freedom of speech and expression."[39] It is, however, worth mentioning that such freedom is not absolute. Instead, it is qualified by certain clearly defined limitations under Article 19(2) in the interests of the public.[40] Specifically, this provision enables the legislature to impose reasonable restrictions on free speech when the content of the speech is considered to pose a danger to the following:

1. Security of the State.
2. Friendly relations with foreign States.
3. Public order.
4. Decency and morality.
5. Contempt of court.
6. Defamation: Clause (2) of Article 19 prevents any person from making any statement that injures the reputation of another. With the same view, defamation has been criminalized in India, the regulations of which could be found in Section 499 of the India Penal Code.
7. Incitement to an offence.
8. Sovereignty and integrity of India

As the provision states, only "reasonable" restrictions are allowed and those reasonable restrictions can be imposed only by a duly enacted law and not by executive action.

The development of freedom of the press in India was not a smooth ride. In fact, for the first half-century of its independence, media control by the state was a major constraint on press freedom. As Mehta pointed out, like other newly independent countries at the time, the Indian government wanted to make sure the media did not publish any materials that could jeopardize the fledging regime, and some government officials did not have a problem expressing that sentiment publicly (1979). For instance, Indira Gandhi famously stated in 1975 that the radio broadcaster All India Radio was the Government's mouthpiece and would remain so for the foreseeable future. As further evidence of her view on the media at the time came out, Indira Gandhi's reign resulted in a huge setback for press freedom in India. By declaring a state of emergency in 1975 in the face of mounting

---

[39] See Constitution of India, Article 19(1)(a).

[40] See Constitution of India, Article 19(2).

accusations of government misconduct, the Indian government effectively suspended all basic rights, including freedom of expression, and a censorship apparatus was promptly set up to control media content (Singh, 1980). Gandhi's justification for the repression of the Indian mass media was based on three major assumptions: 1) Economic productivity and social justice are more important than civil liberties and freedom of expression; 2) The press in India was acting in a manner that seriously hindered the state in its efforts to promote economic productivity and social justice; and 3) A drastic contraction of civil liberties and press rights will advance the state's ability to promote those social causes (Mehta, 1979) .

Some scholars have commented that India's struggle to maintain a sense of press freedom cannot be entirely blamed on Indira Gandhi. They argued that there was an "intrinsic weakness" in the media system and philosophy. More specifically, they believed that the Indian mass media system had already suffered from the following four flaws: 1) a lack of well-defined national mass communication philosophy and policies, 2) a lack of public awareness on the importance of a free mass media in a democratic process of nation building, 3) diffidence of commitment on the part of publishers and editors to oppose relentless attacks by the government, and 4) mass media's dependence on the government for newsprint and advertising, which is its way of controlling the media (Singh, 1980) .

This was a somewhat surprising development because the press participated vigorously in fighting against British rule and later became the main instrument for Indian social reformers and nationalists to gain national independence (Arvind& Rogers, 1989). The early philosophy of the press, thus, was based on a definite and concrete cause: to gain national freedom.

Although the press system has developed significantly since its early days, it has failed to adapt a cohesive philosophy and principles that are vital to maintaining its own goals and tradition. In its absence, the Indian press system was left vulnerable to governmental intrusion and unable to maintain its freedom and responsibility. The lack of a well-defined overarching national mass communication philosophy and policies, therefore, has resulted in very little public support for a strong mass media system in India (Kalhan, 2006) .

Ordinary people in India did not care enough about press freedom, some have argued. Since its inception, the Indian mass media have been tuned to the needs of a small group of intellectual elite rather than the masses of the people, as Kalhan argued (2006). This has also contributed to a weak support by the Indian public for a free and responsible mass media system. Since the Indian mass media has been the playground for the intellectual set, there is little surprise that the media failed to gain much significant public support to battle against Indira Gandhi's press censorship (Kalhan, 2006).

The fault, however, does not lie on the Indian mass media as much as it does on the government with regard to a lack of national mass communication policies, as Singh argued (1980). The Indian government, in the name of planned social and economic development, has made the Indian mass media over-dependent on governmental decisions. This, consequently, has made the media vulnerable to manipulations by the people in political power. Indira Gandhi's successful control of the mass media was a prime example (, 1980); however, the status of press freedom in India has improved in the last couple of decades. With the liberalization starting in the 1990s, private control of media has burgeoned, leading to an increased independence and greater scrutiny of government. Organizations like CNN-IBN, NDTV, and Times Now have been particularly influential in their reports, bringing about the resignations of some very powerful political figures. Courts have also held that prohibiting newspapers from publishing their own views or the views of news correspondents on any topic was a serious encroachment on the freedom of speech and expression (Kohli, 2006). Furthermore, Kohli also pointed out that laws like the Prasar Bharati Act passed in 1997, provides greater autonomy for the media and contributed significantly to reducing the control of the press by the government (2006).

An important aspect of this freer press is the ability to scrutinize and criticize the government. Mere criticism of the government no longer automatically amounts to sedition. If it was not calculated to undermine the respect for the government in such a way as to make people cease to obey it, it could lead to anarchy (Kalhan, 2006).

Overall, India experienced long periods of press oppression. First, in the hands of the British and then in its own newly formed government, under the control of Indira Gandhi, who was instrumental in curbing press freedom when the country was trying to build itself following its independence. Scholars have argued that the lack of a cohesive mass media philosophy has contributed to the country's very modest press freedom condition; however, in the last two decades or so, there has been improvements within press freedom in India, with more and more privatizations of media companies, which freed the media from strict government control.

Four Theories of the Press and India: Although India does have constitutional protection for press freedom in the vein of libertarian tradition, in the last few decades the Indian government attempted to install various authoritarian legal restrictions to control the press, including the law that required the publisher accused of publishing "objectionable matter" to deposit a security bond. (Siebert, 1956.) These days, control over the media has been much tamer than in the not-so-distant past, and although India's press freedom ranking has not been particularly high, scholars have noticed that the philosophy behind the country's media regulations have been moving towards the social responsibility theory.

Singapore

Although Singapore is an economically robust country, to this day the government maintains a firm control over its citizens in many aspects of their lives. The fierce regulations of its press were put into place early on and the government still has the final say as to how the media should behave. In fact, Singapore routinely receives one of the lowest ratings in the Freedom House's Freedom of the press index. In 2008, it was ranked 153 out of 195 countries, tying with Iraq (Karlekar & Cook, 2008).) In the 2011 report, it was still tied with Iraq, albeit with a slightly higher ranking standing at 150.[41]In the latest report that came out in 2012, Singapore was still ranked 150th. [42] Consequently, Singapore's press control regime has attracted persistent criticisms from international organizations for constraining the press from freely reporting on news as they see fit.

---

[41] SeeFreedom House Freedom of the Press 2011: Global Press Freedom Ranking, http://freedomhouse.org/images/File/fop/2011/FOTP2011GlobalRegionalTables.pdf.

[42] See the Freedom House of 2012 ranking at http://www.freedomhouse.org/sites/default/files/Global%20and%20Regional%20Press%20Freedom%20Rankings.pdf

The clause regarding freedom of speech and expression in the Constitution of Singapore was modeled after the Indian Constitution. Just like the Indian Constitution, the Constitution of the Republic of Singapore does not outwardly provide for freedom of the press. Article 14 (1) (a) of the Constitution of the Republic of Singapore guarantees that "every citizen of Singapore has the right to freedom of speech and expression" without explicitly mentioning the word "press." [43] In practice, this provision is interpreted in a very narrow way. Furthermore, to compound the problems for the press in Singapore, numerous measures approved by the legislative and administrative branches of the government were designed to restrain the press and limit the scope of press freedom (Tey, 2008). Generally, under the constitution, the government can impose restrictions it considers necessary to protect the following:

1. The security interest of Singapore.
2. Friendly relations with other countries.
3. Public order.
4. Morality.
5. The privileges of Parliament.
6. The provision against contempt of court, defamation, or incitement to any offence (Tan, 2005).

These restrictions make freedom of the press in Singapore much weaker, than the United States, where the First Amendment to the Constitution says that "Congress shall make no law" abridging press freedom (Tan, 2005). It is also safe to say that the government of Singapore is not afraid to show the journalists exactly who is in control. The history of press freedom in Singapore is littered with woeful tales of arrests of journalists and the shutting down of newspapers for publishing stories that the government did not deem appropriate. Also, the government does not hesitate to insert government officials or former officials into management positions within newspaper companies (Tey, 2008). Given these facts, typical criticisms of the state of press freedom in Singapore reference the following:

1. The prominence of government stories.

---

[43] See the Constitution of the Republic of Singapore, Art. 14 (1) (a).

2. The pro-government stance taken by columnists.
3. The presence of a number of former government officials occupying high ranks in the media business (Hoong, 1998).

To the government in Singapore, the sole purpose of the constitution is to safeguard national interest and well-being of the citizens. To that end, one of the duties of the government was to prevent the newspapers from being used as instruments for rebellion, a sentiment that has been echoed by just about every member of the government (Hoong, 1998).

It should be pointed out that restrictive legislation regulating the local press has always been a part of Singapore's legislative history. The press has been regulated under the Printing Presses Ordinance (and later the Printing Presses Act) since 1920. Singapore has since developed and maintained an elaborate system of press ownership as a result of events in which the government had taken coercive actions against some of the newspapers (Tey, 2008).

Given its reputation of having a highly restricted press, one might be surprised to know that when Singapore first became independent from British rule in 1959, the country actually had a wide variety of independent newspapers that were free to criticize and scrutinize the government's actions and policies with little intervention (Wong, 2001)). This changed after 1961 when the leading party in Singapore, the People's Action Party (PAP) decided to solidify its power (Rodan, 2000).

The most important step toward a regime of total media control the PAP took was amending the Newspapers and Printing Presses Act (NPPA) in 1974. Essentially, this amendment allowed the government to own newspapers. By creating two different kinds of stock for newspaper companies, the government could gain complete control of the news industry by inserting their preferred candidates into management positions within these companies (Rodan, 2000).

To understand why "press freedom" was not a particularly treasured right in Singapore, one has to discuss the Singaporean concept of freedom of the press and the historical development of the country. The historical explanation as to why freedom of the press was not considered a fundamental right in the constitution had to do with long periods of foreign rule in the region until 1959. During the foreign rule period, the PAP felt that the newspapers did not support the independence movement. Instead, the papers relentlessly attacked the party, which severely soured the PAP on the notion of press freedom (Tey, 2008). The country's turbulent past with the British and Malaysian's also explains the reason behind some of the harsher punishments imposed on the press. Back in the 70s, the situation between Singapore and Malaysia could be characterized as constant outbreaks of racial and communist violence. During that period, Singapore still had a tense relationship with Malaysia, from whom Singapore formally separated in 1965. It also did not help the relationship between the two countries that the Communist Party of Malaysia followed the Chinese Cultural Revolution by actively becoming visible again. Additionally, aside from the political complexities, another reason for the exclusion is that the PAP believed that freedom of the press was not an individual freedom, since the press is an institution, not an individual (Hoong, 1998).

The long-time chief of the nation and supreme leader of Singapore, Lee Kuan Yew, often commented on the issue of press freedom in Singapore. Over the years, Lee had stated that the western model for press freedom is not the only model because media in different countries play different roles, which grew out of their different historical experiences, political systems, and national temperaments (Tey, 2008) . He also said that mass media should reinforce instead of undermine the cultural values and social attitudes of Singapore. More importantly, press freedom must play second fiddle to the overriding needs of the integrity of Singapore (Hoong, 1998).

Lee stated that the model for media Singapore should imitate is the Japanese model, which was staying out of partisan politics, but also making an effort to shape public opinion to help build up a national consensus on important issues (Hoong, 1998). One can also claim that Singapore, like several other Asian countries, subscribes to Asian values/Asian Model for press freedom, which is the notion that the press needs to play a positive social role, and that journalists should be more respectful and deferential to-authority (Trilling, 2010). Under this model, the press is an ally, not an adversary of the government and the journalists are "partners" with government officials in building up the nation. In that respect, the Singaporean model more resembles the social responsibility model under Siebert's four theories of the press (1956).

The Singapore government has always held a pragmatic, or practical, approach to governance. In the minds of the Singaporean politicians and policy makers, it is more important to build the nation economically and maintain its effective leadership than granting the press the freedom to report the news with a critical eye. In fact, the role of the press in the eyes of politicians, is to serve an active, participatory, and responsible role of contributing to the strong nation-building model in Singapore. Government officials have always been keenly aware of the strong influence the press could wield and therefore took the view that only through a responsible press will the task of nation-building be successfully utilized in Singapore (Tey, 2008). In other words, the main goal of the press, according to the government, is to conduct simple and straightforward journalism and reporting.

As Tey pointed out, one important method the government in Singapore utilizes to control the media is through the restrictions on media ownership (2008). To have the government's permission to run a newspaper the press must accept the subordinate role given by the government. It cannot be controlled by any individuals or corporations, and it cannot exercise its own editorial independence. It is allowed to report mistakes, corruption, and be critical of some policies, but it is not allowed to ridicule or lampoon the political leadership and erode the public respect for elected office holders or the political leadership. Some issues regarded as fundamental by the government cannot be contradicted by opinion columns in the press. The press must also play its role as the channel for marshaling and readjusting the political attitude of the population. The press has to be an effective communication tool for the executive branch and must be able to clearly convey the government's messages to the masses and engage the public in the conversations on what the government wants the citizens to have (Tey, 2008).

While the government does have an iron grip on the media industry and adopts a press freedom philosophy that is miles apart from the western countries', the government is not the only driving force in the media industry. Newspapers in Singapore generally publish the stories that clearly echo the point of view of the government. Some journalists flat-out rejected the western notion that all newspapers should be anti-establishment watchdogs for the government. They believed that the media should focus on helping a society get organized in a time of great change instead of subscribing to the western notion of press freedom and letting the press undermine the government's effort to build a nation. This is partially due to the fact that the leaders in the newspaper industry in Singapore are the ones who previously served in the government, and journalists are often recruited by the government to work in parliament or the cabinet (Hoong, 1998) . Naturally, this makes it more likely that the press would censor itself so that their reports would not embarrass the government or seem contradictory to the policies advocated by officials.

The fact that Singapore enjoys a strong economy and was one of the countries least effected by the 1997 financial crisis, proved to the leaders of Singapore that they have the right attitude towards freedom of the press. Singapore's government officials would argue that the very impressive economic development in the last few decades was a result of the government's tight control over all forms of media (Rodan, 2000).

Another aspect of press freedom that needs to be addressed is the treatment of foreign press in Singapore. Specifically, foreign media in Singapore are subject to many of the same pressures and restrictive laws as domestic outlets. In March 2009, *Wall Street Journal* editor Melanie Kirkpatrick was found guilty of contempt of court for two articles and an editorial published in the *Wall Street Journal Asia* in 2008. She was ordered to pay a fine of SG$10,000, which came to about US$6,600 (Tey, 2008). Even the revered *Time* magazine suffered the punishment of decreased quota for circulation when it printed a story that was not to the liking of the government. The foreign publications and foreign journalists in Singapore constantly face the fear of being accused by the government of "engaging in the domestic politics of Singapore" simply by publishing stories that were not flattering to the officials of Singapore. So far, the government in Singapore has interpreted the term of "engaging in the domestic politics of Singapore" very broadly (Rodan, 2000). In short, as long as the news stories are related to political, social, and economic policies of the government, they would be considered to be engaging in the domestic politics of Singapore. Under this broad interpretation, if the foreign press imposes their own ideas of press freedom in their reporting without understanding the nature of the Singaporean society, that would qualify. As Rodan pointed out, these foreign publishers and journalists are constantly threatened with deportation and a decrease in circulation of their publications (2000).

In short, it is obvious that the Singaporean government does not share the same view on press freedom and the need for openness and transparency as their western counterparts. In fact, the PAP wanted to avoid the competitive politics common in other democratic countries. The government controlled the media industry directly and indirectly by media ownership, management, and also regulations (Tey, 2008) . With political, regulatory, and structural control over the media by the government, the journalists and reporters have a somewhat curtailed freedom to objectively report on the news, especially unflattering news about the government.[44] Furthermore, the government uses draconian statutes to control the media, and sometimes stifles dissenting voices in the press by accusing the media of libel, defamation, or contempt of court (Rodan, 2000) . Generally speaking, there is censorship in Singapore, but aside from the usual norm of banning obscenity, the government is mainly concerned with the comments voiced by the opposition (Hoong, 1998) .

All of these unfortunately led to an absence of press freedom and diversity in the press in Singapore (Rodan, 2000). This also means that as a result of the heavy restrictions and the threat of lawsuits, there is a very prevalent practice of self-censorship among journalists in Singapore (Tey, 2008). The same oppressive environment also applied to the Internet. Though Singaporeans generally have unrestricted access to the Internet, it is monitored by the government and subject to the same laws as traditional media (Karlekar & Cook, 2008).

In summary, the press in Singapore enjoys very little freedom to do their jobs. The government in Singapore, subscribing to the idea of press being a supporter of the authorities instead of a critic, views the media as a tool to help build the nation and imposes heavy restrictions on the press. Given all the existent evidence, there is no indication that this will change any time soon.

Four Theories of the Press and Singapore: As noted earlier, the Singaporean constitution, including the freedom of expression clause contained inside it, was influenced by the Indian constitution, which in turn was influenced by the United Kingdom. This means that the freedom of expression clause has its roots in the libertarian theory.

---

[44] See James Gomez's 2005 report on "Freedom of Expression and the Media in Singapore", which was part of a series of baseline studies on seven Southeast Asian countries.

Some of the more recent media legislations are considered to follow the social responsibility theory; however, given how tightly the government in Singapore is controlling the media, there is a strong argument to be made that the country is adhering to the authoritarian theory when it comes to media laws.

South Korea

According to Freedom House's most recent Freedom of the Press index in 2012, among the Asian countries discussed in this book, South Korea is ranked 68th.[45] This is a drop from its ranking in previous years. For the first time in years, South Korea is classified as a country that has a "partially free" press. This is related to a number of events suggesting that the government was attempting to curb critical media, including increased state censorship (Lee, 2011). Legislation to deregulate media ownership was passed in 2009, potentially allowing large conservative newspaper companies to take over progressive broadcast outlets that tend to be critical of the current president Lee Myung-bak's administration (Karlekar, 2010).

South Korea's recent decline in press freedom even caught the attention of the United Nations. Frank La Rue, the U.N. Special Rapporteur for Freedom of Opinion and Expression, announced that the government under President Lee severely curtailed the freedom of expression in South Korea (Karlekar, 2010).

Despite this recent setback for the press, South Korea does, at least on paper, have protection for freedom of the press. In South Korea, freedom of the press is *explicitly* guaranteed under the constitution. South Korea's constitution provides for both freedom of speech and the press as fundamental rights; however, aside from giving all citizens the right of freedom of the press, and providing that licensing or censorship of speech "shall not be recognized," Article 21 of the South Korean Constitution also states that neither "speech nor press shall violate the honor or rights of other persons or undermine public morals or social ethics." Freedom of the press in Korea is similar to other basic rights. In other words, freedom of the press in South Korea is not at a superior level to other basic rights (Sa, 2009).

---

[45] See Freedom House Freedom of the Press Index, 2012 for a detailed ranking.

Korean laws are heavily influenced by foreign laws. Korean media laws combine the Anglo-American free press model and the European model, especially Germany's. On one hand, similar to the First Amendment of the United States Constitution, the Korean Constitution guarantees freedom of the press. On the other hand, Korean media laws are more similar to German laws since they both elaborate more on the concept of media and publication and what the media can or cannot do (Choi, 2005). For example, Korean laws stipulate that the media cannot defame other people, or abuse public morals and social ethics. In other words, compared to the First Amendment of the United States Constitution, which is a closed system that stipulates that there should be no law to restrict freedom of the press, the freedom of the press clause in the South Korean constitution guarantees an open system. This means it is possible to create laws to guarantee freedom of the press but also to regulate the media (Park, 2004).

Like several other Asian countries, South Korea has a history of long periods of foreign rule, which has a huge impact on the country's subsequent development, including the creation of laws. Several decades of Japanese rule, American military rule, and military dictatorships have influenced the Korean society and the media politically, economically, socially, and culturally (Park, 2004). Because of this chaotic history, the Korean government has consistently tried to control the media. Throughout the last few decades of Korea's history, it has experienced the brutal Japanese rule, a long period of military dictatorship, and severe poverty and famine caused by the Korean War. As a result of the constant chaos, the Korean government came to view the media as a potentially disruptive force that the developing, unstable, and still insecure nation could not afford to have (Sa, 2009). With no historical tradition of democratic principles in Korea until 1987, the Korean press did not have the opportunity to flourish according to the principles of press freedom long recognized by the West. Some have claimed that because the country does not have a historical tradition of democratic principles the very idea of press freedom is nothing more than a "superficial imposition of a foreign idea which completely lacks indigenous institutional support" (du Mars, 2000).

South Korea's transformation from a mostly authoritarian regime to a blossoming democracy was complete in 1987 reflected by the remarkable change of its new media to a libertarian system (du Mars, 2000). Many factors have contributed to this transformation, with sociopolitical, institutional, and economic forces driving the South Korean press towards becoming a truly free and democratic institution (Youm, 2002). The South Korean government itself had engaged in several legal reforms, including media law reforms, since the 1980s to move the country from a repressive nation to a country that embraced liberalism. The South Korean courts have also played an essential role in this area. The South Korean Constitutional Court's activist view of freedom of expression as a right for all citizens has turned South Korea into a far more participatory democracy (du Mars, 2000). Furthermore, judicial review in general has broadened the notions of freedom of speech and press as constitutional rights in South Korea.

Kim Young Sam, the first non-military president who took office in 1993, recognized the Korean press' contribution to achieving democratic progress in Korea and in fact declared that freedom of the press was the most important goal in achieving true democratization in the country because a free press is the cornerstone of democratization, as Youm noted (1998). However, it should be pointed out that Kim's concept of freedom of the press was based on the "cooperative," not adversarial relationship between the press and the government that is very common in the western world. He prefers a "guided press" to a watchdog press (Youm, 1998).

In recent years, statutory reform and judicial review have combined to produce a more robust and vibrant freedom of the press in South Korea. Laws such as the Public information Disclosure Act and Election Act allow the press to enjoy substantial access to government documents and proceedings, which in turn afford the press the opportunity to keep an eye on the government and inform the public when somebody in the government has abused his/her power. Additionally, the courts in South Korea have established a "right to know" law, which afford the press a wide range of access to official proceedings (Youm, 1998).

There are several issues in terms of press freedom in South Korea. A major problem with journalism in South Korea is that the journalists play a more passive role and do not go out to search for news. Instead, Youm argued that they have a very comfortable relationship with the government and simply publish whatever information the government offers them without much probing and investigating (2002). When the journalists do criticize and question certain government policies, it is usually because the public is already expressing doubts and concerns.

This is a demonstration of the fact that it is actually acceptable that journalists only put forth the minimum effort in their reporting (Youm, 2002).

Another problem with press freedom in South Korea is the cozy relationship between big businesses and the journalists. Due to the existence of this too-close relationship, the journalists' reports are often biased towards these businesses (du Mars, 2000). This is a problem that exists in many other countries.

Scholars have commented that the ideologically weak media industry was the product of both the country's cultural traditions and decades of Japanese colonial and subsequent military rule. The combination of years of totalitarianism and Koreans' devotion to Confucianism have instilled the need to submit to pressure from authority figures and maintain a sense of harmony and consensus in the society in the journalists (du Mars, 2000).

In regards to taboo subjects for the press, North Korea is still a sensitive subject and the No. 1 reason journalists might get into trouble. Even after the country became firmly democratic in 1988, there were still direct and indirect restrictions on freedom of the press because of their incredibly tense relationship with North Korea. Specifically, the Agency for National Security Planning (ANSP), was set up in part to monitor the press' activities. Most notably, the ANSP maintains guidelines on media coverage of North Korea. Now, even though the media coverage of North Korea has increased and diversified since 1987, news stories on North Korea are still selectively published and ideologically manipulated. In fact, the primary source of information on North Korea is still the Naeoe News Agency, which is operated by the ANSP Because of this, to report on the North-South relations, the Korean press often has to rely on the information provided by this Agency because the National Security Act bans South Korean journalists from directly contacting North Korean sources without prior authorization (Sa, 2009).

All things considered, after decades of foreign and military rule marked by tight media control, journalists are free to report on whatever they like. Before it became a true democratic country in 1987, South Korea went through decades of strict censorship where media was simply a mouthpiece for the government. After the repeal of the strict Basic Press Law, censorship had basically disappeared from the statutes, and as long as the journalists stay away from stories that can be construed as pro-North Korea, they can basically write whatever they want without having to worry about being put in jail; however, the government still requests private meetings with journalists if the journalists publish stories that portray the government in a negative light (du Mars, 2000) . Recent developments also indicated that the press freedom in South Korea, a country that does not have a strong foundation for this concept, is declining, mainly due to President Lee's antagonistic relationship with the press.

Four Theories of the Press and South Korea: South Korea modeled its constitutional protection for press freedom after German law, but before 1987, the country was governed by either foreign powers or strong military men, who ruled the country, and by extension its media, under an authoritarian regime. While there are still certain restrictions placed on the media, especially when it comes to reportage on North Korea, the media laws in South Korea are now generally designed to improve the country and better the political discourse. Therefore, the general consensus among scholars is that the country is now following the social responsibility theory.

Japan

Japan has been receiving a total score of 20 or 21 on the Freedom House index for the last five years. While this is still a very good showing, Japan's score has regressed since the early 2000s when it was usually between 17 or 18; however, even with a placement of 37 on the index, Japan still had the highest ranking in East Asia in 2012.[46] Freedom House rated Japan as having a press-friendly legal environment and an economic environment conducive to freedom of the press, but it also concluded that Japan has a relatively poor showing when it comes to its political climate's effect on press freedom.

In Japan, freedom of the press is guaranteed in their constitution. Namely, Article 21 of Chapter 3: Rights and Duties of the People provides, "Freedom of assembly and association as well as speech, press and all other forms of expression are guaranteed." Furthermore, this provision also specifically mentioned censorship. Namely, "No censorship shall be maintained, nor shall the secrecy of any means of communication be violated." It should be noted that despite the

---

[46] See Freedom House Freedom of the Press Index 2012.

language, this clause does not mean that censorship is completely abolished in Japan, nor does it mean that there were no other statutes that place limitations on the press.

The protection for press freedom did not always appear in the Japanese constitution. In fact, prior to 1889 Japan did not have a written constitution that mentioned the press. The first written constitution arose from a group of leaders who had a vision of how to modernize Japan but little tolerance for any opposing voices or political activities. The Meiji Constitution of 1889 was modeled on the German constitution and defined the boundaries of freedom of expression (de Lange, 1998). De Lange also pointed out that early regular publications first appeared in the 1860s, and only in the next few decades did they evolve into newspapers, which were beholden to powerful politicians and their parties (1998). The emergence of militarism, which led to Japan's active role in WWII, was characterized by the stifling of free expression in general and dissident expression (Ourvan, 2002). Thus, it is not surprising to learn that during World War II, the press mostly served as the government's propaganda organs. Some scholars believed that this experience made the Japanese press determined not to repeat the errors of the past, and that this history provides the genuinely Japanese justification of free expression (Horibe, 1985).

Immediately following World War II, the Allied Forces led by the American General McArthur occupied Japan for a few years. During this period, the American's started to enforce a very comprehensive censorship system (Horibe, 1985). Some scholars, such as Eto, even argued that the Americans helped the Japanese write a new constitution (1982). Under this influence, the new constitution guaranteed press freedom, and the Japanese mass media adopted the libertarian model; however, the Japanese press should not be considered a model of the western libertarian press theory, as Eto pointed out (1982).

That is because the Japanese is heavily influenced by Confucianism. According to the ancient Chinese educator, people should seek to create social harmony by envisioning a strict hierarchical society based upon key family relationships that defined everyone's role and impose enormous moral pressure on individuals to conform to their roles (Winfield et al., 2000). The success of this idea depends on respect for authority.

Fundamental to this system of hierarchy is the idea of knowing one's place. The Japanese reliance on order is in stark contrast to the

American faith in freedom and equality. Instead of championing the need of having to question the authority, Japan's confidence in hierarchy is central in the country's whole notion of man's relation to his fellow man and of man's relation to the State (Winfield et al., 2000). This philosophy shaped the concept of freedom of the press for the Japanese.

Although deeply rooted in Asian values, the Japanese are not afraid to embrace some changes. The post-war press system, imported and based on western liberal philosophy, has become successful in Japan. The acceptance of some infusion of western ideas and the adoption of a more democratic Japanese Constitution after the war, however, did not necessarily eliminate the long-standing Confucian and Buddhist values and customs at a practical level. Hierarchy and harmony remain highly valued, and conflicts are usually resolved without having to resort to litigations and lawsuits. In other words, even though modern Japan holds freedom of expression and freedom of the press in high regards, the societal restraints imposed by Asian values seem more important than legal restrictions (Winfield et al., 2000). Despite the introduction of the new constitution and new journalism concepts, these new ideas ultimately did not and could not eliminate the inherent cultural, social, and ethical uniqueness of Japanese society. As in any other country, Japanese interpersonal and mass communications reflect the cultural values of its society (Takeichi, 1997).

In line with the more conservative Asian values, the Japanese press takes a different approach to the selection of news coverage. Although constitutionally independent, the Japanese media are not as aggressive in their coverage of the government as the western press is, which is also the result of the nation's traditions of collectivism and hierarchy (Winfield et al., 2000). Journalists in Japan accept the social responsibility to oversee the wrongdoing of those who hold power, but the press-government relationship in Japan, at the very least, is less adversarial than that of western democratic nations, as Takeichi noted (1997). Many have noticed that the press and other types of media in Japan are not known for their harsh criticism and have argued that the spirit of criticism in the press toward governmental powers is not very strong (Takeichi, 1997). The major news media in Japan are often restrained when reporting critically on governmental conduct or on the affairs of the royal family, and this type of self-regulation and self-censorship is a mechanism that is constantly working in the Japanese media (Horibe, 1985). The custom of self-regulation, according to media law professors in Japan, is based upon a type of social control, not overt punishment, as media self-regulation originated from fear of the authorities (Winfield et al., 2000).

The Japanese press has enjoyed a high degree of freedom since the end of World War II and the media has thrived in a booming economy. Japan has vigorous and free media and boasts the highest daily newspaper circulation per capita in the world (Karlekar & Cook, 2008).) Many national dailies have circulations topping one million and often produce both morning and evening editions; however, there are still troublesome issues that haunt the status of press freedom in Japan. These concerns mainly regard the lack of diversity and independence in reporting, especially in political news.

The major culprit of this problem is the existence of a "press club" system called *kishakurabu*, in which major media outlets have close relationships with bureaucrats and politicians. What is problematic is that reporters are inclined to depend on the press clubs with which they are affiliated as the main venue for news-gathering. Once the clubs decide on a story, all of the members will report on the agreed-club-sanctioned story without investigation. This leads to a decline in the number of original articles based on reporters' voluntary news-gathering activities. Furthermore, the press clubs are prone to become a cartel in which members of the same club would place an embargo on publishing a particular news item or expel reporters who break such embargoes, thus resulting in self-imposed regulations on free competition. Press clubs, which are steeped in Japanese tradition, tend to encourage reporters from their member newspapers to follow identical issues, a practice that was born out of a group mentality. The unfortunate consequence of this practice is that it leads to identical news reporting among rival newspapers. Such a cartel-prone characteristic of the press makes the following common occurrences: 1) The press has collusive relations with the authorities, who serve as a major source of news; 2) off-the-record news quotations become the norm, which would deprive readers of their right to know (Amenomori, 1998).

Evidence of this group mentality, influenced by the cultural traditions, was demonstrated in the agreement in 1993 among the press to refrain from reporting on the developments of the screening of the

Crown Prince's bride, and it is also customary whenever an abduction case occurs, with the press agreeing not to report on the case until the culprits are apprehended (Horibe, 1985). These agreements can be good-intentioned, but it seems as if there is too much of a pack mentality among Japanese journalists today. Exposés by media outlets that belong to such clubs are not welcome and can result in the banning of members from press club briefings. Journalists therefore tend to avoid writing critical stories about the government, reducing the media's ability to pressure politicians for greater transparency and accountability. To avoid any conflicts, most of Japan's investigative journalism is conducted by reporters outside the press club system. In recent years, the exclusivity of the clubs has eroded as foreign journalists with press cards from the Ministry of Foreign Affairs are now guaranteed access to most official press conferences (Amenomori, 1998).

Another problem with the Japanese press is the heavy influence of the United States. As previously mentioned, after the end of War World II, there was a short period of foreign occupation. During this time, most of the major newspapers in Japan had to survive and grow within the framework of Japan's political and economic set-up, which was premised on collaboration with the United States. The papers that came out of that period are still major forces in Japan's press world (Ourvan, 2002). Consequently, even though the United States helped the Japanese achieve a higher level of press freedom, some have argued that close ties with the United States actually restrains the Japanese media to some degree and contributed to the paucity of reports in Japan on negative news about the United States, such as the violence committed by the US soldiers in Okinawa, as Ourvan argued (2002).

To summarize the history of the press freedom in Japan, one can argue that–freedom did not begin until after World War II ended in 1945. Japan went through a period of law overhaul, which also included media laws. For the first time in Japan's history, the constitution guaranteed press freedom. Additionally, up until 1998, the press was granted special treatment in the form of discounted mail rates and tax break (Hamilton, 2000). Another sign of vibrant press freedom is the fact that no government body officially oversees the newspaper industry in Japan, as Hamilton pointed out (2000).

Another influence on the development of press freedom in Japan, are the Asian values and Confucianism, which emphasizes respect for authority and a sense of group harmony. Given the Japanese culture, some scholars have argued that the future of press freedom in Japan does not rest on whether the government would set up new laws to regulate the media or how concentrated the media ownership is in Japan. Instead, it depends on whether the Japanese journalists can resist acting on their cultural tendency to be deferential to the authority and the group mentality (Hamilton, 2000).

Overall, the journalists in Japan enjoy a decent amount of press freedom; however, Japan's concept of press freedom is different from the West and heavily influenced by Asian values and Confucianism. This means that the Japanese press is more reluctant to be critical of the government. Additionally, the prevalent press club system in Japan fostered a cartel and group mentality, which contributed to the lack of diversity in news reports and also self-censorship. This continues to be a concern in Japan.

Four Theories of the Press and Japan: Japan and South Korea have a similar media law history when it comes to freedom of the press. Japan has a west-inspired constitutional protection for press freedom, which was rooted in the libertarian tradition; however, just like South Korea, the Japanese culture is heavily influenced by Confucianism, which emphasizes a respect for the authority. This influence has also led to the Japanese media hesitating to expose the wrongdoings of those in power. Ultimately, the general consensus is that the media must follow certain ethical codes by the press to improve society, which has led scholars to agree that Japan is now subscribing to the social responsibility theory when it comes to media laws.

China

Given its political system, it is no surprise that China maintains a firm control on how the media operates and what information the media can disseminate. Due to this control, the watchdog group, Reporters Without Borders, ranked China 171 out of 178 countries in its 2010 index of press freedom. The organization elaborated that China, despite its increasingly dynamic media and Internet, remains in a low position because of the Chinese government's censorship and control of news reporting.[47] Freedom House typically ranks China below 180, with the

---

[47] See the report on Reporters Without Borders' website.

latest ranking being 187 out of 197 in 2011. Some of the countries that are consistently ranked lower than China are North Korea, Eritrea, Laos, Iran, Belarus, Cuba, and Libya.[48]

Considering the numerous reports on China's tight control of its press and low ranking on both Freedom House and Reporters Without Borders' press freedom indexes, it might be somewhat of a shocking revelation to some that freedom of the press is guaranteed under the Constitution of the People's Republic of China. In the second chapter of the constitution, titled the "Rights and Duties of Citizens," Article 35 provides, "Citizens of the People's Republic of China enjoy freedom of speech, of the press, of assembly, of association, of procession and of demonstration." Although China's constitution does afford its citizens freedom of speech and press, the document contains very broad languages in several articles that the government can use to restrain freedom of expression and freedom of the press. The Chinese Constitution has gone through several incarnations over the years. The 1982 constitution, initiated by Deng Xiaoping following Mao Zedong's death and the end of the Cultural Revolution, refocused the state's attention from class strife to economic development and gave the press more room to do its job (Lam, 2000). In the same document, however, it is made clear that the state maintains a strong role in controlling all kinds of public expression. The Chinese government plays the most central role in shaping the direction of the country's public discourse (Lam, 2000). The state can and does maintain control over unwanted individual expression and public order by citing several articles from the constitution. For example, Chapter 1, Article 22 states: "The state promotes the development of art and literature, the press, radio and television broadcasting, publishing and distribution services, libraries, museums, cultural centers and other cultural undertakings that serve the people and socialism, and it sponsors mass cultural activities."[49] Another example is Article 54, which states Chinese citizens must defend "the security, honor, and interests of the motherland." Contrary political ideas that can be disruptive and threatening are discouraged by constitutional language such as the one in Article 28: "The state maintains public order and suppresses treasonable and other counter-

---

[48] These same countries have been at the bottom of the chart for the last few years.

[49] Constitution of the People's Republic of China, Article 22.

revolutionary activities; it penalizes criminal activities that endanger public security and disrupt the socialist economy as well as other criminal activities." Article 28 would prevail if it were to come in conflict with article 35. These clauses give the Chinese government a lot of leeway to censor the press and control the media industry as a whole. It is safe to claim that although the Chinese constitution provides for freedom of speech and the press, these are not priority rights like they are in the United States. The two main goals continue to be Maosim and economic development for the Chinese government. Ultimately, the protection of the state is the most important goal to the Chinese government, while the press is viewed more as a tool to advance this goal. Mao Zedong, who once worked as a journalist, saw the press as a tool for developing socialist consciousness among the people and for the construction of a socialist state (Yu, 1994). This philosophy has been altered somewhat, but for the most part, his successors all adhere to this in some degree.

Tight control over the press also had to do with the belief among the elite and government leaders that ordinary citizens were generally unworthy of having a forum for expression. According to Houn (1962), the masses weren't capable of direct participation in the country's rule; instead, they had to be "prodded and guided." That "prodding" would come from the Department of Propaganda, which disseminated Chinese Communist Party policy, whether by thought-control, megaphones, or the mass media (Markham, 1967).

The tight control loosened a bit after Mao's reign. In the mid-1970s, President Deng Xiaoping started to encourage the journalists to seek truth from facts instead of merely repeating Mao's ideology (Barnett, 1979). In the 1980s, the Chinese media started to cover broad policy debates that included occasional calls for free speech and press. This wave reached its peak with the 1989 Tiananmen movement when young media workers actively protested control by the Party. Before June 1989, they were allowed to print the truth as they saw it; however, with the June 1989 crackdown, China reverted back to a more traditional relationship between the media and the state to take control of a messy public relations disaster. The dynamics of the mass media in China were forever changed following Deng Xiaoping's rule. His rule proved to be more tolerant towards the media than ever before, but the characteristics of the mass media in China at any given time are still largely determined by the tone of politics in the nation, and the goal of the media in China is still to further the aims of the state. In the aftermath of the Tiananmen Square pro-democracy movement, Chinese leadership felt that there was a threat to the stability of the nation and closed the door on the free flow of political ideas for the time being (Winfield et al., 2000) .

Press freedom came into discussion again a few years later. During the 1990s, there were several efforts put forth by the Chinese government to grant the press more freedom. For instance, in 1998, just prior to President Clinton's visit to China, there was the "Beijing Spring" initiative where the government considered allowing the intellectual elite to form political parties; however, after Clinton's visit, there was a renewed crackdown on the dissenting voices (Lam, 2000).

In the late 90s and early 2000s, China was facing mounting pressure for economic reforms and constant calls for the expansion of civil institutions. The Chinese Communist Party began to allow the media more freedom to do their jobs, including reporting on governmental corruption. Some of the most prominent leaders in the party, including former Premier Zhu Rongji, publicly spoke about the need for the media to be a watchdog in the absence of an opposition party. Of course, this new practice had it limits. Ultimately, the media must get the approval from the higher-ups to run a story about the misdeeds of a government official, (Lam, 2000).

Entering the new millennium, the Chinese government kept getting pressure to provide the press with a freer environment as the nation's economic prowess gets more powerful each year. Consequently, China's media is undergoing a process of commercialization, which is leading to growing competition, diversified content, and an increase in investigative reporting by Chinese news agencies, as Freedom House reported (2008). There are now more than 2000 newspapers, 8000 magazines, and about 374 television stations in the country. China also has over 150 million Internet users and despite restrictions governing online content, domestic and international stories that censors would prefer to control sometimes slip through government information firewalls. Only state agencies can own media in China, but there is some privatization occurring as outlets subcontract administrative operations to the private sector (Karlekar& Cook, 2008).)

A significant turning point in the history of press freedom in China was the 2008 Summer Olympics in Beijing. Prior to the 2008 Summer Olympics in Beijing, the Chinese government was getting more pressure than ever from the rest of the world to grant the media more freedom to cover this big event. In response, the Olympic Games in August 2008 initiated a relaxation of reporting rules for the foreign media, culminating in a decree signed by Prime Minister Wen Jiabao that more or less eliminated the need for journalists to seek government permission before conducting interviews. After the end of the Olympic Games, some complained that the relaxed rules the journalists enjoyed seemed to have tightened up again (LaFraniere & Wong, 2011).)

In the winter and spring of 2011, the North African region went through an incredibly turbulent period where the citizens from several countries, including Egypt and Libya, demanded a political reform from their existing government. Some succeeded in removing their long-time dictators, while others witnessed their leaders take a hard stand to combat the rebels. This called for a change of regime, which made the Chinese government very nervous and prompted the leaders in the Communist party to crack down on reports that might seem sympathetic towards the rebels in those African countries out of fear that they would have another Tiananmen disaster on their hands in the future. In the wake of these revolutions in Africa, keywords such as "Jasmin Revolutions," "Egypt," "Libya," "Tunisia," and "democracy" were blocked in search engines. Demonstrations in Beijing, Shanghai, Canton, and a dozen other cities, organized through online appeals, were squashed by the Chinese government. Journalists were barred from covering them and police turned out in force and online attempts to discuss them were blocked. President Hu Jintao called for new censorship as part of an eight-point social monitoring strategy at a conference, urging provincial leaders to step up online monitoring and develop new ways to "channel online opinion" so as to improve social "harmonization," a term the authorities often use to mean censorship (LaFraniere & Wong, 2011).

While it is true that the press in China currently enjoys more freedom versus a few years ago, various forms of censorship and other types of control still restrain the press today. The government usually relies on regulations and directives, some found in the constitution, some in the standing rules of the Party, and others in governmental statutes, to control the media. Other ways to keep the journalists in line include the appointment and promotion of journalists if they toe the party line, and the rule that editors must submit future plans covering major news to be approved by the central government. (Lam, 2000).

The Chinese government also controls the mass media through other means such as ownership, permitting authorities to control, limit, and restrict information, as well as to disseminate new ideas and values (Winfield et al., 2000) . This kind of control persists in a largely internal and indirect way and usually outsiders would not notice it unless they really look for it, as Winfield and colleagues point out (2000).

When editors and journalists do not follow the Party line, they face serious consequences. Internet and foreign news media, just like Chinese journalists, are subject to censorship by the state (Winfield et al., 2000). Dissidents are arrested, including both Chinese and foreign correspondents, and with the emergence of the Internet, the government also implemented strict controls to limit the transmission of what it considered to be harmful information via the Internet.

Generally speaking, media law is not that important in China because formal regulation is not really required, as Winfield noted (2000). With the combination of the Communist party system, and the Asian values, namely Confucianism, protection for press freedom takes on a whole different meaning for the Chinese compared to the West. All in all, the Chinese mass media primarily remain an educational tool and major propaganda unit of the central government (Winfield et al., 2000).

To sum this up, while the constitution does grant the right of press freedom, the freedom of the press condition in China is actually already determined by the preamble of the constitution. In the preamble of the Chinese Constitution, it was clearly stated that the main goal for the Chinese government is to focus its effort on "socialist modernization" and further build and strengthen the country under the guidance of Marxism- Leninism and Mao Zedong's thoughts. [50] Additionally, mindful of the diverse population of the country and anticipating the difficulties of effectively governing all the distinctively different people when the Chinese Communist Party initially took control, the Chinese legislators made it a point to stress in the preamble of the constitution that "class struggle will continue to exist within certain limits for a long time to come." It is apparent that the ideology guiding the press under the Chinese Communist Party was derived from Soviet Union---Marxism-Leninism (Lu, 1982). Unlike the West, whose press ideology

[50] See the Constitution of the People's Republic of China.

is modeled after the social responsibility theory, the Chinese viewed the press as a tool to carry out class struggle between the proletariat and the bourgeois, including propagating policies and organizing and mobilizing the mass, as Lu pointed out (1982).

In the wake of the rapid emergence of the Internet, which provided a new and effective avenue for dissidents to voice their views, the Chinese government quickly passed "Regulations Governing the Security and Protection of Computer Information Systems" (Lam, 2000). The Chinese government is using the world's most sophisticated censorship apparatus, known as "the Great Firewall," to block certain websites it considers to be inappropriate for the public. With the Internet and social networking websites playing such a big part in the African revolutions of 2011, the Chinese government is now keeping an even more watchful eye on its people's online activities.

China has media regulations with a vague language that authorities use to claim certain stories are endangering the country because they would reveal state secrets. Journalists face harassment and prison terms for violating these rules and revealing classified state matters (Lam, 2000). As a result, it is inevitable that the government's heavy control of the press promotes an atmosphere of self-censorship, especially since the lack of a concrete set of media laws left many Chinese journalists feeling uncertain as to whether a subject was taboo and thus unsuitable for publication (Winfield et al., 2000). If published materials are deemed too dangerous to state security after they appear in the media, the information can then be considered classified and journalists can be prosecuted. Some examples of the stories that caused the journalists who worked on them to receive harsh punishment include the following: 1) criticism of the firing of an investigative reporter by the hands of the government, 2) criticism of the government's version of the 1937-45 Sino-Japanese War, 3) a major government corruption scandal,4) the depreciation of the Chinese currency, and 5) the number of casualties who have perished in the fire or floods (Reporters Without Borders Staff, 2011).

Overall, the freedom of the press conditions in China remain highly repressive today. Authorities increased censorship and the coverage of Communist Party propaganda in traditional and online media during periods of high-profile events that could incite rebellions. Freedom House reported that dozens of detailed party directives curbed coverage relating to public health, environmental accidents, deaths in police custody, and foreign policy. Journalists investigating corruption or environmental pollution faced a growing threat from physical attacks to politicized charges of bribery, while other activists were sentenced to long prison terms for their online writings. Nevertheless, Freedom House also reported that the conditions are slowly improving for journalists, bloggers, and grassroots activists as they continued to push the limits of permissible expression, including the exposure of corruption and the circulation of underground political publications (2008). It was also positive news for journalists and the public in general when the government retracted its order to install Green Dam monitoring and censorship software on all personal computers (Karlekar, 2010).

In 2013, the Chinese government announced that it would allow media outlets to report on the country's notorious air pollution problem. More specifically, on January 13th, 2013, according to a story published by the New York Times, the Chinese news media published "aggressive reports" on what they described as the "sickening and dangerous air pollution in Beijing and other parts of northern China." One account stated that the story appeared in news media ranging from People's Daily to China Central Television. A major reason the story was finally reported was that the Chinese government had recognized that the air pollution problem in China became too serious to ignore and in fact addressed the issue in the 18th Party Congress in the November of 2012. Another major reason the government decided to allow the media to report on this problem, which had been sporadically reported prior but mostly considered to be a taboo topic in the past because it brings to light an issue that would cast a negative light on the country, was because the public's anger and concern over the air quality had reached a level where the Chinese government officials felt that they had to allow the officially sanctioned press to address the growing concerns of ordinary citizens. Prominent Chinese Internet users and especially Northern China's residents had been expressing their concern over the pollution problem in their region by having serious discussions about this issue on Chinese "microblogs" on the Internet in the days leading up to the Chinese government's decision to have the official news media report on this problem. This recent development is a positive sign that the Chinese government has been gradually and selectively loosening its tight control on the media even though the Soviet- communist theory is still the dominant ideology.

Taiwan

Based on the 2008 Freedom House's freedom of the press index, Taiwan is ranked 32nd, the highest placement in East Asia (Karlekar & Cook, 2008)). However, in the most recent index published in 2012, Taiwan's ranking was dropped from 32nd to 47th, resulting in Japan becoming the country in East Asia to have the freest press. In fact, while still categorized as "free," Taiwan's press freedom has dropped every year since 2008. As of 2011, Taiwan is only ranked 7th in the Asia-Pacific region. This is alarming because as recent as 2007, Taiwan was ranked 4th.

Article 11 of the Constitution of the Republic of China (Taiwan) provides that the people shall have freedom of speech and freedom of publication. Article 23 subjects this freedom to a number of restrictions to prevent "infringement upon the freedoms of other persons, to avert an imminent crisis, to maintain social order or to advance the public welfare." Freedom of the press was *not* specifically mentioned in the constitution. To understand this omission, it is important to look back at the history of Taiwan since 1949 and the cultural background of the Island.

Taiwan, like South Korea, was colonized by Japan until 1945. After the Japanese left the island, the Taiwanese media enjoyed a brief period of press freedom; however this freedom was short-lived because Chiang Kai-shek and Kuomintang (KMT, the leading political party at the time the civil war with the Communist party broke out) immediately began their authoritarian rule and imposed tight control over the media following their defeat in the hands of the Chinese Communist Party and their subsequent retreat to the island (Pang, 1998). All cultural institutions, including the media, were basically extensions of the government under the martial law, which lasted for decades. As Pang pointed out, the regulatory philosophy of media law in Taiwan was based on the notion that the government is the protector of the common goods in society, and thus should not be questioned or criticized (1998). Under the rules of martial law, the press was considered a tool for enhancing the power and legitimacy of the ruling bureaucracies, rather than as a medium of dialogue. The press was deemed to be a political educator to promote the solidarity of the people and to strengthen the rule of law in accordance with the Chinese culture and the ideology of anti-Communism. Given the important role the press played during this period for the Nationalist Party (KMT), freedom of expression was subordinated to the larger and more pressing goal of nation-building (Chen, 1998). In other words, like the leading party in South Korea, KMT believed that aside from solidifying its power in Taiwan, another reason for heavy media censorship was so the government could concentrate on establishing infrastructure, and improve the poor, agriculture-based economic conditions of the island without having to worry about media getting in the way.

As Chen noted, during the martial law period, the KMT's tight control over the media was manifested in two ways: 1) legal structural constraints, and 2) control of ownership (1998). Specifically, state licensing and government censorship were the defining characteristics of the Taiwanese media for a long time. What was egregious during this period was that the legal control of the media was enforced by either political or military authorities instead of the judicial branch of the government (Rawnsley, 2007).

The peak of the government's effort to crack down any dissenting voices was the infamous "white terror" period, which lasted from 1949 to the mid-1950s (Rawnsley, 2007). During this time, anyone who criticized the Chiang government or expressed sympathy towards the Chinese Communist Party, even in the comfort of their own homes, could be hauled out of their houses in the middle of the night and never be heard from again. Phones were widely tapped and people's every move was closely watched by the secret police. A lot of highly educated intellectuals lost their lives because the government believed that they had voiced unflattering opinions about General Chiang and the KMT. This unfortunate piece of history in Taiwan contributed to the tense relationship between the native Taiwanese and the mainlanders who came to the island after 1949, a tension that still exists to this day (Yang & Engbarth, 2000).

As Chen pointed out, during the martial law period, Taiwan Garrison Command was the most powerful regulatory body that monitored the opposition publications (1998). They used several tactics such as seizing magazines in printing shops, sending police to patrol newsstands to prevent the sale of banned publications, and requiring typesetters to submit photocopies of the manuscripts of opposition magazines (Chen, 1998).

Some of the stories did not pass the censor test and therefore landed the publishers and journalists in hot water during the martial law period. On top of this, most of them failed the test because they either portrayed KMT in a not-so-positive light or gave the Chinese Communist Party too much coverage (Chen, 1998). These stories included a protest against alleged rigged vote counting in an election, front page stories about the achievements of athletes from China during the 1984 Summer Olympics, and the formation of the first real opposition party, the Democratic Progressive Party (DDP.) Before the democratization of Taiwan, magazines and underground radio stations were the main outlets for oppositions. The more mainstream forms of media, television and newspapers, were all owned and controlled by the government, either by the ruling KMT party, or the powerful military; however, the government still made every effort to shut down these underground magazines and radio stations, which gradually caused enormous economic hardships for the magazine publishers, many of whom became political prisoners and were behind bars for many years (Yang & Engbarth, 2000).

The press freedom conditions in Taiwan eventually improved. After years of authoritarian rule by the Chiang family following their retreat from mainland China to Taiwan, the long-standing martial law was lifted in 1987. Since Taiwan has become democratic and the thriving economy catapulted the island to the "Four Tigers of Asia" status, there really was no reason for the KMT to place any restrictions on the press (Pang, 1998) . The media market seemed to have opened up overnight with numerous new media outlets springing up, especially after 1999, when the government repealed the Publication Law, the last of the restrictive press law. This meant that everybody in Taiwan could own or publish newspapers and magazines (Rawnsley, 2007) . Additionally, the good news for journalists in Taiwan is that there were no longer limits on foreign ownership and censorship (Yang & Engbarth, 2000) .

Today, Taiwan's media environment remains one of the freest in Asia, with a vigorous and diverse press that reports aggressively on government policies and alleged official wrongdoing. The constitution of Taiwan provides for freedom of speech, which ultimately encompasses freedom of the press for all intents and purposes, and the government and independent courts generally respect these rights in practice. Nevertheless, Freedom House reported that actions by media owners, a revival of "embedded marketing" amid economic difficulties, and government influence over the editorial content of publicly owned outlets all posed threats to media independence since 2009. Each of these contributed to Taiwan's drop in Freedom House's Freedom of the Press rankings (Karlekar, 2010).

As mentioned, a worrisome trend that helped to downgrade Taiwan's freedom of the press ranking is the increase of "embedded marketing." This refers to the marketing/advertising disguised as news reports, which happens when big companies "bribe" the news outlets to publish positive reports about their products that masquerade as news (Karlekar, 2010). This deplorable practice obviously lowered the qualities of journalism in Taiwan, but more importantly, these bogus "reports" take up precious space in the newspapers or television news programs that could be occupied by far more pressing and legitimate news stories that the public deserves to know, thus damaging press freedom. However, Freedom House has noted in its report that the Taiwanese government recently attempted to rectify this problem by enacting a statute that could outlaw this practice (Karlekar, 2000).

Another potential threat to press freedom in Taiwan is its increasingly close economic ties with China. As commercial ties between Taiwan and mainland China deepened in 2010 with the signing of the Economic Cooperation Framework Agreement, press freedom advocates expressed their worry that media owners and some journalists would censor their news reports about China to protect their own financial interests (Lowther et al., 2011).

In regards to legislating the Internet, which is accessed by about 72% of the population in Taiwan, the Taiwanese government has been taking a relaxed approach to regulating this new medium. In fact, it has refrained from restricting the Internet so far; however, that is not to say that the Taiwanese government is allowing Internet activities to go completely wild (Karlekar, 2010). In the cyber-piracy chapter later in the book, Taiwan's effort to crack down on Internet piracy is discussed.

Overall, Taiwan's history is not unlike other nations in the Eastern Asian region that had the same history of foreign occupation and dictatorship. In the wake of its defeat in the civil war in the hands of the Chinese Communist Party, the Nationalist Party, led by General Chiang Kai-Shek, retreated to Taiwan and began a long period of authoritarian rule and heavy media censorship. By all accounts, Taiwan did not become a real democracy until his son, Chiang Ching-kuo, who succeeded him as the leader, abolished martial law in 1987 (Rawnsley, 2007). Bolstered by the constitutional protection, press freedom really started to flourish afterwards. Generally, the media enjoys wide range of freedom, but in recent years, economic concerns seemed to have taken precedence over journalistic integrity, thus threatening the status of freedom in Taiwan.

Hong Kong

Hong Kong is a unique case. Technically, it was handed back to China after a long period of British rule in 1997 but to this day Hong Kong is governed on a different playing field than the rest of China. This includes how the control of the media is handled and how much press freedom the press enjoys.

According to the Freedom House index, the press in Hong Kong enjoys much more freedom than its counterpart in China. Even after the handover, it is still categorized as a "free-press" territory; however, in the Freedom House index that came out in 2010, the press in Hong Kong is now considered only "partly free." In the latest ranking that came out in 2012, Hong Kong is ranked 70, tying with Italy.

Under Article 27 of the Basic Law, the Constitution of Hong Kong, Hong Kong residents enjoy freedom of speech, press, and publication, and these rights are generally upheld by the territory's independent courts. Under the highly controversial Article 23, the existence of which sparked a large-scale protest, the government is granted a great deal of leeway to punish publications and expressions that could be construed as violating national security.[51] Generally speaking, the state of press freedom in Hong Kong is at risk of being undermined by the power of the Chinese National People's Congress to make final interpretations of Hong Kong's Basic Law and the Chinese surveillance in the territory (Cheung, 2003).

The good news is that even though there are harsh laws regarding the publication of state secrets such as Article 23 of Basic Law, for the most part, the media in Hong Kong have experienced little interference with the Chinese government since the handover in 1997. Some scholars have argued that the reason for the Chinese government's reluctance to censor the media is because the economy in Hong Kong is very dependent on overseas investment, and press freedom is still very important to foreign investors. This does not necessarily mean that the

[51] See Hong Kong Basic Law Art. 23.

journalists in Hong Kong enjoy the same amount of press freedom as they did under the British rule; however, Some journalists have admitted that even though there has been no outright change in the amount of freedom with their jobs, they felt the "psychological pressure" to choose what stories they could publish and the words they use had to be chosen very carefully after 1997 (Cheung, 2003) .. In other words, the Chinese government might not have outwardly altered the press freedom landscape of Hong Kong, but that is not to say that self-censorship is not alive and well.

The most prominent feature of journalism in Hong Kong is somewhat unflattering and could potentially have a more lasting impact on the status of freedom of the press than the Chinese government does. Hong Kong, perhaps influenced by the British has a very sensationalism-oriented media environment (Yeung, 2000). Under British occupation, journalists in Hong Kong enjoyed a great degree of freedom, but during this period, the British brought its popular tabloid journalism to the island. Yeung noted that the ironic thing about the media in Hong Kong is that before the handover to China in 1997, Hong Kong journalists were worried about the loss of press freedom, but that fear has been replaced by concern for the quality of reporting and the irresponsibility of the media (2000). Interestingly, this means that the major threat to press freedom comes from the pervasive tabloid nature of newspapers, which many agreed has gotten out of control in terms of sleaze and sensationalism. Due to this, many worry that the government will step in and punish the media for their irresponsibility. Although some have stated that they do not like that such law would decrease the level of press freedom in Hong Kong, they would welcome it because it is necessary (Karlekar, 2010).

While press freedom remains alive and well in Hong Kong, political and economic pressures, including from Beijing, have narrowed the scope of freedom in recent years. The number one concern for Hong Kong journalists is that they face restrictions and intimidation when covering events that occur on the mainland, thus limiting their ability to provide national news to the local population. In contrast to the loosened regulations for foreign journalists in China, which were extended indefinitely before the 2008 Beijing Olympics, mainland authorities issued more restrictive conditions for Hong Kong media workers in February 2009. The regulations require journalists to obtain 1) temporary press cards from Beijing's liaison office in Hong

Kong every time they visit the mainland for a report and 2) the prior consent of anyone they would like to interview (Karlekar, 2010). Several journalists have said that they were generally able to obtain the desired press card on the day of the application, but also expressed fears that they could run into obstructions by mainland authorities if and when they attempt to cover a breaking story that was not mentioned in their documents they submitted. Journalists from Hong Kong who had worse luck have reportedly been subject to surveillance, threats, beatings, and occasional jail time when reporting on the mainland (Karlekar, 2010).

A major problem since 1997 for the development of press freedom in Hong Kong is self-censorship. Increasing media self-censorship poses a serious threat to free expression in the territory (Cheung, 2003). In recent years, Beijing's influence over the news, publishing, and film industries has increased, prompting greater restraint on issues deemed sensitive by the central government (Karlekar & Cook, 2008). The Hong Kong University Public Opinion Program reported in September 2009 that over half of the citizens interviewed believed the media practiced self-censorship. In one incident during 2009, top managers of the Hong Kong edition of *Esquire* magazine barred the publication of a 16-page feature about the June 4, 1989, Tiananmen Square incident. The feature's author was subsequently fired soon after (Karlekar, 2010).

Despite the increasing self-censorship, Hong Kong's media remained outspoken. As Freedom House reported, there is a high degree of professionalism and political debate is vigorous in the diverse and partisan press. Hong Kong has numerous news outlets that attract a large number of readers and the media industry remains strong and vibrant. In recent years, however, publications known for their criticism of the central government, such as the *Apple Daily* and the *Epoch Times*, have reported difficulties in attracting advertisers because of their fear that these publications would harm their economic interests on the mainland (Karlekar, 2010).

Chapter Conclusion

The aim of this chapter was to analyze whether there is constitutional protection for freedom of the press in the countries examined in this book. The findings show that most of them do have some type of constitutional protection for freedom of the press, but in various degrees. There are commonalities and differences among the countries across all three continents. Additionally, this chapter also presented a brief history of the development of press freedom in every country, which serves as the answer to Research Question 2 for the purpose of finding out what cultural, economic, and political factors have played a part in these developments. In Chapter 10, a detailed comparison and analysis of these constitutional freedom of the press protections and the factors that have affected the developments of press freedom over the years are presented.

Chapter 4

Press Freedom Laws and Censorship in America

The constitutional guarantee of freedom of the press is just part of the picture in the grand scheme of things for the media. As the findings show, just because a country has an explicit constitutional guarantee for freedom of press does not automatically mean that the country has a free press environment. Other statutes regulating the media also have long and short-term consequences for freedom of the press. In the next three chapters of this book, laws and statutes in every country examined in this book that have an impact on the journalists' freedom to do their jobs are discussed and analyzed. It should be noted that while there is such a broad range of laws that govern this subject, this book mainly focuses on two areas of press laws: 1) laws regarding censorship and what the press can or cannot publish, and 2) laws regarding reporters' privilege (or shield laws), which determine whether reporters have the right not to reveal their news sources when testifying in courts. These two areas were chosen because they encompass the dual concerns journalists have about their jobs: First, whether they have freedom to publish certain stories or have access to certain important information and second, whether or not their personal freedom would be affected by protecting their sources or publishing certain sensitive stories.

Censorship regarding the press in the United States does not seem like an issue these days, but this does not mean that in the history of the United States, censorship of the press has not been an important issue that seriously hindered freedom of the press. In the United States, it is believed that the first famous censorship case occurred in 1735, when newspaper publisher John Peter Zenger published a story criticizing the British ruler at the time. This story began in 1733, when Zenger began publishing a newspaper in New York to express his displeasure with the policies of newly appointed colonial governor William Cosby. After a while, Cosby issued a statement condemning the newspaper's publication of scandalous falsehood. Soon after that, Zenger was charged with seditious libel and taken to court, but thanks to his lawyer, Andrew Hamilton the court ultimately found him not guilty. This case paved the way for freedom of the press in the United States to be adopted into the constitution (Foerstel, 1998).

Since the Zenger case, there have been several other attempts to enact seditious laws that outlaw criticisms of the government. There have been a number of attempts in the United States to forbid speech that has been deemed "seditious." In 1798, President John Adams signed into law the Alien and Sedition Acts. One part of the law, the Sedition Act, or "An Act for the Punishment of Certain Crimes against the United States," set out punishments that could last up to two years' imprisonment for "opposing or resisting any law of the United States" or writing/publishing "false, scandalous, and malicious writing" about the President or Congress. The act expired in 1801 after the election of Thomas Jefferson. More than a century later, another seditious law, the Sedition Act of 1917, was passed when the United States joined the Allied Powers during the First World War. This version of the seditious law was a particularly controversial law because it allowed the government to imprison many prominent individuals for opposing the war or the draft. During this period, state laws prohibiting seditious acts were also passed and used to prosecute and persecute alleged "seditionists," including many people guilty of being members of the Wobblies (the Industrial Workers of the World), which is an international industrial union that formed in 1905 and promoted the following ideas: 1)"one big union," 2) all workers should be united as a social class, and 3) capitalism and wage labor should be abolished. This Sedition Act expired shortly after the end of the First World War.

History has shown that censorship is particularly rampant during war time, as the United States government often attempted to withhold certain sensitive information from the public and the press during these periods. For example, wide-spread xenophobia during WWI led to a period where press censorship was in full force and criticisms of the government in any way could mean trouble for the reporters. During this time, war correspondents and their reports were subject to advance censorship to preserve military secrets. The extent of such censorship was not generally challenged, and no major court case arose from this issue. Even the Supreme Court found it constitutional on the grounds that it "protected free speech from tyranny." During World War II, censorship again reared its ugly head. While the government at the time no longer charged the journalists who voiced criticisms of the authority with seditious libel, it achieved the same result of censorship by withholding certain governmental information from the press, who relied heavily on the government to supply information for news stories (Foerstel, 1998). Moreover, the Office of Censorship, an emergency wartime agency, heavily censored reporting during World War II. In December of 1941, President Franklin Roosevelt signed Executive Order 8985, which established the Office of Censorship and appointed the director the power to censor all international communications. Additionally, censorship was not limited to reporting. Letters were also subject to being opened and inspected during this period. When the United States was engaged in the Cold War with the Soviet Union, President John Kennedy publicly asked the press to exercise voluntary censorship to prevent sensitive information from getting into the hands of the enemy. In the last two decades, President George H. W. Bush and George W. Bush also practiced censorship when they were engaged in their respective wars with Iraq by requiring the press to not reveal any confidential information regarding military actions. Since 9/11, there has been a growing effort to censor the press when it comes to information pertaining to national security in efforts to fight terrorism; however, overall, censorship is not a serious threat to freedom of the press in the United States, especially since the Supreme Court ruled in *Near v. Minnesota* that prior restraint, is unconstitutional, except in extremely limited circumstances, such as when national security issues are involved (Johnson, 2003).

Freedom of Information Act in the United States

In" the United States, a journalist does not have the First Amendment right enabling them to access government information; however, he/she may inspect public records pursuant to freedom of information statutes. One of the most important statutes that supplement the First Amendment to bolster freedom of the press in the nation is the

Freedom of Information Act " (FOIA). FOIA is a federal law that allows for the full or partial disclosure of previously unreleased information and documents controlled by the United States government.[52]The United States Congress passed this law because of their belief that access to information is essential to citizenship in a representative democracy and that ordinary political processes do not necessarily produce an adequate flow of information to the people or their representatives. In short, FOIA was intended to enforce the constitutional "right to know" by creating a presumption in favor of disclosure.[53] At the time FOIA came into existence, the primary objective was to "unlock government secrets and open up channels of information."[54]The Act defines agency records that would be subject to disclosure, outlines mandatory disclosure procedures, and grants nine exemptions to the statute. It was signed into law by President Lyndon Johnson in 1966 and went into effect in 1967.[55]

While FOIA" gave the public the right to have access to governmental information, arguably the more important parts of this law are the aforementioned exemptions. Oftentimes these exemptions give rise to problems and discrepancies. Broadly speaking, the nine exemptions to the FOIA address issues of sensitivity and personal rights. They are:

1. a: Information specifically authorized under criteria established by an Executive order to be kept secret in the interest of national defense or foreign policy and
   b. is in fact properly classified pursuant to such Executive order;
2. Information related solely to the internal personnel rules and practices of an agency;
3. Information specifically exempt from disclosure by statute (other than section 552b of this title), provided that such

[52] Seethe Freedom of Information Act for more details.
[53] See Barry Sullivan, FOIA and the First Amendment: Representative Democracy and the People's Elusive Right to Know, 72 Md. L Rev.1 (2012).
[54] Id.
[55] To this day, this Act remains in force, and many Americans have taken advantage of the law.

statute (A) requires that the matters be withheld from the public in such a manner as to leave no discretion on the issue, or (B) establishes particular criteria for withholding or refers to particular types of matters to be withheld;

4. Trade secrets and commercial or financial information obtained from a person who is privileged or confidential;
5. Inter-agency or intra-agency memoranda or letters which would not be available by law to a party other than an agency in litigation with the agency;
6. Personnel and medical files and similar files the disclosure of which would constitute a clearly unwarranted invasion of personal privacy;
7. Records or information compiled for law enforcement purposes, but only to the extent that the production of such law enforcement records or information (A) could reasonably be expected to interfere with enforcement proceedings, (B) would deprive a person of the right to a fair trial or an impartial adjudication, (C) could reasonably be expected to constitute an unwarranted invasion of personal privacy, (D) could reasonably be expected to disclose the identity of a confidential source, including a State, local, or foreign agency or any private institution which furnished information on a confidential basis, and, in the case of a record or information compiled by a criminal law enforcement authority in the course of a criminal investigation or by an agency conducting a lawful national security intelligence investigation, information furnished by a confidential source, (E) would disclose techniques and procedures for law enforcement investigations or prosecutions, or would disclose guidelines for law enforcement investigations or prosecutions if such disclosure could reasonably be expected to risk circumvention of the law, or (F) could reasonably be expected to endanger the life or physical safety of any individual;
8. Information contained in or related to examination, operating, or condition reports prepared by, on behalf of, or for the use of an agency responsible for the regulation or supervision of financial institutions; or
9. Geological and geophysical information and data, including maps, concerning wells.

Since 1966, Congress has regularly updated the original statute through legislative amendments. In 1976, as part of the Government in the Sunshine Act, which was designed to make the government more transparent, exemption 3 of the original FOIA" was amended so that several exemptions were specified. These include the following:

1. Information relating to national defense;
2. Related solely to internal personnel rules and practices;
3. Related to accusing a person of a crime;
4. Related to information where disclosure would constitute a breach of privacy;
5. Related to investigatory records where the information would harm the proceedings;
6. Related to information which would lead to financial speculation or endanger the stability of any financial institution;
7. Related to the agency's participation in legal proceedings.

In recent years, FOIA" has gone through further alterations. In 2007, Congress passed the OPEN Government Act of 2007, which addressed several procedural issues that concern FOIA administration. Specifically, the law strived to make the following changes to FOIA:

1. Establishing a definition of "a representative of the news media;"
2. Directing that required attorney fees to be paid from an agency's own appropriation rather than from the Judgment Fund;
3. Prohibiting an agency from assessing certain fees if it fails to comply with FOIA deadlines; and
4. Establishing an Office of Government Information Services (OGIS) in the National Archives and Record Administration to review agency compliance with FOIA.

Detailed changes to FOIA under this new version include the following:

1. The new version recognizes electronic media and defines "News Media" as "any person or entity that gathers information of potential interest to a segment of the public, uses its editorial skills to turn the raw materials into a distinct work, and distributes that work to an audience." This includes freelance journalists.
2. It extends the 20-day deadline by allowing up to 10 days between the FOIA office of the agency and the component of the agency holding the records and specifically allows for clarification of requests by the FOIA" office (this became effective on 12/31/2007).
3. It calls for each agency to designate a FOIA" Public Liaison, "who shall assist in the resolution of any disputes" (this became effective on 12/31/2008).
4. It requires agencies to assign "tracking numbers" to FOIA requests that would take longer than 10 days, and to provide systems determining the status of a request.
5. It codifies and defines annual reporting requirements for each agency's FOIA program.
6. The reporting requirements shall be "expressed in terms of each principal component of the agency and for the agency overall." Moreover, the data used to compile the reports must also be made "available electronically to the public upon request."
7. It expands the definition of an agency "record" to include information held for an agency by a government contractor. This provision makes clear that records, in the possession of Government contractors for purposes of record management, are considered agency records for purposes of the FOIA.
8. It establishes an Office of Government Information Services (OGIS),) which will offer mediation services to resolve disputes as a non-exclusive alternative to litigation. This office may also "issue advisory opinions if mediation has not resolved the dispute."
9. It requires agencies to make recommendations in regards to personnel matters related to FOIA such as whether FOIA performance is a merit factor.
10. It requires agencies to specify the specific exemption for each deletion or redaction in disclosed documents.

Overall, the Open Government Act of 2007 addresses a range of administrative and procedural issues affecting FOIA administration. In several instances, it codifies what practices already exists, such as the assigning of tracking numbers to the requests for information. Other areas of the law established new reporting requirements, such as the additional statistics/data required in agency annual FOIA reports. Additionally, it also specifies procedures for the calculation of the FOIA's time periods and limits the assessment of search and other related fees for certain information requests not responded to by government agencies within the applicable time period.

More recently, the OPEN FOIA Act of 2009, which revised the requirements of FOIA exemptions, offered more clarification of the law. Specifically, it amended the Freedom of Information Act" to require statutory exemptions to its disclosure requirements-exemption No. 3 mentioned above-to specifically cite its provision that authorizes such exemptions mainly to "ensure an open and deliberative process in Congress by providing for related legislative proposals to explicitly state such required citations, and for other purposes."[56]

To briefly summarize the evolutions of FOIA", it should first be noted that FOIA explicitly applies to executive branch government agencies. Under the Act, these agencies are under several mandates to comply with public solicitation of information, along with making public and accessible all bureaucratic and technical procedures for applying to gain access to certain documents. Agencies are also subject to penalties for hindering the process of a petition for information. Yet, as mentioned above, there are nine exemptions in the statute that range from "withholding information specifically authorized under criteria established by an Executive Order to be kept secret in the interest of national defense or foreign policy" and "trade secrets" to information if revealed would constitute "clearly unwarranted invasion of personal privacy."[57] After 9/11, it is understandable that this was the first exemption to receive a lot of attention since it's in regards to sensitive information involving national security. It should also be noted that the 2007 amendment of Freedom of Information Act "finally recognizes electronic media and defined "news media" as "any person or entity

[56] SeeFOIA Resources, the Department of Justice Official Website, http://www.justice.gov/oip/foia-resources.html.

[57] Freedom of Information Act, 5 U.S.C. § 552.

that gathers information of potential interest to a segment of the public, uses its editorial skills to turn the raw materials into a distinct work, and distributes that work to an audience." Essentially, this new amendment recognized the fact that bloggers and on-line reporters could be legitimate journalists and "representatives of a news media." It is worth mentioning that in an effort to reverse the trend of the Bush administration's secrecy, the 2007 amendment was designed to toughen the Freedom of Information Act and increase penalties on agencies that do not comply with legitimate requests (Williams, 2007) . Under this new version of FOIA, agencies would be required to meet a 20-day deadline for responding to FOIA requests. If they fail to meet the 20-day deadline, agencies would have to refund search and duplication fees for noncommercial requesters (Williamson, 2007). Overall, while on the surface, the revised FOIA" seemed to demand the government to be more specific when it attempts to refuse the disclosure of certain information, some scholars have noticed that in recent years, the government has cited "national security" as a justification numerous times over the years for objecting to the disclosure of certain information.

For journalists in the United States, another statute that pertains to access of information is the Privacy Act of 1974. The historical context of the law is crucial in understanding its purpose. Specifically, in 1974, Congress was concerned with curbing the illegal surveillance and investigation of individuals by federal agencies that had been exposed during the Watergate scandal. Furthermore, it was also concerned with potential abuses presented by the government's increasing use of computers to store and retrieve personal data.[58]To speak in broad terms, the purpose of the law was to balance the government's need to maintain information about individuals while also protecting the rights of individuals against unwarranted invasions of their privacy stemming from federal agencies' collection, maintenance, use, and disclosure of personal information about them.[59]

This statute establishes a "Code of Fair Information Practice" that governs the collection, maintenance, use, and dissemination of personally identifiable information about individuals that is maintained

---

[58] More information can be found on the US Department of Justice's website, http://it.ojp.gov/default.aspx?area=privacy&page=1279

[59] Id.

in a system of records by federal agencies.[60] The Privacy Act of 1974 prohibits the disclosure of information from a system of records without first obtaining the written consent of the subject individual, unless the disclosure falls under one of the 12 statutory exceptions, which include the Census Bureau Statistics, the Bureau of Labor Statistics, information obtained for law enforcement purposes, and congressional investigations.

PROTECTION OF SOURCES

Another issue journalists today face everywhere is the protection of their secret sources. The laws granting this protection are often called the "reporters' privilege" or "shield laws." The problems associated with protecting the anonymous sources journalists use arises when the journalists have confidential information that pertains to an ongoing court case. In such a scenario, the courts would sometimes compel the journalists who have that relevant information to testify in court. In that process, from time to time, the identities of these confidential sources would become so crucial to resolving the ongoing court case that the judges would order the journalists to reveal who those sources are. If the journalists do not comply with the order, they could be put behind bars for long periods of time. It is unfortunate that while such outcomes are still rare in the United States, the imprisonment of journalists has happened enough in the country that the protection of sources has become an ongoing topic of journalistic concern.

WHY SHIELD LAWS ARE NECESSARY AND THE CASE OF MISSING FEDERAL SHIELD LAWS IN THE US

Crucial to the rationale behind having a "reporter's privilege" is the belief that the press must not only be insulated from government interference, but also free from governmental assistance because either would compromise its independence (Alexander & Bush, 1997). In short, this privilege promotes 1) the autonomy of the press required to serve as a check on the government's actions and 2) society's interest in a newsgathering process free from interventions and interruptions. This

---

[60] See Privacy Act of 1974 on the Department of Justice Official Website, http://www.justice.gov/opcl/privacyact1974.htm.

is why Justice Potter Stewart stated in his dissenting opinion in the famous case *Branzburg v. Hayes*, that his fellow justices' distorted view of the First Amendment reflected a disturbing insensitivity to the critical role of an independent press in American society and that journalists should not be required to divulge the names of confidential sources who have provided them with information. If they are required to do so, journalists would turn into investigators for law enforcement agencies, which is not the point of journalism (Watkins, 1994).

The seminal Supreme Court case dealing with reporters' rights not to reveal his/her confidential sources is the case mentioned above, *Branzburg v. Hayes*. This case involved Paul Branzburg of *The (Louisville) Courier-Journal*, who in the course of his reporting duties, witnessed people manufacturing and using hashish. Soon after his discovery, he wrote two articles regarding this drug use in Kentucky. In that first article, he mentioned unidentified people holding hashish, while the second article used marijuana users as his major source. Not surprisingly, these sources asked not to be identified in his articles; however, subsequent to their publications, both of the articles were brought to the attention of law-enforcement, and Branzburg was subpoenaed before a grand jury and ordered to name his sources. Branzburg refused to comply, citing his privilege under the Press Clause in the First Amendment, and was held in contempt. The case then went to the Supreme Court, and in a split decision, the Court ruled 5-4 against the existence of reportorial privilege in the Press Clause of the First Amendment. Justice Byron White declared that Branzburg and the journalism community were asking the Court to grant journalists a testimonial privilege that other citizens do not enjoy, and that was something that he would not agree to do. While Justice White acknowledged that refusing to recognize such a privilege would undermine the ability of the press to gather news, he also contended that "from the beginning of the country the press has operated without constitutional protection for press informants, and the press has flourished."[61] Ultimately, the Court held that reporters had no First Amendment privilege to refuse to respond to the grand juries' inquiries or to refuse to attend their sessions. The silver lining for journalists was that although the Court rejected an absolute privilege, it also left room

---

[61] From the decision for Branzburg v. Hayes, 408 U.S. 665 (1972).

for development of a qualified privilege for protection of confidential sources.[62]

The *Branzburg* decision was a highly complex one. Although the majority did not recognize a reporter's privilege to withhold hi/her sources, over the years, Justice Stewart's dissent actually offered a test that other lower courts had adhered to when dealing with reporter's privilege. In his opinion, in order for the courts to compel a journalist to reveal their sources in court, the government must meet three criteria:

1. Show that there is probable cause to believe that the newsman has information that is clearly relevant to a specific probable violation of the law.
2. Show that the information sought cannot be obtained by alternative means less destructive to First Amendment rights.
3. Show a compelling and overriding interest in the information: The information is of critical relevance to the matter at hand, whether it be a grand jury investigation, or civil/criminal trial.

Despite the fact that there is still no official federal law to protect reporters' privilege, after *Branzburg*, the lower federal courts and most state courts recognized a qualified First Amendment privilege allowing journalists to protect their confidential sources and unpublished information. Nowadays, 40 states and the District of Columbia have some form of shield laws that protect the journalists from having to reveal their confidential sources.[63]

Generally speaking, the amount of protection the courts allow journalists to have in a reporter's privilege case is lowest when the journalists are called upon to testify in front of a grand jury and asked to provide confidential sources or information in criminal cases (Watkins, 1994). The courts always reject a reporter's privilege claim when the reporter observed his/her sources or other persons engaging in criminal activity or when his/her unpublished notes and background materials might lead the law enforcement officials to suspected

---

[62] Id.

[63] Seean article from the Reporters' Committee for Freedom of the Press, Reporter's Privilege. Retrieved from http://www.rcfp.org/privilege/.

criminals. Compared with criminal cases, the amount of protection for journalists in civil cases is much larger (Alexander & Bush, 1997) .

As noted earlier, most states, have passed state shield laws. These 40 states include: Alabama, Alaska, Arizona, Arkansas, California, Colorado, Connecticut, Delaware, Florida, Georgia, Hawaii, Illinois, Indiana, Kansas, Kentucky, Louisiana, Maine, Maryland, Michigan, Minnesota, Montana, Nebraska, Nevada, New Jersey, New Mexico, New York, North Carolina, North Dakota, Ohio, Oklahoma, Oregon, Pennsylvania, Rhode Island, South Carolina, Tennessee, Texas, Utah, Washington, West Virginia, Wisconsin. Even though they vary to a certain degree, under almost all state shield laws, a journalist is entitled to the privilege if he/she receives information from sources within the course of newsgathering activities. Therefore, sources who provide materials to a reporter in some capacity other than his/her role as a journalist would be subject to disclosure.[64]

One of the most famous Supreme Court cases involving reporter's privilege is *In re Farber*. Myron Farber, a reporter for the *New York Times*, wrote a very provocative article about the alleged mishandling of patients by a hospital which lead to the deaths of these patients. In the wake of the publication of this article, a doctor was indicted for murder for those deaths. During the trial, the defendant subpoenaed Farber in order to force him to produce his records of interviews with several unnamed witnesses, and Farber refused to comply. After the trial court ordered Farber to turn over the materials in question, Farber appealed, and the case went to the Supreme Court, where the Justices declined to hear the case. It was made clear by the justices that freedom of the press does not trump a defendant's right to a fair trial, and that neither the constitution or existing state shield laws provide journalists with an absolute privilege to refuse to provide information demanded in a criminal case by a defendant. Farber therefore became one of the few journalists who were put behind bars for refusing to name his/her sources.[65]

More recently, the issue of a reporter's privilege came to the forefront of media attention in the case *In re Miller*, involving reporters Judith Miller, who worked for the *New York Times* at the time, and

---

[64] Aside from the 40 states, a few other states are now also considering implementing some type of shield laws.

[65] See the decision for In re Farber, 439 U.S. 997 (1978).

Mathew Cooper, who worked for *Time* magazine. Miller and Cooper were both served with grand jury subpoenas to testify and provide information, including notes and documents pertaining to conversations they had with confidential sources relating to the revelation of former CIA agent Valerie Plame's identity. Both invoked state reporter's privilege and refused to comply with the subpoenas.[66] The federal district court held both Miller and Cooper in contempt of court, and the United States Court of Appeals for the District of Columbia Circuit upheld the ruling.

Miller and Cooper, in their appeal to the appellate court, pleaded several defenses including a First Amendment reporter's privilege and a common law reporter's privilege, but the appellate court rejected both the First Amendment and common law claims for privilege. The court held Miller and Cooper in civil contempt of court and sentenced both to 18 months in prison. The sentence, however, was stayed pending an appeal to the U.S. Supreme Court. Ultimately, the U.S. Supreme Court refused to hear the case, so Judith Miller ended up serving the remaining 4 months of the original 18-month sentence. On the other hand, Matthew Cooper was lucky enough to have his confidential source release him from their confidentiality agreement, so he chose to comply with the subpoena and agreed to testify before the grand jury (Natta et al., 2005).

These two cases demonstrated that to this day, the Supreme Court has not deviated far from its decision for *Branzburg*. In the end, it still is unwilling to recognize the existence of a federal reporter's privilege. This signals that there is a long way to go for journalists to truly protect their confidential sources, and that there is always the risk for them to go to jail if they refuse to comply with the order to testify in court. There seems to be two main reasons for the Supreme Court's persistent unwillingness to recognize this right. First, it feels that a person's right to a fair trial is just as important as the First Amendment right of a free press. Second, it does not want to grant the press special treatment of not having to testify in court when subpoenaed, something everyone else has to do. Additionally, it does not want to open the floodgate and have any writer who is working on a story claim him/herself a journalist and thus entitled to the privilege (Fargo, 2006). The issue of

[66] See the decision for In re Miller, 397 F.3d 964, 966-68 (D.C. Cir. 2005).

"who qualifies as a journalist and thus would be entitled to the shield law protection in this Internet age" is garnering a lot of attention currently, and in the absence of a unifying federal shield law, states that do recognize their own state shield laws have expressed different opinions as to whether an online blogger should be considered a journalist. In *Obsidian Finance Group, LLC v. Cox*(2011), which was a defamation case, an Oregon district court decided that a blogger who published a fact-based article in which she accused a businessman of corruption was *not* considered a journalist and therefore liable for libel. The court further noted that to qualify as a reporter, a standard of professionalism must be met, including but not limited to, being associated with a traditional news print or television media outlet or obtaining a degree in journalism. However, a subsequent opinion in the same case clarified that these criteria were "examples" rather than requirements. Therefore, bloggers could potentially qualify and the denial of media status in this particular case could be attributed to the fact that the defendant reportedly offered to remove accusations she alleged in her article for $ 2,500. On the other side of the coin, the website *The Mortgage Specialists, Inc. v. Implode-Explode Heavy Industries, Inc* (2010), was sued by a mortgage lender for publishing confidential documents given by an anonymous source. The New Hampshire Supreme Court decided that Internet news outlets should be treated like print media and receive the same legal privileges granted to traditional journalists. Similarly, the court found that the publication of these confidential documents could not be restrained and that the identity of the anonymous poster was protected unless the plaintiff could prove harm. This case set a precedent for protecting the legal rights of online media at the state level and reiterates the high legal hurdle required to restrict the free flow of information. This increased recognition of the right of online bloggers/journalists not to reveal their sources on the state level is in stark contrast to the Supreme Court's continuing reluctance to recognize a more universal shield law.

The US Congress, on the other hand, seems to be more eager to pass a federal shield law. In 2004, two significant bills were introduced into the United States House of Representatives and into the United States Senate to create a federal shield law. The first bill was introduced in an identical form in both the Senate and the House by two Republican congressmen. Separately, Democratic Senators also introduced another legislation that created a seemingly broader protection than the previous bill (Jackson, 2008). However, due to several factors, including the 2010 reveal of a massive amount of confidential information on the website Wikileaks, up until early 2013, these proposals are still "under consideration."

In May of 2013, however, the issue of a federal shield law has once again become a hot topic in the media in the wake of the news that the calling records of journalists for Associated Press (AP) were subpoenaed by the Justice Department in an effort to find the source of a leak threatening national security. After the news broke and the AP expressed their outage, the Obama administration sought to revive legislation that would provide greater protection to reporters in keeping their sources and communications confidential. Specifically, President Obama asked New York senator Chuck Schumer to reintroduce a version of a bill that he had pushed in 2009 called the Free Flow of Information Act, which would be the federal shield law.

So exactly what is in the federal shield law proposed by Schumer in 2009? If we use the AP case as an example, the 2009 legislation would have created a presumption that when the government was pursuing the AP journalists' phone records from a telephone carrier, and AP would be notified ahead of time, which would allow it to fight the subpoena in court. However, the proposed bill would also have allowed the government to seek a 45-to-90-day delay in notification if a court determined that such notice would threaten the integrity of the investigation.

Under the proposed bill, the scope of protection for reporters would vary depending on whether it was a civil case, a criminal case, or a national security case. It's not surprising to learn that the greatest protection would be given to civil cases in which litigants are seeking to force reporters to testify or in which they are trying to obtain their calling information to show why their need for the information outweighed the public's interest in a free press. Criminal cases would function similarly, but the burden would be on the reporter seeking to quash the subpoena to show that the public interest in the free flow of information should prevail over the needs of law enforcement. On the other hand, in cases involving the disclosure of classified information, the government's interest is generally favored. For instance, judges could not quash a subpoena through a balancing test if the government presented facts to show that the information might help prevent a terrorist attack or other acts likely to put national security in danger.

We should keep an eye on how this latest development on the federal shield law will turn out. Will this finally bear fruit to the creation of a federal shield law, or will this effort once again fizzle out like all the previous versions of the law?[67]

Ultimately, journalists will always have to rely heavily on anonymous sources to provide them with confidential information. Without those confidential sources, a lot of important stories would not be told, such as the Watergate scandal. That is why the journalists should be legally protected from having to reveal their confidential sources. Without this protection, journalists would have to divulge the names of their sources in court or face serious jail time. This would have significant implications on the journalists' ability to adequately do their jobs and tell important stories. The "chilling effect" that would result without the reporter's privilege is significant because some sources will refuse to talk to them out of fear of being publicly exposed (Banisar, 2007).

Chapter Conclusion

Overall, the United States has allowed journalists ample freedom to do their jobs with little to no censorship apparatus to control media content. This is especially true after the Supreme Court ruled in the landmark case of *Neal v. Minnesota* that prior restraint, except in special circumstances involving national security, of the press is unconstitutional. This is not to say that there is absolutely no censorship in the US. In the past, there had been several versions of Sedition Acts. In a more recent development, after the tragedy of 9/11, information that could be considered threatening to national security could be withheld from the public; however, the 2007 Amendment of FOIA seemed to be reversing the trend of government secrecy set by the George W. Bush's administration by not only recognizing online reporters as legitimate journalists but also giving out harsher penalties when the agencies fail to comply with a FOIA" request for information. This is an encouraging development for journalists and press freedom advocates (Banisar, 2007).

---

[67] Reports on the development of the renewed effort to enact a federal shield law in May 2013 can be found all the major news outlets.

The protection for confidential sources is another issue that has been of constant discussion in recent years. Since the decision of *Branzburg*, 40 states and the District of Columbia have enacted shield laws to protect journalists from having to reveal confidential sources in courts. While there is still no federal shield law today, several proposals have been in circulation in the US congress for consideration since 2004; however, given how many versions there have been and the Supreme Court's continuing reluctance to recognize a reporters' privilege, the authors are predicting that there will not be a federal shield law in the United States any time soon, if ever.

Chapter 5

Press Freedom Laws and Censorship in Europe

Similar to the previous chapter, this chapter discusses censorship, laws granting access to official documents, and the existence or absence of shield laws in the five European countries examined in this book. Each of the countries is discussed separately.

FRANCE

Freedom of the press is now guaranteed by the French Constitution and instances of governmental censorship are relatively limited today; however, France had a long history of governmental censorship, particularly from the 16th to 18th centuries.

As in many European countries, during periods before the 19th century, France's censorship regulations mainly concerned books and other publications that were related to the topic of religion. In France, however, the state began to take a greater interest in censorship. The main concern for censors was "heresy, sedition, and personal libel" at the beginning. After 1629, the French government started to also focus their censorship efforts on immorality and indecency. All things considered, the government still mostly wanted to control people's thoughts.[68]

[68] This information was taken from the Wikipedia entry, Censorship in France. Retrieved from http://en.wikipedia.org/wiki/Freedom_of_information_in_France#cite_note-Pottinger.2C_supra.2C_p._59-8.

The press freedom in France faced a breakthrough in 1881 when the Press Law of 1881 was passed. This law not only provided a legal framework for publications but also regulated the display of advertisements on public roads. Since its passage, it has been amended several times and remains in force to this day. It is often regarded as the foundational legal statement on freedom of the press and freedom of speech in France, but at the same time, the law imposes legal obligations on publishers and criminalizes certain specific behaviors, particularly behaviors concerning libel and slander (Kuhn, 1995). In recent years, French courts have ruled that this law also applies to content on the web.

Similar to many other countries that tightened their press control and strengthened the censorship laws when they are engaged in wars, France is no exception. During World War I, postal censorship was in force because the French government at the time believed it was necessary to control the public's morale and thus engaged in a kind of psychological warfare. Censorship laws were revoked with the founding of the Fifth Republic in 1958. Although cases of censorship still occurred from time to time, especially during war time, such as during the Algerian War, which lasted from 1954-1962 (Kuhn, 1995).

Today, the press is largely unrestricted by the law in France. Nevertheless, indirect pressures are sometimes applied to prevent publication of materials against the interests of the government or influential industries. According to Freedom House's report, involvement of the government and major industrial groups, sometimes with political ties with certain press organizations often raises questions as to the ability of the press to remain truly independent and unrestricted. For instance, the Agence France-Presse (AFP), an internationally prominent news agency whose reports are picked up by the media all around the world, is a public corporation supposedly independent from the government. However, the agency derives a lot of its revenue from sales to the government, which could potentially have an impact on how the content and tone of the stories is decided. Another such example is Radio France International (RFI), which is financially supported by the Minister of Foreign Affairs. Aside from that, most of the press depends on advertising to generate revenue, and there is a persistent concern about the media's independence from advertisers (Karlekar & Cook, 2008).

Furthermore, French law specifically proscribes certain publications. Generally speaking, the proscriptions can be classified into five categories:

1. Confidential information and related matters.
2. Privileged judicial or administrative information.
3. Press sensationalism.
4. Certain types of litigation, either to protect the content of the proceedings or the identities of the parties involved.
5. Interests related to national security (Errera, 1985).

In terms of access to governmental documents, the French press has not always been able to have this access to official documents, and as Errera pointed out, the history of France indicated that the French government has a tradition of secrecy (1985). In fact, while freedom of the press was generally practiced in France, there was no general law providing for disclosure of official documents and the right of access to official documents, a right that is closely related to freedom of the press, until the 1978 reform (Errera, 1985).

The Law of 1978 provided that all those subject to French jurisdiction have a right of access to all general official documents. With the exception of a list of enumerated official documents and confidential information, all other documents should be accessible to the public. Included on the list of exemptions under the law are "documents established in the process of justice," "documents which are already available to the public," "internal deliberations of the national executive," and "documents with secrets regarding national defense or national foreign policy." When a person is denied access to documents, he/she must be notified with a written document setting forth the reasons why (Errera, 1985). He/she can also challenge the denial in front of the administrative court. The bad news is these courts are always overbooked and citizens must often wait several years to have their rights examined in a fair trial. Consequently, France has been declared guilty of excessive delays many times by the European Court of Human Rights (Banisar, 2007).

In France, there is legal protection of confidential sources. Specifically, the confidentiality of the sources is protected under the 1881 Press Law, which provides that any journalist called to testify about information obtained in the pursuit of his profession is free not to reveal his/her confidential sources (Reporters Without Borders Staff, 2011b).

Generally speaking, the protection of confidential sources is very important for press freedom in Europe. It is defined by Article 10 of the European Convention on Human Rights and shaped by the constant case law of the European Court of Human Rights (ECHR) (Banisar, 2007). In France, a special law was enacted in 2010, stipulating that it is illegal to attempt to discover a journalist's sources by investigating any person who, because of his/her usual relationship with a journalist, may hold information identifying these sources. The major provision in this new law includes the following: 1) The formal right for journalists to hide sources; 2) Stricter rules for searches by investigators; 3) Invalidation of information obtained through phone taps; and 4) A ban on trying to obtain sources from journalists' relations. There can be exceptions, however, if there is an overriding public interest. Moreover, it also provides that in a criminal case, the right to keep sources secret can only be infringed upon if the nature and gravity of the offense justify it (Atwell, 2010).

Overall, the new law strengthens the protection against government searches of journalists' homes, offices, or cars when the searches are related to their professional activities. When this kind of search is allowed to happen, it requires the presence of a magistrate during those searches (Atwell, 2010). One aspect of this law that is worth pointing out is that bloggers are not protected under this law.

Despite having a long history of strong source protection law, journalists are still being arrested and forced to reveal their sources in recent years. Throughout 2007, authorities detained journalists in order to pressure them into revealing their sources and attempted to search media offices and personal premises for documents and sources. In a serious violation of free speech in late 2007, counterterrorism authorities detained *Le Monde* reporter Guillaume Dasquie for 48 hours after searching his Paris apartment and trying to make him reveal his sources. Dasquie was targeted for this search because he had published state secrets pertaining to the terrorist attacks of September 11, 2001 (Karlekar & Cook, 2008).

In 2010, there was another sensational case that involved the protection of sources. In this instance, it was alleged that presidential aides directly violated the source protection law by using a domestic intelligence agency to identify an official who was leaking information about a judicial investigation involving labor minister Eric Woerth and L'Oréal heiress Liliane Bettencourt. The case was prompted by a September 2010 report in *Le Monde* that claimed police had searched Bettencourt's home. When Bettencourt's lawyer complained that the confidentiality of a judicial investigation had been violated, the prosecutor ordered the police to scour the journalists' phone records in an effort to identify who had told them about the raid (Reporters Without Borders Staff, 2011b).

In summary, France does have a history of censorship and secrecy, especially during war times such as WWI, but French press today generally operate without government interference. On the other hand, the close ties between the press, the government, and corporations creates a potentially toxic environment that is conducive to press self-censorship. In regards to the press' access to official documents, the Law of 1978, a similar law to the United States' Freedom of Information Act, granted the public the right to ask for those documents. Unlike the US though, France does have statutory legal protection for the right to protect confidential sources, and this law underwent a revision in 2010 that strengthened it. This does not mean that police searches of reporters' homes to find the identities of confidential sources or the imprisonment of reporters for refusing to testify in courts do not still happen from time to time in France.

SWEDEN

Sweden strongly protects freedom of the press and was a pioneer in officially abolishing censorship. In 1766, Sweden became the first country to introduce a constitutional law where censorship was eliminated and freedom of the press was guaranteed (Strömberg, 1985).

In Sweden, the constitutional prohibition against all forms of censorship has been in place since and a cornerstone of Sweden's freedom of the press (Strömberg, 1985). A censoring system is considered illegal, and so are all other forms of measures by the authorities to suppress or restrict a book or a newspaper before its publication. Simply put, as Strömberg pointed out, the injunctions that in many countries are sought by lawyers or officials, and given by the courts to stop the publication or broadcasting of certain stories, are not possible in Sweden (1985).

However, just as in any other country in the world, it is also inaccurate to say that Sweden has always been immune to censorship. As in many other countries, a form of censorship was set up during war times in Sweden. During WWII, pressure from Germany caused the Swedish government to "recommend" Swedish publishers not to publish stories that Germany would find biased. Specifically, the Swedish government revived an old law that made it illegal to "publish offensive writings about a foreign state." Invoking this law during the war, meant the Swedish court sentenced several journalists to jail for their anti-Hitler and anti-Nazi writings.[69]

Another area that has censorship implications in Sweden is military information. In Sweden, it is illegal to photograph or describe in writing or publish pictures or documents of military installations and other "protected objects." The term "protected objects" can be applied to anything from the facilities to military aircraft when it is considered to be in the interest of national security to do so. Sweden also prohibits "hate speech," which is defined as publicly making statements that threaten or express disrespect for an ethnic group or similar group regarding their race, skin color, national or ethnic origin, faith, or sexual orientation (Kent, 2008). Overall, though, censorship is not a concerning threat to the press freedom in Sweden.

In regards to the public's access to official documents, Sweden has a long history of granting access. In fact, the Freedom of the Press Act of 1766 granted public access to government documents and later became an important part of the Swedish Constitution. This was the first ever piece of freedom of information legislation in the world and some have argued that all Freedom of Information Acts" in the world have grown out of an application of this Swedish principle, albeit in somewhat diluted forms (Banisar, 2007).

Freedom of the Press Act explicitly identifies the right to publish official records as one element of press freedom that the Act protects. A person who is seeking to gain access to official information is ordinarily not required to reveal his/her reason or name. Although another statute, the Secrecy Act, limits the types of information that the public has access to, generally speaking, access to official records may

---

[69] This information was taken fromDepartment of State's report on Sweden. Retrieved from http://www.state.gov/j/drl/rls/hrrpt/2006/78841.htm.

be limited only if it is requested with respect to records relating to sensitive information. Some of the examples of the restricted information are 1) national security and foreign affairs, 2) the central financial, monetary, and foreign exchange policy of the state, 3) administrative action concerning inspection, control, or other supervision, and 4) the protection of personal privacy or economic data. A denial of access, however, can usually be challenged in court and then appealed to a higher court (Banisar, 2007).

Another aspect of the interaction between the Freedom of the Press Act and the Secrecy Act is that in regards to the restricted official records, the Secrecy Act only allows a specific maximum period of secrecy ranging from 2 to 70 years. More importantly, the Secrecy Act does not authorize the imposition of secrecy solely to protect authorities from criticism. The Swedes recognize that secrecy generally inhibits free debate and comprehensive enlightenment, and therefore, any restrictions on the access to official records should be carefully tailored to balance the public's right to know with the government's legitimate needs to keep certain sensitive information out of the public's watchful eyes (Strömberg, 1985).

When it comes to the protection of sources, Sweden also has strong laws for this protection. Swedish laws concerning source protection are described in the Freedom of the Press Act and the Law on Freedom of Expression, two of the nation's four fundamental laws, which together make up the country's constitution. Just as the U.S. constitution, no other law or act of the state is allowed to infringe on the rights described in fundamental laws (Hendler, 2010).

These laws forbid what is routine in the United States. For example, government entities cannot investigate or even ask about the identity of an information leaker presumed to be on their staff, unless the leaker is suspected of a national security crime such as treason, or of knowingly leaking a properly classified document (Hendler, 2010).

Swedish law also offers an unusual protection to sources inside and out of government. Unlike reporter's shield laws—which, in the United States, offer journalists some protection for refusing to comply with a subpoena—Sweden's Freedom of the Press Act, actively forbids journalists to reveal a confidential source. Naturally, there are exceptions to this rule, as in cases of high treason, or where a source intentionally disclosed classified information (Hendler, 2010).

These protections apply when the journalist involved works for a constitutionally protected media outlet. After various amendments, revisions, and clarifying regulations, Sweden has extended the act's obligations and protections to properly registered radio, television, and websites. However, websites and other electronic media are not automatically covered under the act, as Hendler pointed out (2010). In order for websites to obtain a certificate and registration, which would entitle them to this protection, they have to show the following: 1) Material on the site can only be modified by employees or agents of the media organization; 2) The site's name must be distinct from other registered outlets, and must maintain a more or less consistent design identity throughout its pages; and 3) The site must be able to designate a responsible editor. As one can see, these are not difficult criteria to meet (Hendler, 2010) .

As stated above, the Swedish protection of confidential sources is one of the strongest in the world. The constitution protects people who share information to the media from being sought by the authorities. This is precisely why the controversial website Wikileaks decided to base part of its operation in Sweden. In 2010, Wikileaks was thrust into spotlight because of its publication of Afghan War logs, which led to one of the largest and most controversial intelligence leaks to date. Wikileaks claimed that Swedish law protects their sources, but the problem was Wikileaks had no publication license in Sweden; therefore, this disqualified the website from enjoying the constitutionally recognized right of source protection (Jonasson, 2010).

Not only is censorship rare, but the Swedish constitution actually provides for the right of access to official documents and the protection of confidential sources. Every citizen has the right to access government records except in rare occasions. On top of this, journalists would actually be penalized if they reveal the identities of their confidential sources. Now, reporters on the web can also be protected under this law. This speaks to the fact that Sweden has always been a pioneer when it comes to freedom of the press, forward thinking and quick to adapt the law to keep up with the times. All things considered, the authors see no indications that Sweden, which has a proud libertarian tradition when it comes to the media, would stop being the press freedom pioneer that it is in the future.

GERMANY

In German history, censorship has unfortunately been more of a rule than an exception. It was introduced by the Catholic Church in the form of the inquisition. As Humphreys noted, in the German Empire period, media were under imperial control and the government had the right to censor materials before their work was published (1996). After the start of WWI, the military took control of censorship with the goal of mobilizing German support for the war. A police official was instated in every city for this purpose, and restrictions on materials became much harsher. Materials could be banned because of their association with a particular person or country (Humphreys, 1996).

During the Weimer Republic period, the Weimar Constitution forbade censorship, but the Nazi party soon took over the country and began to implement a strict form of censorship (Humphreys, 1996). Censorship under Nazi rule was implemented by the Minister of Propaganda, Joseph Goebbels. All forms of media, including literature, music, and newspapers, were censored. Attempts were also made to censor private communications, such as mail and private conversations. The goal of censorship under the Nazi regime, as Humphreys pointed out, was to reinforce Nazi power and to suppress opposing viewpoints and information (1996). Punishment under the censorship laws ranged from banning the presentation given by journalists and publishing of works to deportation, imprisonment, or even execution in a concentration camp (Humphreys, 1996).

Following Germany's defeat in WWII, the West German media were subject to censorship by the Allied Occupational forces. During this short period, criticism of the allied forces and the emerging government were not allowed. Publications that were expected to have a negative effect on the general public were not printed. When the official government of the Federal Republic of Germany took over, these limitations on freedom of speech and press were greatly relaxed in West Germany under the new constitution, while East Germany experienced severe censorship under the communist regime. The new constitution, which was still in use following the unification of Germany and enacted under this new government granted its people the right of freedom of the press/expression and prohibited censorship. However, there is a limiting provision stating that these rights could be restricted under the provision of general laws, in provisions for the protection of personal rights, in provisions for the protection of young persons, and in the provision of the right to personal honor (Kohl, 1985) .

Undoubtedly related to the turbulent history of Hitler and Nazi rule, in today's Germany, membership in a Nazi party, incitement of hatred against a segment of the population, and Holocaust denial are illegal. In short, the provision in German Criminal Law that bans the incitement of hatred against a segment of the population is often applied in trials relating to Holocaust denial in Germany. Publications that express sympathy towards Nazi Germany and question the existence of the Holocaust results in the authors of these publications facing legal consequences that may include jail time.[70]

In terms of access to official documents, Germany was slow, by European standard, to allow the public to have access to these documents. In fact, along with Luxembourg, Germany was the only country in the EU, without an access to an information law until 2005, when the federal government of Germany passed a freedom of information law on September 5th of that year. The law, called the German Freedom of Information Act", grants each person an unconditional right to access official federal information. No legal, commercial, or any other kind of justification is necessary and the information must be provided within one month (Banisar, 2006).

Just as other freedom of information legislations around the world go, there are several exemptions to this new law in Germany. Those exemptions include information on the disclosure of which would have a detrimental effect on international relations, information on military interests and internal or external security interests, information on the duties of regulatory authorities, and information that could cause harm to public safety. Similar to other freedom of information acts "in other countries, if a person's request for an official document is denied, he/she has the right to appeal that decision (Banisar, 2006).

Perhaps due to the law's relative newness, the high cost of obtaining the documents, and the lack of advertisement by the German government, so far, the number of requests for official government

---

[70] SeeGerman Criminal Law, § 130 Public Incitement. There have been several high-profile cases where German scientists were sentenced to jail because they were Holocaust deniers. One of them actually fled to the United States but was later deported back to Germany.

documents is still relatively small (Schwanitz, 2007). It remains to be seen whether this law will have any future impact on freedom of the press in Germany.

Protection of sources in Germany is granted by law. In fact, Germany has found that protection of sources is part of the constitutional right to freedom of expression and press. In Germany, the Constitutional Court first ruled in 1966 that freedom of the press also includes a certain degree of protection for the confidential relationships between the press and its private sources of information. The Court recognized that such protection is absolutely indispensable for freedom of the press. In 2007, the Constitutional Court ruled that searches of newsrooms in investigations of state secrets cases impaired the right of freedom of the press under the Basic Law and were constitutionally illegal in preliminary investigations (Banisar, 2007).

Overall, Germany had a long history of censorship. While the current German Constitution states that there should be no censorship, that rule has several restrictions. This includes instances when the publications in questions are deemed to be harmful to the youth or detrimental to national security. A unique feature in censorship in Germany today is the topic of Hitler and the Nazi Party. Specifically, Holocaust denial is illegal in Germany, and any person who expresses that view could be sent to jail.

Regarding people's right to have access to official documents, Germany was surprisingly one of the slowest countries in Europe to adopt an official Freedom of Information Act", which came into effect in 2006. Like similar laws in other countries, this Act allows several exemptions, including documents that could reveal national security secrets. In terms of protection of sources for the press, Germany's Constitutional Court recognized that this protection is part of the right of freedom of the press; therefore, journalists in Germany normally do not have to reveal their sources.

ITALY

Italy has one of the lowest levels of press freedom in Europe. A 2009 report by Freedom House classified Italy as "partly free",", making Italy the only country in Western Europe to be classified as such. Italy's ranking also made it fall behind many former communist states of Eastern Europe. Part of the reason for this low ranking is the censorship and self-censorship system that is rampant in the media in Italy.

Under the Mussolini and Fascist rule from 1922-1944, censorship was in full force. During this period, censorship was enforced in the following methods:

1. Control over the public appearance of the regime. Censorship was obtained with the deletion of any content that could allow opposition, suspects, or doubts on fascism.
2. Constant check of the public opinion as a measuring instrument of consensus.
3. Creation of national and local archives in which each citizen was filed and classified depending on his ideas, his habits, his relationship and his eventual shameful acts or situations (Bonsaver, 2007).

Judging from these guidelines, for the Fascist regime, the main goal for censorship was to root out ideological and defeatist contents. Just like any authoritarian dictatorship regime, it wanted to utilize a censorship system to make sure that no anti-government content could be used to undermine its authority (Bonsaver, 2007).

After the fall of the Fascist regime, the rules were relaxed and there was more freedom of expression. Article 21 of the Constitution of Italy provides that everyone has the right to freely express thoughts in speech, writing, and by other communication, and that the "press may not be controlled by authorization or submitted to censorship."[71] In other words, censorship was abolished and outlawed in Italy more than sixty years ago. Freedom of the press and of personal opinion is not only established by the Constitution, but also deeply rooted in custom and in all perceptions of civil society. This does not mean, however, that there is no longer any censorship in Italy to hinder freedom of the press, as there have been some worrisome developments. As Freedom House's reports showed, the most disturbing trend in the Italian media industry is the concentration of media ownership, with only a handful of media moguls who own and control the media outlets. This created a highly centralized landscape of the dominant culture that is "partly deliberate manipulation and partly borne out of sheer ignorance"

[71] See The Constitution of Italy, Article 21.

(Bonsaver, 2007) . Under this kind of media culture, Italian press self-censored itself before any censorship commission could do it. In other words, even though there is no formal censorship system to monitor the press activities, because of the high concentration of media ownership, which former prime minister Silvio Berlusconi was a major player of, and the existence of a kind of "group think" among the journalists, they actually self-censor themselves when it comes to reporting the news, which could be just as potent, if not more so, than any formal censorship system (Karlekar & Cook, 2008).)

Another very effective form of censorship in Italy is the defamation law in Italy. The libel law system in Italy is considered unfriendly to the media and could send journalists to jail for printing "defamatory" comments about public figures. This subject is discussed in a later chapter.

Compared with other European countries, Italy has a somewhat weak protection for access to official documents. Chapter V of Law No. 241 of 7 August 1990 provides for access to administrative documents. However, the right to access is limited. The law states that those requesting information must have a legitimate legal interest. The subsequent 1992 regulations required that the people who were requesting the documents have a personal concrete interest to safeguard in legally relevant situations. The courts have ruled that this includes the right of environmental groups and local counselors to demand information on behalf of those they represent (Banisar, 2006). The statute was amended in 2005, and the revision appeared to adopt the court rulings and relaxed the interest requirement to allow access when an individual can show they represent a more general public interest. Once a request is filed, the government agencies must respond within 30 days; however, they can delay release if releasing the information would prevent or severely impede the performance of administrative action.[72]

As stated above, there are limitations and exemptions to this law. In particular, the statute provides that information relating to state secrets, fiscal procedures, development of policy, and the rights of third parties is excluded. Restricted to a lesser extent is information relating to national defense, international relations monetary policy, public order and prevention of crime, and personal privacy and professional

---

[72] See details in Chapter V of Law No. 241 of 7 August 1990.

secrets, which can be withheld but must be given when it is necessary to defend their legal interest. The 1992 regulations mandate that non-disclosure be justified in terms of damage to the public interest, but they also state that access may be denied if there is specific, identified damage to national security and defense or international relations.

Once again, compared with other countries in Europe, Italy has a relatively weak legal protection of sources, which does not speak well of its press freedom environment. In Italy, the press law of 1963 assigns the journalists and the publishers the obligation to "respect the professional secret related to the sources of their information." [73] However, according to the Italian criminal procedure code, a judge in charge of a criminal case can ask a journalist to reveal his/her informant's identity if the information is crucial to the resolution of the case and if the information's authenticity can only be confirmed by the informant's identity. In recent years, Italy, similar to almost everywhere else, has enacted new security laws that appear to be threatening the protection of journalistic sources (Banisar, 2006).

Italy, a country that was ranked as one of the lowest on multiple freedom of the press charts, earned those dismal rankings, which are lower than a lot of former Communist countries. Despite the constitutional provision that states there should be no censorship to hinder freedom of the press, there is a prevalence of self-censorship, mainly due to the heavy concentration of media ownership controlled by a few moguls, including former Prime Minister Berlusconi, and a sense of "group think" among the journalists. In terms of access to government information, there is a law in place that allows the media to request official documents, but there are various limitations and restrictions to this rule. Unlike other European laws regulating this access, the Italian law demands the people who request the documents to justify their requests. Regarding the protection of confidential sources, the press law in Italy grants this right to journalists; however, journalists could still be hauled into court to testify if the judges feel it is necessary and several newsrooms were searched in order for the police to identify confidential sources.

---

[73] See an article from European Federation of Journalists (EFJ) about policy document on protection of sources. The article retrieved from http://www.ifj.org/assets/docs/056/155/eaea138-b943c9b.pdf.

THE UNITED KINGDOM

The United Kingdom has a long and rich history of censorship. Depending on the time, the laws could be lax or harsh. A big, important player in the censorship history of the United Kingdom was the Ministry of Information. As Supperstone pointed out, it was set up during World War I, and again came into life during World War II, for obvious propaganda purposes (1985). As such, the Ministry was responsible for keeping a lot of information out of the public domain during the years of war, mainly because the British government felt that the revelation of the information would have been harmful to the national sentiment. It also censored many press reports that were not deemed to be sufficiently patriotic, or reports that might have revealed too many details of the British military operations that could benefit enemies. Following the end of WWII, the Ministry was officially dissolved in 1946 when the Central Office of Information took over some of the Minister's old duties (Supperstone, 1985).

A major and recurrent justification for censorship is protection of national security. In the United Kingdom, there were several Acts passed by the British parliament for the protection of official information, and they are mainly related to national security. The latest revision of this Act is the Official Secrets Act 1989, which eliminated the public interest defense by repealing section 2 of the Official Secrets Act 1911.[74] Additionally, the previously mentioned DA notice, the official request to news editors not to publish or broadcast items on specified subjects for reasons of national security, can also be considered a form of censorship.[75]

On the other end of the spectrum, the Freedom of Information Act "was adopted in November 2000 and went into full effect January 2005.The Act gives any person a right of access to information kept by over 100,000 public bodies. Those bodies are required to respond within 20 working days. This deadline can be extended to allow for consideration of release on public-interest test grounds as long as it is within a time period that is deemed reasonable under the circumstances (Banisar, 2006).

---

[74] See Official Secrets Act 1989.

[75] See more details from the DA Notice System website. Retrieved from http://www.dnotice.org.uk/index.htm,

The British Freedom of Information Act contains an astonishing 13-page long list of exemptions divided by 3 categories. Under the absolute exemption category, court records and information that is about the personal life of individuals, the security services, or is protected under another law cannot be disclosed. Under the "qualified class exemption" category, information can be withheld if it is determined to be within a broad class of exempt information relating to government policy formulation, safeguarding national security, or if it was received in confidence from a foreign government. A "public-interest test" applies and provides that information can be withheld only when the public interest in maintaining the exemption outweighs the public interest in disclosure. The last category is a more limited exemption where the government must show harm to specified interests, such as defense, crime prevention, or international relations, to withhold information. The public interest test also applies to information in this category.[76]

The implementation of the Act moved at a very slow pace. Although it is called Freedom of information Act 2000", the right to demand information from the government did not go into effect until January 2005, nearly five years after the adoption of the Act, which was the slowest of any country in the world. Rather than implementing the Act in phases, all national and local departments simultaneously provided access. Probably owing to the long wait in adopting the Act and its implementation, there was tremendous interest in the law once it came into force, with the government agencies receiving literally thousands of requests for information (Banisar, 2006).

The reviews on the implementation of the Act have generally been positive. The biggest problems with the Act thus far has been delays on responses and decisions, as there are no fixed time limits for the government to decide on whether a request should be granted. Many users also report problems with the excessive use of exemptions by public bodies, but as with other similar laws in other countries, applicants can repeal the decisions if their requests for information that is denied (Banisar, 2006).

When it comes to the protection of confidential sources in the United Kingdom, there is one statute that grants this protection for the journalists; however, the provision has a clause that provides the courts

---

[76] See the British Freedom of Information Act for more details.

a lot of leeway to strip away this protection from the journalists who want to keep the identities of their sources secret. Section 10 of Contempt of Court Act of 1981 provides that no court can require a person to disclose, nor is any person guilty of contempt of court for refusing to disclose the source of information contained in a publication for which he/she is responsible, unless it is established to the satisfaction of the court that disclosure is necessary in the interests of justice, national security, or for the prevention of disorder or crime.[77]

The interpretation of section 10 of the Contempt of Court Act 1981is affected by three considerations: 1) As a matter of principle, the necessity for disclosure must be convincingly established and the basis upon which production of information is ordered in any particular case must not negate the right to freedom of expression; 2) Limitations on confidentiality of journalistic sources call for the most careful scrutiny by the Court; and 3)Disclosure must be demanded in order to meet a urgent social need and should be proportionate to a legitimate aim which is being pursued with no less invasive alternative available (Supperstone, 1985).

The bad news for the news-gatherers in the UK is that in practice, the courts have often taken a broad view of the "interests of justice or national security or for the prevention of disorder or crime" clause, particularly when influenced by legislation such as the UK Terrorism Act 2000 that created a new offence of "withholding information on suspected terrorist offences."[78] In other words, the courts in the UK have held that journalists have no immunity to protect them from their obligation to disclose their sources in court when it is decided that such disclosure is absolutely necessary in the interest of justice.[79]

Although there is no formal system of censorship in the United Kingdom now, the country has had a long history with censorship. In terms of censorship of the press, it usually occurred when the country was engaged in a war for propaganda purposes, while in recent years, press censorship would be justified in the name of national security or anti-terrorism, as when the Official Secrets Act of 1989 is invoked. The United Kingdom was also late in enacting an official statute to grant

---

[77] Contempt of Court Act, 1981, §10.

[78] See Terrorism Act 2000.

[79] See the rulings for British Steel Corp. v. Granada [1980] 3 W.L.R. 774.

access to official documents, as the Freedom of Information Act 2000" was not fully implemented until 2005. The Act has a surprisingly long list of exemptions and requests for information can be denied if it is determined that it is in the public's best interest for that information not to be revealed. As for protection of confidential sources, the journalists in the UK can invoke section 10 of the Contempt of Court Act 1981, which provides a reporter's privilege, when ordered to reveal their confidential sources; however, courts have been known to sidestep this right when they determined that revealing the source is in the best interest of national security and prevention of crimes.

Chapter 6

Press Freedom Laws and Censorship in Asia

This chapter discusses censorship, laws granting access to official documents, and the existence or absence of shield laws in the five Asian countries (plus Hong Kong and Taiwan) examined in this book. In order to present a fuller picture, all these countries are discussed separately.

INDIA

On the whole, censorship in India mainly targets religious issues. The Constitution of India does guarantee freedom of expression, but also places certain restrictions on content. These restrictions are mainly because the government wants to maintain communal and religious harmony so that the history of tension in the nation will not happen again.[80]

There is no outright press censorship law to regulate the journalists in India, but this does not mean that the Indian government has not tried to silence news representatives. A good example of press censorship in India occurred during the "State of Emergency" period from 1975-1977. This 21-month long controversial period in India was brought about by political unrest in the country. To take control of an increasingly chaotic situation where the oppositions were accusing the ruling party of election fraud and gaining credibility by the minute, the government declared a state of emergency and suspended elections and

[80] See the Constitution of India.

civil liberties (Mehta, 1979). The liberties that were suspended included freedom of the press, as the government imposed censorship on the press, who could no longer publish any stories that portrayed the Indira Gandhi-led ruling party in a negative light, as Mehta pointed out (1979).

There are also legal statutes that although not exactly about censorship, could be used to censor the press. Such laws include the Official Secrets Act 1923 and Prevention of Terrorist Activities Act (PoTA), both of which have been used to limit press freedom. Under the decades-old Official Secrets Act, the disclosure of any information that is likely to affect the sovereignty and integrity of India, the security of the state, or friendly relations with foreign states, is punishable by this act.[81] Under PoTA, a person could be detained for up to six months for being in contact with a terrorist or terrorist group. PoTA was repealed in 2006 and reinstated in 2008, but the Official Secrets Act 1923 has been in effect since its inception.[82] The journalists were naturally concerned by these laws, as they had to worry about whether talking to a certain person or revealing certain information could be considered as breaking the law.

The Supreme Court ruled in 1975 that access to government information was an essential part of the fundamental right to freedom of speech and expression. The Court ruled in 2002 that voters have a right to know information about candidates for elected offices and ordered the Election Commission to make candidates publish information about criminal records, assets, liabilities and educational qualifications (Banisar, 2006).

The Indian Right to Information Act (RTI Act) was passed by the Indian Parliament on 15 June 2005 to give the Indian people that right. Under this law, all Indian citizens have a right to ask for information not only from central government public authorities, but also from public authorities under the jurisdiction of the states. This includes local level bodies. It also stipulates that all government departments or government-funded agencies have to designate a Public Information Officer (PIO). The PIO's responsibility is to ensure that information requested is disclosed to the petitioner within 30 days or within 48

---

[81] See Official Secrets Act 1923. This law was also influenced by the British.

[82] See Prevention of Terrorist Activities Act.

hours in the case of information concerning the life or liberty of a person.[83]

Like other similar laws around the world, the Act includes a list of exemptions. They include disclosures that would prejudicially affect the sovereignty and integrity of India, the security, strategic or economic interests of the State, trade secrets, and personal information which has no relationship to any public activity or which would cause an unwarranted invasion of privacy.

Since the Act came into existence, there have been a number of high profile disclosures that revealed corruption in various government schemes, such as scams in disaster relief and construction of highways (Banisar, 2006). The law itself has been hailed as a landmark in India's drive towards more openness and accountability. However, the Act also has certain weaknesses that hamper implementation, such as the lack of speedy appeal and non-compliance to requests, as Banisar's research shows.

In India, the protection of sources did not receive a great deal of attention. Although this protection is somewhat recognized under the Constitution of India as part of the freedom of expression/press guarantee, it is limited (Srinivasan, 1998).

Aside from the limited constitution-provided right of the protection of sources, there was another law adopted for the protection of sources in India. Namely, the Newspaper Rule, which allows for newspapers to withhold the identities of their sources in libel cases prior to trial, has been recognized at least once. Generally speaking, there have been very few cases where Indian journalists were forced to disclose their sources (Banisar, 2007).

Currently, press censorship is imposed for for national security reasons. The Official Secrets Act 1923 played a major part in press censorship in India by penalizing the journalists for publicly disclosing information that the government considers to be state secrets. India's freedom of information act", the Indian Right to Information Act gives people the right to have access to official documents, and since it came into effect, it has been credited with helping to disclose misdeeds in the government. Regarding the right for protection of confidential sources, the Indian constitution gives limited protection. However, there has not

---

[83] See India's Right to Information Act 2005.

been that many instances where the journalists in India were asked to reveal their sources.

SINGAPORE

In Singapore, there is an official government group that was set up to deal with censorship issues. The Censorship Review Committee (CRC), which meets every 10 years, was formed to review and update the nation's censorship objectives and principles to meet the long-term interests of Singaporean society.[84] The recommendations are submitted to the Ministry of Information, Communications and the Arts (MICA) and Media Development Authority (MDA), who are responsible for the implementation of the recommendations. These are subsequently reviewed regularly to ensure that they keep up with technological, social, and industry developments.

The fact that the government in Singapore set up a committee to review censorship issues demonstrated how important censorship is in this nation. The government often justified having a censorship system by arguing that censorship of political, racial, and religious content is necessary to avoid upsetting the balance of Singapore's delicate multi-racial society (Tey, 2008). As previously mentioned, Singapore is a nation that has an abysmally low freedom of the press ranking with severely tight media control, so it's no surprise that there are several statutes that essentially serve the purpose of press censorship. Specifically, the Newspapers and Printing Presses Act (NPPA), the Defamation Act, the Internal Security Act (ISA), the Sedition Act, and the Official Secrets Act all in one way or another constrain press freedom, allowing the authorities to restrict the circulation of news that is deemed to incite violence, arouse racial or religious tensions, interfere in domestic politics, or threaten public order, the national interest, or national security (Banisar, 2006). Furthermore, the Sedition Act outlaws seditious speech, the distribution of seditious materials, and acts with a "seditious tendency."[85]

Out of these laws, the Internal Security Act, the Sedition Act, and the Official Secrets Act are particularly harsh on the press. Recognizing

---

[84] See the Media Development Authority website. Retrieved from http://www.mda.gov.sg/Public/Consultation/Pages/CRC.aspx.

[85] See Singapore's Sedition Act.

and conceding that these laws were inordinately draconian, the Singaporean government softened slightly on its treatment of the press by amending the Newspaper and Printing Presses Act in 1986 (Banisar, 2006). Over the years, these highly repressive laws had not often been enforced and served more as a deterrent back-up and symbolism, as Banisar observed (2006). In fact, the last time one of these laws was used against the media was in 1971, when the police detained four executives of a Chinese language newspaper for allegedly printing articles that promote communism. However, from time to time, the political leaders would come out and remind the press that those laws would be used against journalists or people who work in the media who are considered to be a threat to national security (Banisar, 2006). In other words, the Singapore government came up with a more subtle and insidious way to control the press that allowed it to keep its eyes on the press without having to constantly resort to legal action.

It should also be noted that subsequent to the press crisis of 1971, the Newspaper and Printing Presses Act made it mandatory in 1974 for newspaper corporations to be publicly listed and to create management shares allocated to banks and other establishment figures. These shares have 200 times the voting rights as ordinary shares and serve as a critical mechanism for the government to influence a newspaper's workings without having to directly interfere with ownership and provide effective control over the board and top editorial positions (Tey, 2008). In short, it is a subtler mechanism of press control and press censorship.

Foreign journalists in Singapore are also subject to strict press control. Under the Newspaper and Printing Presses of 1986, the government can declare any newspaper published outside Singapore to be a newspaper engaging in the domestic politics of Singapore (Tey, 2008). The term "engaging in domestic politics" was broadly defined, and the foreign publications could easily find themselves in hot water if they published stories that were critical to the government of Singapore, with the penalty being having their circulation quota reduced. Some very prominent publications, *the Economist* and *Time*, were among those that had been censored (Hoong, 1998). The government justifies its harsh position on the fear of political chaos and the adverse economic repercussions that an unrestrained circulation of foreign newspapers might bring to the country, as Hoong remarked (1998).

On the whole, there is press censorship in Singapore, but the government is mainly concerned with the comments voiced by the opposition. When the media allows opposition parties, civil opponents, and foreign journalists to comment on what are perceived as local issues, the government usually pays extra attention to these comments. Censorship of the press is usually achieved through a mixture of ownership, legislation, defamation suits, harassment, and self-censorship on the part of the media.

More than 85 countries around the world have implemented some form of Freedom of Information Act to allow their citizens to have access to official documents, but Singapore is not one of them (Banisar, 2006). There is usually an information gap between citizens and the government, which is privy to a wealth of information unavailable to the public. Currently, citizens have no legal right to have access to official documents and the government agencies have no obligation to provide those documents.[86]

Similarly, there is also a lack of protection for confidential sources in Singapore. Aside from formal legal guarantees for this protection in several countries, there is also a rule of practice known as the "Newspaper Rule," which states that newspapers will not be compelled to disclose sources of information in pre-trial discovery. Simply put, this rule protects the confidentiality of a newspaper's sources. It originated from England, but so far, the courts in Singapore are not receptive to this rule. In fact, Courts in Singapore have rejected the Newspaper Rule twice. Their reasoning was that even though it was widely adopted in common law countries, it was not the law for Singapore (Banisar, 2007). It was also noted that the courts in Singapore expressed concern that adoption of this rule would encourage unseen character assassins and other troublemakers.

Singapore is ranked near the bottom of Freedom Houses' Freedom of the Press Index year after year for valid reasons. There is an official censorship committee that deals with press censorship issues, and several of Singapore's harsh laws, including the Internal Security Act, the Sedition Act, and the Official Secrets Act, more or less function as press censorship tools. Given the conservative nature of Singapore and

---

[86] See a relevant article on the subject onTemasek Review Emeritus. Retrieved from http://www.temasekreview.com/2010/05/07/pushing-for-freedom-of-information-laws-in-singapore,

the long-time rule of the People's Action Party, which has a strong hold on the media, it should be no surprise that there is no law in Singapore granting citizens access to government documents. Additionally, there is also no reporter's privilege for journalists in Singapore, which puts the journalists in danger of having to reveal their confidential sources. Taking all of this evidence into consideration, there are no signs that the government in Singapore, who has been controlling the press for so long, will change its course any time soon.

SOUTH KOREA

South Korea has a turbulent history with press censorship in the last few decades. In the early 1900s, Japan occupied the country and ruled it with an iron hand. After the Japanese left, South Korea went through a long period of military dictatorship when the country was trying to establish itself economically. During these times, the Korean government restricted, freedom of the press on the grounds that it should be subordinate to national security interests (Youm, 1998). There were various instances where journalists were arrested and tried for publishing stories that the government considered to be detrimental to South Korea's national security. In fact, the National Security Act, which was enacted in 1948, provided a statutory mechanism for this purpose. Some examples of the application of the statute include the following:

1. The name 'People's Republic of North Korea' shall be referred to as the 'North Korean Puppet Regime.'
2. Reports on the withdrawal of US troops that might cause political anxiety among the people shall be avoided.
3. Editorials or articles that slander the US military presence in Korea shall not be published.
4. Reports that might have a bad influence on the people by sympathizing with rebels or the North Korean army, or by dealing with them as heroes shall be prohibited (Youm, 1998).

Since military rule came to an end in 1987 and the country became a true democracy, the media has been enjoying much more freedom. From 1988 on, freedom of expression increased noticeably and political authorities lost their control over the media. Censorship was officially eliminated, and the media were therefore freer than ever to criticize the government and to address formerly taboo issues, such as the massacres of civilians carried out by both American and Korean soldiers, scandals involving high-level officials, and even Communist ideology (Youm, 1998). Several restrictive laws, including the Criminal Code, have been revised since 1987 in an effort to reduce press censorship and to expand freedom of the press (Park, 2002).

This does not mean that the press has not experienced instances of press censorship since the end of military-controlled rule in 1987. Overall, South Korea has fluctuated between liberal and restrictive administrations in the last 20 years or so. In recent years, under the rule of President Lee Myung-bak, the country has dealt with periods of media tightening, evidenced by the arrests of journalists and a prominent bloggers (Karlekar, 2010).

Additionally, North Korea continues to be a sensitive subject for South Korea. As Lee noted, any news stories that express sympathy toward North Korea could still get journalists arrested (2010). In-line with the disturbing trend of increasing Internet censorship since 2009, there has been an effort to take down pro-North Korea comments in the web. This may be in response to an increase in the North Korean government's attempts to enter the online debate, but some also contribute this to the general anti-Internet sentiment of the Lee administration (Lee, 2010). All these recent developments led to South Korea's fall in the Freedom House Freedom of the Press ranking and is surely a step in the wrong direction for South Korea's press freedom.

In 1989 the Constitutional Court in South Korea ruled that there is a constitutional right to information as part of the right of freedom of expression, and it also held that specific implementing legislation to define the boundaries of the right was not a prerequisite to its enforcement (Banisar, 2006). A few years afterward, the Act on Disclosure of Information by Public Agencies was enacted in 1996 and went into effect in January 1998. It allows citizens to demand information held by public agencies, and the agencies must decide within 15 days.[87]

[87] See Act on Information Disclosure by Public Agencies, Act No. 5242, 31 December 1996.

Under the Act, there are eight categories of discretionary exemptions, which include the ones commonly seen in other countries' freedom of information acts", such as secrets, information that could harm national security, defense, unification or diplomatic relations, information that would substantially harm individuals, property or public safety, and information on the prevention and investigation of crime.

So far, the applications of this Act have seen mixed results. Specifically, there have been problems with frequent improper denials of requests, the failure of government agencies to publish lists of available documents, and a disregard and non-enforcement of the Act (Banisar, 2006). Additionally, aside from this Act, there is also a sunshine statute which grants access to sessions of the legislature and other elected bodies, or regulatory hearings (Youm. 2002).

In regards to the journalists' right to protect their confidential sources in South Korea, our research showed that there has been very little discussion of the journalist's privilege as a legal right for the Korean press (Youm. 1998). Although there have not been significant instances where journalists were jailed for refusing to reveal their confidential sources in South Korea, it remains to be seen whether journalists and bloggers will be forced to do so in an environment where Internet censorship is rising.

All in all, after long periods of oppressive regimes where press censorship was the norm, South Korean journalists have been enjoying press freedom since it was democratized in 1987; however, with the succession of each president since then having a different ideology towards freedom of the press, press censorship reared its head from time to time, especially regarding reports on national security and North Korea. In the last two years, under President Lee's rule, the government has been trying to tighten Internet censorship, which is unfortunate, since South Korea is one of the most Internet-penetrated countries (Karlekar, 2010).

In 1998, the Act on Disclosure of Information by Public Agencies came into effect allowing the public to have access to official documents; however, there have been some problems with the applications of this Act. Regarding the right to protect confidential sources, there has not been much discussion about this issue in South Korea.

JAPAN

Japan is no stranger to press censorship. During the Empire of Japan period, the government practiced heavy censorship of Western ideas or any articles which dared to criticize the government. As in other countries examined in this book, censorship was especially forceful during war time. At one point, the death penalty was actually an option as the punishment for violating censorship laws (Amenomori, 1998). In 1941, right in the middle of WWII, the government eliminated freedom of the press entirely and controlled the media by forcing papers in each prefecture to either merge into one paper or cease publication, with all news articles having to be screened by government censors before they could be published, as Amenomori noted (1998).

After WWII ended, the allied forces occupied Japan and abolished all forms of censorship and controls on the freedom of speech, the concept of which was integrated into Article 21 of the 1947 Constitution of Japan (Horibe, 1985). Specifically, Article 21 of the Japanese Constitution guarantees freedom of expression and prohibits formal censorship. Regardless, censorship remained present in the post-war era, especially in political matters deemed subversive by the American government during its occupation of Japan. One interesting fact about censorship during this period was that even the mention the word "censorship" was not allowed (Amenomori, 1998).

Japanese journalists now enjoy a wide range of freedom to do their job, but censorship does still exist today and it is often carried out through Article 175 of the Criminal Code of Japan. Nowadays, self-censorship is much more prevalent than government censorship. This is mainly because of the existence of the aforementioned press clubs in Japan, which are attached to a variety of government ministries, political parties, and business groups. The only way for newspapers, wire services, and broadcasting companies to gather news is to become a member of these clubs. Since these clubs monopolize information sources, reporters are pressured into choosing to cover stories that show these institutions in a positive light or risk having their press club memberships revoked if they write negative stories (Freeman, 2000). This press club phenomenon and group think mentality could have contributed to the lack of criticism on the Japanese government in 2011 after the aftermath of the disastrous nuclear crisis. This example demonstrated the fact that self-censorship is sometimes just as effective as the formal censorship system.

In terms of giving the public the right to have access to official documents, Japan enacted a legal statute that grants that right. The Law Concerning Access to Information Held by Administrative Organs was passed in 1999 and enforced in 2001 (Banisar, 2006). This law gives any individual or company, Japanese or even foreign, the right to request administrative documents held by administrative agencies and the Departments must respond within 30 days following the request.[88]

Like any other similar laws in other countries, there are exemptions to this law; however, compared with India and South Korea, who have long lists of exemptions, the list in the Japanese statute is relatively short. There are only six broad categories of exemptions, which are also similar to other countries'. For instance, documents can be withheld if they contain information about a specific individual unless the information is made public by law, information that puts national security, international relations or negotiations at risk, or information that could hinder law enforcement business. The number of requests has been fairly high, around 100,000 annually, even though the cost for requests are quite high (Banisar, 2006).

In Japan, there is no explicit legal protection for news sources, but protection of sources has been partially recognized for many years in court decisions. In 2006, the Japanese Supreme Court strongly affirmed the right, describing it as an "important social value" which must be considered when determining the balancing of interests. The Court stated that Article 21 of the Constitution, which grants freedom of the press, should be interpreted as encompassing the need to protect the identities of secret sources, which is a major part of news gathering. However, the Court also stipulates that this protection would only apply when several criteria are met: 1) The report in question relates to public interest; 2) There are no special circumstances where the means or methods employed for gathering news conflicts with any provision of general criminal law; or 3) The disclosure is no longer necessary to have a fair trial. If these criteria are met, then the journalist may, in principle, refuse to testify about their confidential sources (Banisar, 2007).

---

[88] See Law Concerning Access to Information Held by Administrative Organs.

Japan had a long history with press censorship until the allied forces left the country a few years after the end of WWII. Since then, Japanese journalists generally have freedom to do their jobs. Censorship is still employed occasionally today through the Criminal Code; however, the real hindrance to achieving true freedom of the press in Japan is self-censorship on the part of the journalists. The prevalent self-censorship in Japan is the product of close ties with the government and the group mentality brought on by the system of press clubs. The impact of press clubs is still huge today, as evidenced by the lack of negative reports on the nuclear disaster in the spring of 2011. In other aspects of press freedom, Japan has a law in place which allows the public to view official documents and the Japanese Supreme Court has recognized that the constitution provides at least some protection for journalists not to reveal their confidential sources in courts. All in all, Japan has a reasonably healthy press freedom environment, but the self-censorship situation is worth keeping an eye on in the future.

CHINA

China, just as any other nation with a prominent Communist political system, has a long history of press censorship that restricts media content. This occurs because one of the key features of totalitarianism is the combination of promotion of one singular ideology and the monopolistic control of mass media (Su, 1994). Censorship in China encompasses a wide range of subject matters. The rationales behind each type of censorship are varied, some stated outright by the Chinese government itself, while others more self-evident to observers both inside and out of the country.

All evidence suggests that censorship in China is largely used as a tool to maintain the rule of the Chinese Communist Party. As Su noted, censorship helps prevent unwanted reformists, political dissidents, and revolutionaries from organizing themselves and spreading ideas that are detrimental to the central government (1994). Additionally, censorship prevents Chinese citizens from discovering or learning about potentially unflattering news about the Communist Party that could create or inflame anti-government sentiment (Su, 1994). Aside from political reasons, censorship is also practiced in China to protect its economic interests (Reporters Without Borders, 2007). Some even suggested that China ban Facebook, Youtube, and Twitter not just because these websites might lead to people organizing protests and causing troubles for China politically, but also because the Chinese government wanted to give a business advantage to these websites' Chinese competitors (New York Times Staff, 2010).

Freedom House noted that China's Internet censorship is regarded by many as the most pervasive and sophisticated in the world. This practice was achieved by building one of the most technically sophisticated Internet firewalls. According to a study, at least 18,000 websites are blocked from within the country (Karlekar & Cook, 2008)). Banned sites have included those mentioned above, YouTube, Facebook and Twitter. A long list of search terms, including democracy, Dalai Lama, and human rights, are blocked as well, and 52 cyber dissidents are reportedly imprisoned in China for their online communications (New York Times Staff, 2010). Websites in China are required to employ people who monitor and delete objectionable content; tens of thousands of others are paid to "guide" bulletin board web exchanges in the government's favor, according to a New York Times report. In 2010, Google had a major dispute with the Chinese government and actually closed the Google-China website after some Chinese dissidents' gmail accounts were hacked. However, six months later, not wanting to leave this gigantic market, Google had its license renewed and the website was back up again in China (Levy, 2011).

Censorship guidelines are often circulated weekly from the Communist Party propaganda department and the government Bureau of Internet Affairs to all the prominent editors, and those guidelines are enforced through directives issued to heads of media outlets, demanding that they kill controversial stories and instructing them on how to cover sensitive topics. Journalists face harassment and even prison terms for violating those guidelines. Laws such as the State Secrets Law and the Maintenance of State Secrets Law Implementing Procedures have given the government a lot of leeway in putting journalists behind bars (Sun, 2001). When standing trials for violating one of these laws, the Chinese journalists, unlike many of their western counterpoints, cannot defend themselves by saying that the stories are of public interest, as Su noted (2001).

Notwithstanding the strong censorship apparatus, there are signs that the media in China is enjoying more freedom in recent years due to an increase in globalization. China's media industry is undergoing a process of commercialization, which is leading to growing competition, diversified content, and an increase in investigative reporting by Chinese news agencies, including exposés on government corruptions. Additionally, while only state agencies can own media in China, there is increasing privatization in the media industry (Bennett, 2011).

In terms of giving people access to government documents, China has opened up a bit in this area as well. In 2007, the State Council of the Republic of China enacted the "Regulations of the People's Republic of China on Open Government Information," which officially came into effect in 2008. Some have argued that the main motivations underlying the OGI Regulations are largely domestic: broader sharing of government information in the service of economic development, improving people's lives, enhancing trust between the public and the government, curbing government corruption, and promoting better governance at all levels of government (Horsley, 2007). Government information, as referred to in the OGI regulations, includes "information made or obtained by administrative agencies, in the course of exercising their responsibilities," but not information from the National People's Congress, and the People's Court system.[89] The law also stipulates that administrative agencies must set up mechanisms to examine the appropriate level of secrecy in regards to the information requested and that they should not disclose information that involves state secrets or commercial information or that compromises individual privacy.

There is no equivalent of a shield law/reporter's privilege in China. It remains to be seen whether the Chinese government would give the right to protect confidential sources any weight in an age when investigative reporting is increasing.

To conclude, China has a reputation of practicing heavy censorship, with a long list of topics that the journalists are not allowed to touch in their reports and a guideline that they have to follow. Internet censorship is also prevalent and one of the most sophisticated in the world, with firewalls blocking websites that have undesirable content. When a number of revolutions occurred in Northern Africa in early 2011, China put forth even more effort to censor the Internet out of fear that the news from Africa might incite people to start their own revolt. Some people tried to organize some sort of demonstration via social

---

[89] SeeRegulations of the People's Republic of China on Open Government Information.

networks, but their efforts were quickly quashed by the Chinese police. In recent years, the Chinese government has loosened up their tight grip in some respects, such as allowing more investigative reporting, including reports on government official corruptions.

In 2007, the famously guarded Chinese government enacted the "Regulations of the People's Republic of China on Open Government Information," giving people access to some official documents. On the other hand, there is still no legal protection to prevent journalists from having to reveal their confidential sources.

HONG KONG AND TAIWAN

Censorship in Hong Kong has been fairly lax since the 1970s when the British government negotiated the sovereignty of Hong Kong with the Chinese government. Since then, freedom of speech is considered an integral Hong Kong value, as protected by the Basic Law of Hong Kong. After Hong Kong was handed over to China in 1997, the media in Hong Kong started to enjoy the same kind of press freedom they had under British rule, but in reality, there has been increasing self-censorship among the journalists in Hong Kong (Yeung, 2000).

There are several reasons for this self-censorship. First, several media outlets have been acquired by big businesses who have very close economic ties with China and thus do not want to damage that relationship by reporting stories that might offend China, as Tao pointed out (2006). Second, the media outlets that are not subject to control and self-censorship are not allowed to send reporters to gather news in mainland China. Third, some reporters are suppressed, arrested and imprisoned. Fourth, journalists are now controlled by their editors and managers and the reports that they file are often heavily revised or distorted. The most obvious form of self-censorship is refraining from reporting negative news about mainland China (Tao, 2006).

Taiwan had its own history with censorship as well. In much of the martial law period of Taiwan, which lasted from 1948–1987, the ruling party KMT led by General Chiang Kai-shek, as an authoritarian state, exercised strict control of the media. No opposition parties were allowed and media advocating either democracy or Taiwanese independence was banned (Rawnsley, 2007). For a few years after KMT retreated from China to Taiwan, there was even a period called "White Terror" when the government and the police put the whole island under surveillance and haul people who dared to criticize KMT away from their home. Those who were taken away often disappeared, never to be heard from again. After Taiwan's democratization in 1987, the regulations that control the media were greatly relaxed and the Taiwanese press has been enjoying a high level of press freedom since then. Even with this freedom, the residuals of past press censorship still exists, particularly when it comes to China-related stories (Chen, 1998).

Hong Kong does not have an official statute that allows the public to have access to government documents; however, the 1996 Code on Access to Information was created to serve the same purpose. Since the Code is not a statute, it has minimum legal weight. Taiwan, on the other hand, does have a law titled the 2005 Freedom of Government Information Law that grants freedom of information. It does, just as any other similar laws, have exemptions built into it, such as national secrets or information if made public could hinder an ongoing investigation or prosecution.[90]

Hong Kong has no statutory law offering any protection against the disclosure of journalistic sources. It is up to the judges to decide whether journalists would be forced to reveal the names of their sources (Weisenhaus, 2007). Similarly, Taiwan does not have legal recognition for protection of journalists' sources either, and journalists have been fined by the courts for refusing to reveal their sources (Banisar, 2007).

Overall, journalists in Hong Kong and Taiwan are enjoying fairly high levels of press freedom, particularly Taiwan, despite its turbulent past concerning freedom of the press and freedom of expression. However, there is a growing concern in Hong Kong that despite the lack of a formal censorship system, journalists are practicing self-censorship for political and economic reasons, both related to China. In terms of freedom of information, Hong Kong does not have an official law that grants people access to official documents, while Taiwan just passed such a law in 2005. Finally, neither Hong Kong nor Taiwan has laws that protect journalists from having to reveal their confidential sources as of yet; however, there is evidence that the Taiwanese government has been thinking about enacting a law to protect confidential sources.

---

[90] See The Freedom of Government Information Law, Article 18.

Chapter 7

Libel Law Issues

Defamation is a big topic in the world of media law. Or rather, the threat of being sued for defamation and how to defend oneself when such a defamation suit occurs is a huge and important subject for any working journalist. That is because defamation and other restrictive press laws are used to intimidate the press, quiet political opposition, and deter investigative journalism. Media also could potentially face harsh punishment for perceived personal attacks on government officials. In a way, defamation lawsuits can function as a form of press censorship if the burden of proof is on the journalists, and if they constantly have to face such lawsuits.

There are two main forms of defamation: libel and slander. Libel is defined as the defamation of a person, business, group, product, government, or nation that is made in written or printed words or pictures. In respect to libel, the claim must be in writing, it must be false and the person making it must state or imply that it is factual. In other words, libel means printing or implying something negative as if it were true when it is not. The publication where libel occurs is assumed to be read by people other than the person defamed.[91]

Slander, another legal term, is also a false, defamatory, and often malicious statement. The major difference between slander and libel is that slander is spoken and libel refers to written words and pictures.

---

[91] A useful article on the subject can be found on the website of FreeAdvice. Retrieved from http://injury-law.freeadvice.com/injury-law/libel_and_slander/libel.htm.

Libel covers any form of defamation other than spoken words or gestures.[92]

Since this book mainly deals with the press, this chapter discusses the laws of libel in all the countries examined and their implications to the journalists of those countries; however, given that libel and slander are very similar, often times the justifications and machinations of these two laws are alike. The following section compares the libel laws by looking at a few aspects of the law, such as "Who has the heavier burden of proof in a libel suit? The plaintiffs or the defendants?" Do plaintiffs who are government officials and public figures such as athletes and celebrities have a better chance of emerging victorious than private citizen defendants in a libel suit? What are the defenses available in a libel suit? Is there a legally sanctioned "right of reply" option for the allegedly defamed plaintiffs?

THE LAW OF LIBEL

There are several ways an allegedly defamed person can go about proving that libel has indeed taken place. In the United States, libel is generally defined as a malicious statement expressed either in print or writing or by signs or pictures tending to injure a person's reputation and expose him or her to public hatred, contempt, or ridicule. The plaintiff in a libel suit first must prove that the statement in question was false. Second, that statement/story is published. Third, that person must prove that the statement actually caused him/her harm. Finally, they must prove that the statement was made without adequate research into the truthfulness of the statement, meaning mere negligence (Anderson, 1974). This rule does not apply to people who are in the public eye.

The United States libel law is unique in its treatment of public officials and public figures. In short, if public officials and figures feel like they have been injured by a statement or a story in the press, they bear the extra burden of proof. Specifically, they must prove the four steps outlined above, and must also prove the statement was made with actual malice (Anderson, 1974).

---

[92] Most countries distinguish between slander and libel, while others combined these two as one offense.

This rule came from the influential Supreme Court case, *New York Times v. Sullivan,* which took place back in the 60s. This case concerns a full-page advertisement in *the New York Times,* which alleged that the arrest of the Rev. Martin Luther King, Jr. for perjury in Alabama was part of a campaign to destroy King's efforts to integrate public facilities and encourage blacks to vote. L. B. Sullivan, the Montgomery city commissioner, filed a libel action against the newspaper and four black ministers who were listed as endorsers of the advertisement, claiming that the allegations against the Montgomery police defamed him personally. Under Alabama law, Sullivan did not have to prove that he had been harmed and a defense claiming that the advertisement was truthful was unavailable since the advertisement contained factual errors. Sullivan won a $500,000 judgment, and later the case went all the way to the Supreme Court.[93]

In the decision of *New York Times v. Sullivan,* which would come to define the scope of libel law in the US, the Court held that because the First Amendment contemplates a system of freedom of expression in which debate on public issues should be uninhibited, robust, and wide-open, it is necessary to protect even some falsehood. In other words, the Court believed that the press should not be obligated or expected to make no mistake in their reports because that requirement would limit the journalists' ability to do their jobs and consequently constrain public debate on certain issues. This marked the first time the Supreme Court held that defamatory statements enjoy some first amendment protection (Anderson, 1974).

Most importantly, the Court declared a key test in the decision for *Sullivan*: press would be held liable for defamatory falsehoods against public officials only if these officials could prove "actual malice." The Court further defined this term to mean publication of falsehood "with knowledge that it was false or with reckless disregard of whether it was false or not."

Another rule of law from the case that's worth noting is that the Court held that false charges of the following would make the publishers of these statements more susceptible to a libel law suit: Criminal conduct, sexual impropriety/immoral behavior, loathsome disease, particularly venereal diseases, professional incompetence or

---

[93] See the rulings for New York Times v. Sullivan, 376 U.S. 254, 270 (1964).

misconduct in one's trade or business, poverty or financial irresponsibility.

Three years after *New York Times v. Sullivan*, the Supreme Court decided another case, *Curtis Publishing Co. v. Butts*, which expanded the scope of the *Sullivan* ruling. In particular, after the Butts ruling, plaintiffs who were public figures, not just public officials, should also have to overcome the same hurdle in order to emerge victorious in a libel lawsuit.[94]

In another 1974 landmark case *Gertz v. Robert Welch, Inc.*, the Court further clarified that a public figure includes a person who achieves that status by his/her position alone or by thrusting himself/herself into the middle of public controversy.[95]*Gertz* also held that those who are not public figures could prevail on the question of intent simply by showing negligence on the part of the media defendant. However, private plaintiffs would be unable to recover punitive damages unless they could prove actual malice.

In short, following *New York Times v. Sullivan*, the most important first question to ask in a libel suit in the US is whether the plaintiff is a public or private person. This distinction makes a huge difference in a libel case because the plaintiffs in these two categories have different levels of fault they have to establish. Under the "public person" category, there are three sub-categories: 1) Public Officials, 2) public figures, which can be divided into all-purpose public figures and limited public figures, and 3) involuntary public figures, who have not purposefully taken action that results in their fame and notoriety (Anderson, 1974).

The category of libel plaintiffs most difficult to define is with a limited public figure. The courts usually have to apply a two-step test to determine whether someone who is neither a public official nor a famous public figure can still be considered a "limited public figure" because he/she is involved in a public controversy. This means the courts will have to decide whether a controversy actually exists and then whether the plaintiff is sufficiently involved in it (Soifer, 1985).

---

[94] See the rulings for Curtis Publishing Co. v. Butts,388 U.S. 130 (1967).

[95] See the rulings for Gertz v. Robert Welch, Inc., 418 U.S. 323, 345 (1974).

An important case that made the rules for the definition of this category is *Time, Inc. v. Firestone*, in which the Supreme Court held that in deciding whether a libel plaintiff is a "limited public figure" because of a controversy, the courts shouldn't deem an event "public controversy" simply because the media consider it newsworthy or that the public happens to be interested in it. Instead, the question is whether it is something the public *should* be interested in.[96]

U.S. libel laws reflect the belief that robust public debate provides the best weapon against tyranny (Smith, 1993). The harm suffered by an individual due to an untrue comment published in the press is generally viewed as an unfortunate by-product of free speech and the country's commitment to democracy (Anderson, 1991). This philosophy and mentality is the reason why the plaintiffs in a libel suit have the burden of proving varying degrees of negligence or actual malice.

As mentioned above, this heavier burden of proof placed on libel plaintiffs who are public officials and public figures is a unique feature for the United States. None of the other countries examined in this book, with the possible exception of Germany, have the same standards and tests for libel litigations. In fact, in some of the countries, libel plaintiffs who are public officials and public figures actually have a better chance of winning a libel case precisely because they are public officials and public figures.

LIBEL IN EUROPE

In Europe, the United Kingdom has a completely different rule when it comes to the burden of proof in a libel case involving public officials and public figures. In contrast with the American law, there is no English doctrine that entitles expression that exposes governmental misbehavior to a higher level of protection than other expression. In fact, the libel law in the UK, which on the whole strongly favors the plaintiffs, has had a chilling effect on press freedom (Supperstone, 1985).

One famous libel case in the United Kingdom that perfectly demonstrated the disadvantages the UK journalists face in a libel case and has recently re-appeared in the headlines in early January 2013 was the libel lawsuit between the infamous cyclist Lance Armstrong and the London newspaper the *Sunday Times* that lasted from 2004-2006.

---

[96] See the rulings for Time, Inc. v. Firestone, 424 U.S.448 (1976).

In 2004, the *Sunday Times* published an article, which was an excerpt from a book, titled LA Confidential - The Secrets of Lance Armstrong, about the doping allegations surrounding the cyclist. It was written by Times journalist David Walsh and a French writer Pierre Ballester, and they basically alleged that Armstrong took performance-enhancing drugs to help him win all of his Tour de France titles. Armstrong and his legal team soon sued the newspaper and Walsh in the United Kingdom (Cozens, 2004).After a drawn-out two-year battle, the two parties settled out of court, resulting in the Sunday Times having to pay 1 million pounds for publishing the story. Regardless of the outcome of the case, the Armstrong doping rumors have continued to persist over the years, and this story took a dramatic turn when the United States Anti-Doping Agency (USAD) determined that Armstrong did indeed use performance-enhancing drugs throughout his cycling career and thus stripped him of all seven of his Tour de France titles in 2012 despite Armstrong's vehement denials of any sort of cheating (Macur, 2012). When the USAD announced its decision, Armstrong remained defiant and continued to vehemently proclaim his innocence, as he had done since he won his first Tour de France title in 1999. After he was stripped of all his titles, he even tweeted a now notorious picture of him lying on a couch right in front of the 7 Tour de France winner's jerseys, which were framed and displayed on his walls. Another twist to this story came when Armstrong decided to participate in a high-profile interview with talk show host Oprah Winfrey in early 2013, in which he finally came clean and admitted to not only using performance-enhancing drugs throughout his career but also ruthlessly attacking anyone who dared to accuse him of doing so. The irony about this latest development-and a true testament to the media-unfriendly libel law in the UK-is that while Armstrong now admitted to cheating, which was exactly what the newspaper articles accused him of doing, legal experts in the UK believed that the Sunday Times would not recoup any of the damages it paid to Armstrong back in 2006. This is because the burden of proof in a libel case in the UK falls on the defendant media, and in this instance, when the newspaper published the story back in 2004, it did not conclusively prove that Armstrong used drugs. (O'Carrol, 2013).

In most legal systems, the courts give the benefit of the doubt to the defendant. In criminal law, he or she is presumed innocent until the prosecution can prove guilt beyond a reasonable doubt, whereas in civil law, he or she is presumed innocent until the plaintiff can show liability on a balance of probabilities. However, the common law of libel, which the British practice, reverses the traditional positions: A defamatory statement is presumed to be false, unless the defendant can prove its truth. This means that if someone thinks that what you write about them is either defamatory or damaging, the onus will be entirely on you to prove that your comments are true in court. In other words, if you make the claim, you have to prove that the claim is true. This rule gives the plaintiffs, often public officials and public figures, a huge advantage in libel suits in the United Kingdom (Supperstone, 1985).

In recent years, Internet libel has become another problem for journalists in the UK because the global nature of the medium means that anything published anywhere could quite easily be claimed to lead to damages under the UK libel law. In recent years, plenty of print and website editors have faced daily threats of libel by not publishing a piece or removing material from a website. In addition, the United Kingdom operates a "multiple publication rule," whereby every time the statement is downloaded or accessed it constitutes a fresh publication. On the Internet, it is hard to imagine how many publications of a statement could be out there if it catches the interest of people around the world (McManus, 2009).

LIBEL TOURISM CAPITAL OF THE WORLD?

In general, English libel laws heavily favor the plaintiffs, placing the burden of proof on the defendants. As a result, the country has become an increasingly popular destination for "libel tourism," in which foreign plaintiffs bring libel actions against foreign defendants in British courts. In fact, the UK has long been known as the "defamation capital of the world" (McManus, 2009). Indeed, defamation is one of the UK's growing "export industries." UK jurisdiction awards the highest damages in Europe, and with costs often running into the millions, has the dubious accolade of being the most expensive place to bring a defamation claim, per McManus' report (2009). This has led to a call for libel law reform in the UK. Advocates for a libel reform in Britain usually pointed out the following aspects of the law problematic:

1. There is an imbalance against defendants. Claimants can pursue actions where publications have caused them no

substantial harm and corporations can threaten expensive actions against individuals, NGOs and newspapers.

2. The available defenses for libel defendants, such as justification and fair comment, are too complex. The courts are unpredictable when establishing what the defendant's words mean, and whether they are expressions of opinion or statements of fact. Moreover, there is no reliable libel defense for discussion of matters in the public interest.[97]

In the spring of 2011, the British government introduced a libel reform bill that addressed the problems within the current libel law and sought to end the unflattering phenomenon of "libel tourism," in which foreigners who have barely any connections with the country can come in and sue another foreigner for libel in the UK court (Barr, 2011).

The good news for the United Kingdom is that its reputation of being the "libel tourism" capital of the world may not stand much longer because there is evidence that France might overtake as the top destination of "libel tourism." Suing for defamation in the U.K. has grown expensive and slow, with outcomes hardly worth the effort. Many defendants don't show up and plaintiffs have a tough time collecting damages. Although the monetary reward is far less lucrative for a libel conviction in France, the process is much quicker. In France, defendants have three months to appear before a tribunal and 10 days from receiving a notice to file evidence in defense (Gardner, 2011). As in England, it is up to the defendant to prove a statement is true instead of a plaintiff having to prove a statement is false, as in the United States. Losing defendants do not get prison time, but they do get a criminal record and a court order that they must publish a prompt retraction, as Errera noted (1985). Perhaps this explains why we are beginning to see France emerge as the forum of choice for foreigners battling over alleged defamation.

Two libel cases that occurred helped to explain why Paris might overtake London as the hot spot for libel tourism. In 2011, a court in Paris actually considered taking a case of supposed criminal libel in a book review. Karin N. Calvo-Goller, a senior lecturer at the Academic

---

[97] See an article on the British libel law reform retrieved from http://www.senseaboutscience.org/data/files/Libel/What_should_a_defamation_bill_contain.pdf,retrieved

Center of Law and Business in Israel and the author of "The Trial Proceedings of the International Criminal Court" is suing Thomas Weigend, a law professor at the University of Cologne, who wrote a negative four-paragraph review of her book, and Joseph Weiler, a law professor at New York University, who published the review as editor of the website, Global Law Books. In this case, the plaintiff also decided to file a lawsuit in a country which she seemingly had no connection. Also in 2011, Prince Albert of Monaco sued an American in a Paris court who accused him of breaking International Olympics Committee rules by accepting lavish gifts from Russia before and after the IOC awarded the 2014 Winter Olympics to the Russian city of Sochi (Gardner, 2011).

It's not surprising to learn that in defamation/libel cases in France, the usual presumption of innocence is reversed, meaning the burden of proof is on the accused. Furthermore, in France, libel is just one of many causes of action that can be brought against journalists (Eisendrath, 1982).

Some scholars, such as Eisendrath, have argued that the many differences between French libel law and American libel law are basically of degree. Given the major differences between the two countries' libel laws, we do not agree with this statement. Observe the following differences between the two:

1. The more powerful a person is, the more protection granted by law in France. The American libel law basically has the exact opposite approach, as public figures have a much tougher time winning libel cases.
2. In France, there is a category in libel law called "no fault libel," which allows the courts to punish the media for publishing something that is true (Eisendrath, 1982). In America, truth is an absolute defense in a libel case.
3. "Outrage:" materials/expressions considered to diminish the moral authority of a public function, or the purpose for which it is exercised, would get journalists into trouble. This means that all the reports on "Watergate" would have been considered illegal in France.

All things considered, French libel laws provide public officials quite a lot of protection, just like the UK libel law, which is why there are more foreigners who want to go to Paris to commence a libel suit. Ample protection for public officials is justified on the grounds that officials deserve to be well-protected from attacks on account of the burdens their public duties already impose on them. The implication is that they are serving the people for the greater good of the country; therefore, they do not deserve to have their reputation sullied. In reality, public officials rarely resort to legal means when libel allegedly occurs (Errera, 1985).

Germany has a defamation law that applies to slander and libel, which are not distinguished from one another. The country has a list of relevant defamation offences under Germany's Criminal Code, including §90 (Denigration of the President of State), §90a (Denigration of the State and its Symbols), §90b (Unconstitutional denigration of the Organs of the Constitution), §185 ("insult"), §186 (Defamation of character), §187 (Defamation with deliberate untruths), §188 (Political defamation with increased penalties for offending against sections 186 and 187), §189 (Denigration of a deceased person), §192 ("insult" with true statements). Paragraph 188, in particular, has been criticized for allowing certain public figures additional protection against criticism.[98]

Despite the fact that a journalist can be charged with criminal libel under Sections §90, §90a, and §90b of the Criminal Code, in reality, those provisions are hardly ever used to prosecute people for libel.[99] When litigation concerning the reputation of public figures, whether public officials or celebrities, does occur, it usually takes place before the civil rather than the criminal law court, although technically speaking, sections §90, §90a, and §90b of the Criminal Code provide more legal protections for public officials who think their reputations are damaged in the press. In other words, if a politician feels as if his/her reputation was damaged and wanted to sue in criminal court, he/she would have a more difficult time succeeding. This is because Article 5 of the Constitution allows the press to have a wide range of freedom to criticize public officials–and Section 193 of the Criminal Code provides that no defamation exists if critical statements are made

---

[98] See a relevant article on World Law Direct about defamation, slander, and libel. Retrieved from http://www.worldlawdirect.com/forum/law-wiki/12227-defamation-slander-libel.html.

[99] See note 87.

for justified reasons. The good news for journalists in Germany is that among the courts and scholars, there is a common agreement that critical supervision of public officials by journalists constitutes as one of those "justified reasons." In addition, another reason public officials and public figures would have more success in a libel suit in a civil court in Germany is because of the civil court's recognition of an individual's "right of personality," which includes a right not to be defamed and a right to privacy (Kohl, 1985) .

Aside from monetary damages, the plaintiff of a libel suit in Germany can ask for an injunction. To obtain an interim injunction, the plaintiff has to persuade the court that the statement is false, defamatory or relates to his/her private life. The defendant usually does not have the chance to challenge the plaintiff's evidence until after the injunction has been granted. Publication in Germany generally occurs if the alleged false and/or defamatory material is read, heard, accessed or seen. In Germany, a simple instance of publication may be enough to successfully bring a defamation case against the publisher. Overall, Germany's defamation law is considered to be on the neutral side. Their defamation law is not as overly favorable towards the plaintiff as in UK libel law and it is certainly not as friendly towards the media like US libel law.

Sweden, compared with other European countries, has a more general rule for defamation/ libel. In Sweden, libel could be a criminal offense, just as in Germany and the UK. The criminal offense of "denigration" is regulated in Chapter 5 of the Criminal Code. Article 1 regulates defamation, which includes pointing out someone as a criminal or as "having a reprehensible way of living," and providing information about someone with the intention of causing disrespect toward that person. If one is found guilty of denigration, the penalty is a fine. While "truth" can be used as a defense in a libel case, over the years, the courts' rulings have shown that it is generally not a requirement that the statements be untrue. It is enough if the statements are meant to be defamatory (Strömberg, 1985).

Given how much the Swedish embrace the concept of freedom of the press, its defamation/libel laws have not produced many outrageous libel cases against journalists. This is especially true when comparing Swedish libel law cases and the far more plaintiff-friendly libel laws of France and the United Kingdom, who have been competing for the title of "libel tourism" capital of the world.

In Italy, there are different crimes against reputation and personal dignity. The crime of injury (Article 594 of the Penal Code) refers to offending one's honor and is punishable for up to six months in prison or up to 516 Euro in fines. If the offense refers to the attribution of a determined fact and the crime is committed in front of many people, penalties are doubled up to a year in prison or up to 1032 Euro in fines. In addition, the crime of defamation (Article 595, Penal Code) refers to any other situation involving offending one's reputation before many people, and has a penalty of up to a year in prison or up to 1032 Euro in fine, doubled to up to two years in prison or a fine of 2065 Euro if the offense consists of the attribution of a determined fact. When the offense happens by means of the press or by any other means of publicity, the penalty is imprisonment for six months to three years, or a fine of at least 516 Euro.[100]

It has been pointed out that the Italian libel law is inconsistent with the idea of press freedom, as journalists could face harsh punishments under the law for merely doing their jobs. This is because Article 595 of the 1930 Penal Code of Italy was drawn up at a time when freedom of expression/press was not regarded as a right. The original aim of all criminal defamation laws at the time was to make criticism against monarchs a criminal offense and to silence dissent. Today, harsh punishments under the Italian libel law are considered inappropriate.

Italian courts are often inundated with libel cases. In recent years, there have been quite a few high profile cases involving public officials suing journalists for statements they considered defamatory. In 2009, former Italian Prime Minister Silvio sued the British magazine *the Economist* for libel for printing a story that portrayed him as unfit to lead Italy. He lost the case and was ordered to pay a fine.[101] In another libel case in 2011, three Italian journalists, who were not as fortunate, were sentenced to one year in prison for writing a story about the suspicious activities of a mayor in Italy (Trionfi, 2011). Also in 2011, the parents of Amanda Knox, the American student who was convicted of murdering her roommate in Italy, was sued for libel, along with a dozen other journalists, by the Italian police for portraying the Italian

---

[100] See Italian Penal Code, Articles 594 & 595.

[101] See a news article on Forbes website regarding Berlusconi's loss in a libel suit against The Economist. Retrieved from http://www.forbes.com/feeds/afx/2008/09/07/afx5396729.html.

police in a negative light (Kennedy, 2011) . The Italian Court indicted Amanda Knox's parents for defamation for alleging in a 2008 newspaper interview that Italian police abused their daughter Amanda and was subjected to physical and verbal abuse during a police interrogation in 2007.

Overall, Italy has a very healthy amount of libel cases and journalists are routinely threatened with the possibility that they could be sued for libel and sent to prison if they write stories that could be construed as dishonoring the reputations of public officials and public figures. Compared with the U.S. libel law, Italian courts tend to protect the nation's public figures and even national organizations and institutions such as the judiciary and the police. They believe that overly critical statements about public figures can be viewed as defamatory because those statements can "undermine the public's confidence."[102] The Italian libel law then undoubtedly contributed to Italy's consistent low ranking on the Freedom House's Freedom of the Press Index.

LIBEL IN ASIA

In Asia, evidence suggests that the majority of countries discussed in this book have similar views to the United Kingdom and France on libel law, especially when the plaintiff in a libel suit is a public official. That is to say, the burden of proof in a libel case is placed more heavily on the media defendants and it is more likely than not that the public official plaintiffs come out victorious in the end.

Singapore is a prime example of this. Singapore has perhaps the world's strongest libel laws. The law governing defamation in Singapore is the Penal Code and the Defamation Act. Defamation/libel law is designed, most fundamentally, to protect a person's reputation and a person's social standing and image in the eyes of reasonable people. Regardless of one's intentions, one is liable of being sued for defamation (Tey, 2008). The reasoning reflects the fact that the vindication of the plaintiff's reputation in the eyes of the public before

---

[102] See the report on Italian libel law in International Defamation Law database, which can be found at http://kellywarnerlaw.com/italy-defamation-laws/

which he/she was defamed is featured prominently in the determination of a libel case.

Perhaps reflecting the culture in Singapore, their judiciary has placed determinative weight on the public interest of maintaining the public reputation of public men as sensitive and honorable men. The judiciary further sought to ensure that the public's perception of their leaders' integrity would remain unaffected so as to promote effective governance, rather than protecting free speech and critical reporting. Therefore, unlike the politicians in jurisdictions ascribing to the public figure doctrine similar to the US, the Singapore public figure is "twice as blessed" (Tey, 2008). Politicians receive just as much protection as private citizens when it comes to defamation liability and critical speech injurious to their individual reputation. At the same time, as Tey pointed out, it allows them to receive much greater punishment than private citizens (2008).

When it comes to news people, it is not just the writer of an allegedly libelous article, or the editor, that can be sued. The libel law in Singapore reaches far and wide. Even those who are indirectly involved, such as the printers and the news vendors, can be sued as well. For example, in a libel lawsuit by the then Prime Minister Lee Kuan Yew against the *Far Eastern Economic Review* in 1987, the publishers and printers were both sued.[103] To adapt to the age of the Internet, the country's leaders indicated to the public that libel on the Internet will not be tolerated and that those they deem responsible will be severely punished. In fact, in 1996, the government made providers and publishers liable for the content placed on the Internet. Even the owners of cyber cafes may be held liable for libelous statements posted or possibly viewed on their establishments (Tey. 2008) .

However, plaintiffs also have to prove a few things: 1) That the statement or words are defamatory; 2) That the defamatory statement or words refer to the plaintiff; and 3) That the remarks were in fact exposed to a third party (Ang & Yeo, 1998). These are similar to the requirements in Western libel law. Nevertheless, despite what the plaintiffs have to prove, Singapore is still a country that gives the plaintiffs in a libel suit a far better chance of winning, especially if they

---

[103] See a useful article on Singapore Press and defamation at http://singaporepress.pbworks.com/w/page/11489265/Defamation-Act.

are public officials. The need to preserve one's reputation is placed on a much higher pedestal than the need to give the press freedom to criticize the government.

What is interesting, but perhaps in-line with our previous discussion about the dynamics among the government, the local press, the foreign press, and the media-related libel actions in Singapore is that the local press usually do not need to worry about libel actions levied against them. As Ellis pointed out, it is the foreign press that usually faces the constant threat of being sued for libel (2002). What is even more astounding is that no foreign press publisher has ever successfully defended a defamation action brought forth by a governing Singapore political leader in the Singapore courts.

India is another country that has a libel law system resembling the United Kingdom's. In India, tort law system was obtained from the British Common Law (Mehta, 1979). Therefore, the existing law relating to defamation places restrictions on the fundamental right of freedom of speech and expression conferred by Article 19 (1)(a) of the Constitution. Section 499 of the Indian Penal Code regulates defamation, and just as the British libel law, libel can be both a criminal and civil offense in India.[104]

Defamation is a relatively new tort for Indian Law. Not many defamation suits were filed in the country until recently; however, after the media revolution in this country, and with people becoming more aware of their rights, the frequency of defamation suits is increasing. In the last couple of years, there has been some journalistic reports on government corruptions and these politicians are now taking advantage of the libel law, Section 499 of the Indian Penal Code, which places a heavier burden of proof on the defendant media.[105]However, so far, it does not seem like Indian libel law has the same degree of favoritism toward the plaintiffs.

Japan and Korea together present another curious case of libel jurisdiction. Both their constitution and libel law are very similar;

---

[104] A useful online article about the libel law in India could be found at JurisOnline.in. The article, Tort of defamation: An analysis of the law in India and the United Kingdom was retrieved from http://jurisonline.in/2010/10/the-tort-of-defamation-an-analysis-of-the-law-in-india-and-the-united-kingdom.

[105] See note 89.

however, this does not mean that they take the same approach to libel litigations.

In Japan, reputation plays a big part in the advancement of libel law. While Americans define reputation in terms of their rights as individuals, the Japanese mostly view reputation within the context of their membership within a family or group (Ourvan, 2002) . Drawing mostly from the Confucian tradition, the Japanese perceive a defamatory accusation as a "loss of face" to their group rather than harm to their individual rights. Japanese law defines defamation as reducing the respect of another in the community or lowering such a person in the estimation of his or her peers. This definition is based on Japan's traditional cultural emphasis on group cohesion over personal autonomy (Smith, 1998). Succinctly put, the Japanese define defamation as reducing the respect of another in the community or lowering him in the estimation of his fellows. This emphasis on reputation and the respect for individuals combined with the recognition that a free press is vital to society leads to Japan's striving both constitutionally and statutorily to strike a balance between protecting the media's freedom of expression and protecting an individual's right to a good name (Ourvan, 2002) .

Consistent with such philosophy, the Japanese libel laws concentrate more on restoring the injured individual's place in its society, which is historically more homogeneous and cohesive than that of the U.S.. Consequently, these laws are more sensitive to the effect libelous statements have on reducing the respect for the individual in the community (Ourvan, 2002) .

A libel plaintiff in Japan can pursue a libel suit under both Japan's Civil Code (MINPO) and (KEIHO). Article 230 of the Penal Code provides that defendants who are found guilty of libel could face up to three years in prison. However, if the matter in question relates to public concern or public interest, the person or entity making the statement would not be punished if the truth of the statement is established.[106] The test for matters of public concern depends on the extent of that person's social activities and his or her influence on society (Ourvan, 2002).

Although available as an option, libel suits under the Penal Code are rare for several reasons: 1) The prosecutors are not eager to contest

---

[106] See KEIHO Art. 230.

them; 2) Prison sentences tend to be suspended by judges; and 3) Plaintiffs are unaware of the option. For these reasons, in the past, most of the libel suits in Japan are filed under the Civil Code (Ourvan, 2002).

Under the Japanese Civil Code, the defendants with the burden of proof, must prove the following: That the matter reported was of public interest; The information was reported with the purpose of benefitting the public good; and The reported information was true or the defendant had a good reason to believe that it was true. In 1969, the Supreme Court of Japan held that in both civil and criminal cases, a media defendant only needs to show that the alleged libelous statement was made under the mistaken but reasonable belief that it was true (Horibe, 1985).

Overall In Japan, libel suits are not that common. Youm believes that there are several reasons for the rarity of libel suits (1990). First of all, monetary compensation awarded by the court for civil libel law is extremely small. Second of all, the fact that the time and expense required for judicial litigation is usually too enormous for the nominal damage awards to offset. Third, the Japanese tend to hesitate challenging the media, which seemingly is too powerful to sue even for a justifiable reason. This unwillingness on the part of many Japanese to sue the mass media for defamation is in no small measure related to the sentiment that it is morally wrong to question authority, of which the media could be seen as a part. Fourth, Japanese are still less conscious of their rights as individuals than as family members.

In recent years, however, the number of libel suits is rising. This is partially because criminal libel laws have become vital tools in policing injurious speech on the Internet. Defamatory posts have led to police intervention and even arrest (Mehra, 2007). Considering how penetrated the Internet is in Japan, and how easy it is to post defamatory comments online, it's not surprising that the Japanese, who put a heavy emphasis on an individual's reputation, made it an important issue to deal with carefully, as Mehra pointed out (2007). Criminal libel now thrives in Japan. Hundreds of people are arrested for criminal libel every year and even the national police take an active part in arresting perpetrators.

The Korean legal system has been enormously influenced by Japan, and the Japanese influence is particularly strong in the area of libel law; however, unlike the Japanese, the Korean defamation law was developed without regard to the importance of a free press, because the media is perceived to have an alliance with the government (Youm, 1990).

As noted, unlike the Anglo-American concept of reputation as an individual right, Koreans and Japanese perceive their reputational interests in relation to the groups to which they belong. In other words, instead of viewing a defamatory statement as a harm to the general social relations of an individual, Koreans and Japanese consider the statement a loss of face to the individual's familial group on the basis of their Confucian tradition (Youm, 1990).

In South Korea, the statutory recognition was manifested in the Criminal Code in 1953 and the Civil Code in 1958. Under Article 309 of the Criminal code, a person who commits the crime of libel can be punished by penal servitude, imprisonment, or a fine. To constitute criminal libel, publication of the statement must be made with the intent to defame. This requirement is protective of the rights of the press because it reflects a recognition that the press should only be punished if it acts with malice. It should be noted, however, that the press should not be punished if the allegedly defamatory statement is truthful. If the statement is false, then there is no need to show criminal intent (Youm, 1990).

As in Japan and other countries, whether a statement would be considered to be related to public interest is a determining factor in libel cases in South Korea (Youm, 1990). Specifically, Article 310 of the Criminal Code provides an affirmative defense to prosecutions of libel, stating that if the facts in the alleged libelous statements are true and solely for the purpose of public interest, the defendant will not be punished.[107]

The Korean Civil Code also protects individuals from defamation. Although the Criminal Code is largely intended to ensure the social interests of public peace and order, the Civil Code is primarily aimed at safeguarding the rights of individuals in their reputations. The Civil Code provides victims of defamation with two possible means of redress. First, article 751 authorizes monetary compensation for damages resulting from the defamation.[108] Secondly, Article 764 authorizes the court, upon the application of the injured party, to order

[107] See Korean Criminal Code Art. 310.

[108] See Korean Civil Code Art. 751 (1), (2)

the defamer "to take suitable measures to restore the injured party's reputation, either in lieu of or together with compensation for damages."[109] Korean courts recognize several "suitable" measures for restoring the reputation of the injured party, such as retraction of the defamatory statement or publication of a notice of apology (Youm, 1990). Courts can also issue injunctions against publishing the challenged libelous material when they are justifiably requested by the complainant, as Youm pointed out (1990).

There have been relatively few libel lawsuits in South Korea, and as Youm pointed out, there are several reasons why. First, the deeply-rooted Confucian system of ethics in Korea contributes to the relative scarcity of libel actions in Korea. Koreans, who have long been taught by Confucianism to place harmony and conciliation before legal battle, still regard it as beneath their dignity to seek legal remedy through the judicial process. Consequently, they are usually reluctant to sue for defamation without an exhaustive attempt to resolve their differences themselves. Similar to Japan, rights of individuals as understood in the West hardly exist in Korea except when they are framed within the context of family (Youm, 1990). This "familial" concept of rights considerably discourages Koreans from asserting individual rights to protect their reputation from unjustified violation by the press.

Secondly, the rarity of libel cases may stem from a traditionally undemocratic political structure in Korea, which for a long time was without any judicial independence. As such, Koreans do not view the courts as protectors of their political rights and civil liberties. Instead, they see the Korean judiciary as an institution serving the ruling elite of Korea in that it is beholden to political and social power instead of taking on the role of a counterbalance to the Korean government (Youm, 1990). Furthermore, when it comes to the operation of laws in the country, Koreans have little confidence in the validity and fairness of the judicial process (Lim, 1974). This lack of confidence is a significant factor that discourages libel victims from going to court to seek a remedy through judicial intervention.

Finally, the general public's prevailing view of the Korean press make it a rare phenomenon for the news media to be subject to attacks by those damaged by news stories. Koreans generally view the mass media as too powerful to challenge. Accordingly, they frequently give

---

[109] See Korean Civil Code Art. 764.

up their right to fight (Youm, 1998).This helps others understand why actual or potential victims of negative press coverage are reluctant to assert their rights to damages for injury to their reputation.

The libel laws in South Korea require the defendants using "truth" as their defense to substantiate their claim with evidence to support their case. Therefore, the defendants in a libel suit carry a heavy burden of proof. A defamation law that strongly favors the so-called "victims" of defamation could hinder press freedom. In fact, when politicians, prosecutors, police officers, and high-ranking government officials bring libel lawsuits against the press for unflattering stories they publish, the news media lose almost every time. This harsh reality for journalists led some scholars to lament that these unfavorable judgments against the media create an unfriendly environment in which the press will be considerably discouraged to do what they should do, which is to keep a watchful eye on the government (Youm, 1990).

China also has a libel system in place that is different from others. In China, the legal framework governing defamation claims is built on three primary statutes: 1) Article 246 of the Constitution of the Criminal Statutes stipulates: "Anyone who, by violence or other methods, publicly insults a person or fabricates facts to defame a person shall be sentenced to not more than three years in jail, criminal detention, public surveillance or privation of private rights."[110] 2) The 1987 General Principles of the Civil Law ("General Principles") provides the initial authorization for defamation claims. Article 101 of the General Principles provides that citizens have the right to reputation, that respect for the personal dignity of individuals shall be protected, and that insult or slander that harms citizens or legal people is prohibited, and 3) Article 120 provides that in cases where reputation is harmed, citizens may demand the cessation of the tort, restoration of reputation, elimination of defamatory effects, apology, and compensation (Liebman, 2006).

In 1993, the Supreme People's Court (SPC) ruled that there are three general circumstances where a libel suit could appear: 1) When the content of the news reports are seriously mistaken, the basic content of such reports is incorrect, and such mistakes led to the harm of an individual's reputation, or 2) when the insulting or derogatory language used results in harm to reputation, and 3) when

[110] See The Constitution of People's Republic of China, Article 246.

unauthorized revelations of personal details causes harm to reputation (Liebman, 2006).

Although there were libel suits before 1987, soon after the libel law principles were formally established in China, there was a growth in libel lawsuits, and scholars such as Liebman espoused that the reason for the increase in defamation/libel cases was the gradual awareness of the people's legal rights in China (2006). They also believed that another reason for this rise in libel suits was the fact that local government officials have been suing the increasingly aggressive media, which has been putting out more and more stories on low-level government corruptions and incompetence (Liebman, 2006).

In some instances, humiliation alone is enough of a justification for filling a defamation lawsuit, even if the information published is true (Liebman, 2006). Additionally, unlike the United States, Chinese libel law does not distinguish between a public and a private figure, which means everyone is on equal footing. Accordingly, there is no extra "actual malice" test that a plaintiff who is a public official or public figure will have to satisfy. However, there have been discussions about applying a "public person" standard in libel cases both in courts and in academia (Winfield et al., 2000). So far, the plaintiffs seem to have a higher success rate in libel cases litigated in China, which might suggest that the defendants have a heavier burden of proof.

Overall, there has been a rise in libel litigations in the wake of a more commercialized and aggressive media environment. The growth in defamation litigation reflects the recent development of Chinese news media. The Chinese media have undergone rapid commercialization over the last two decades, with a number of publications increasing dramatically. As a result, news in China is much more widely disseminated than it was in the early 1990s, which has lead to a serious competition in the media market. This in turn lead to more aggressive reporting and then more libel cases. The increase in the number of defamation cases has also reflected the expansion of civil litigation more generally in China over the past decade (Liebman, 2006).

In Hong Kong, the defendants in a libel suit have the burden of proof. This means that the burden is on them to have to prove that the content of the offending publication is true (Wisenhaus, 2007).

In Taiwan, Article 310 of the Criminal Code of the Republic of China regulates defamation/libel. The Criminal Code provides that "to the extent that a statement is defamatory, an accused must be found not guilty if the accused is able to show that the statement is true." [111] This provision prescribes the elements of a defense; that is, a perpetrator who originated or circulated a defamatory statement may be found not guilty of criminal defamation if the statement is true. Nevertheless, it does not necessarily imply that the accused must carry the burden of proof that the defamatory statement stated. In the case where the accused has no way of showing the truthfulness of the statement, the court must state the accused not guilty when the evidence proffered for the court's review shows that the accused has reasonable grounds to believe that the statement was true at the moment of dissemination. Furthermore, this provision does not exempt a prosecutor from his/her statutory burden to prove that the accused has intended to damage another person's reputation, a burden mandated by the criminal procedures, nor does the provision exempt the court from its duty of discovering the truth.[112]

DEFENSES FOR LIBEL

When faced with a libel lawsuit, the defendant can fight charges with the options of several defenses. Libel defenses are usually more or less the same in the countries examined in this book. Therefore, in the following section, all of the common libel defenses are listed and discussed. It should be noted that not all of the countries have the same mentalities towards these defenses, and they often have different interpretations/applications of the defenses or other unique defenses.

Truth is an absolute defense in the United States (Watkins, 1994) , while in the majority of the countries discussed here, truth alone is not enough to get the defendants off the hook. For example, in other countries such as South Korea and Japan, it is also necessary to show a benefit to the public good in having the information brought to light (Youm, 1990).Specifically, in Japan, the defense of "truth" is permitted only in cases where the alleged defamatory statements relate to matters of public concern and have been made solely for the purpose of promoting public interest, as Youm pointed out (1990). Generally, statements made in good faith and reasonable beliefs that they were

---

[111] See Taiwan's Criminal Code, Art. 310.

[112] See more details on Judicial Yuan Interpretation, No. 509.

true are treated the same as true statements; however, the court may inquire into the reasonableness of the belief. The degree of care expected will depend on the defendant: An ordinary person might safely rely on a single newspaper report, while the newspaper would be expected to carefully check multiple sources.[113] It is worth noting that in the UK, it is not considered a defense if the defendant is only quoting/repeating what he/she had heard (Supperstone, 1985) .

Privilege is a defense when witness testimony, attorneys' arguments, and judges' decisions, rulings, and statements made in court, or statements by legislators on the floor of the legislature, or statements made by a person to his or her spouse, are considered to fall under the "privilege" category. These statements are said to be privileged and cannot be causes for defamation claim.[114]

Opinion is a defense recognized in most jurisdictions. If the allegedly defamatory assertion is an expression of opinion rather than a statement of fact, defamation claims usually cannot be brought forward because opinions are not false by nature. However, some jurisdictions decline to recognize any legal distinction between fact and opinion. The United States Supreme Court, in particular, has ruled that the First Amendment does not require recognition of an opinion privilege.

Fair comment on a matter of public interest, statements made with an honest belief in their truth on a matter of public interest (official acts) are defenses to a defamation claim, even if such arguments lack logic. If a reasonable person could honestly entertain such an opinion, then the statement is protected.

Innocent dissemination is an available defense when a defendant has no actual knowledge of the defamatory statement or no reason to believe the statement was defamatory. Thus, a delivery service cannot be held liable for delivering a sealed defamatory letter.[115]On the other hand, the defense can be defeated if the lack of knowledge was due to negligence.

---

[113] See a useful article onWorld Law Direct about defamation, slander, and libel. Retrieved from http://www.worldlawdirect.com/forum /law-wiki/12227-defamation-slander-libel.html.

[114] Most nations examined in this dissertation offer this defense in a libel suit.

[115] The United Kingdom, for example, offers this defense in a libel suit.

As noted, these are the most common defenses. Depending on the jurisdictions, they could also be applied in different ways. For example, in Asia, unlike the United States, truth is not an absolute defense. The libel defendant who asserts this defense often has to combine the "truth" defense with another defense in order to plead his/her case.

RIGHT OF REPLY

One other element of libel law that has a large impact on the press is the right of reply rule. A "right to reply" rule affords people who feel they have been unfairly criticized or defamed by a media outlet the right to respond and have their response published through the same media outlet. In other words, if this rule applies, then the newspapers being sued for libel would have to publish a response from the plaintiff. This rule is frowned upon by the media and journalists because giving the libel plaintiff a guaranteed forum to express his or her views means they have to relinquish their editorial controls and job autonomy and perhaps discard or delay stories that they are interested in publishing (Hayes, 2004).

The United States is one of the countries that does not recognize a right of reply. Unlike many other countries discussed in this book, there is no right of reply law in the United States. In *Miami Herald Publishing Co. v. Tornillo*, the Court rejected the claim that a newspaper is obligated to grant space to people wishing to respond to its coverage or editorial positions on public issues. The Court found that the statute granting this right violated the freedom of press clause in the First Amendment. The statute was an "intrusion into the function of editors," and it imposed "a penalty on the basis of the content." It further ruled that the "right to reply" statute limits the variety of public debate, and was therefore unconstitutional.[116] The United Kingdom also does not have a statutory provision for right of reply (Supperstone, 1985).

In other countries, however, right of reply plays a big part in libel litigations. In Germany, the right of reply was first incorporated into law in 1874 and is still in the statute today. For the Germans, the rationale for having this law was to safeguard individuals against false

---

[116] See the rulings for Miami Herald Publishing Co. v. Tornillo, 418 U.S. 241 (1974)

press reports. The protection afforded, however, is rather limited. The press only needs to print the reply if they publish supposedly factual statements about a person that turned out to be inaccurate and the reply is limited to corrections of these facts. Moreover, the law detailing the right of reply is quite complex, which makes it rather difficult for a person unfamiliar with the law to force the press to print the reply (Kohl, 1985) . The libel law in France affords public officials who consider their reputations damaged by the press the right of reply. The offended officials or the government itself can also bring a lawsuit against the press that published the offending stories/images (Eisendrath, 1982) .

In Asia, while India and China do not appear to have an official law regarding the right of reply (Liebman, 2006) , most of the countries examined here give the plaintiff in a libel suit the right of reply. In Singapore, the right of reply is employed frequently. Singapore is a strong advocate and enforcer of "right of reply, "and the government is keen on exercising this right with the newspapers and news magazines which have published any information deemed to be politically incorrect or different from what the political leadership understands the facts to be (Tey, 2008) . In Japan, the Newspaper Act contained a statutory provision, which recognized the right of reply. However, the Act was repealed in 1949. Since then, Japan has not had a similar statutory provision. This is not to say that other statutes do not provide a plaintiff the right of reply. In particular, Article 723 of the Civil Code, which allows a court to order suitable measures for the restoration of an injured party's reputation, may provide a basis for asserting this right (Youm, 1990). South Korea, influenced by the German law press law, also provides the plaintiffs in a libel suit the right of reply (Youm, 1993).

Judging from which countries have a "right of reply" statute, it could be argued that on the whole, the countries who place a premium on personal reputation such as France and most of the Asian countries are more likely to have a right of reply law in place, while countries such as the United States, which value freedom of the press tremendously, do not recognize such a right for a libel plaintiff.

In conclusion, libel law is closely related to freedom of the press because if not applied appropriately, it could be utilized as a weapon to penalize the press for printing negative or unflattering stories. The countries examined here all have libel laws in place, but how they apply these laws differs greatly. For the United States, the burden of proof in a libel case is placed on the plaintiff, while in most of the countries examined here such as France, Singapore, South Korea, and Germany place a heavy emphasis on personal reputation and the burden is squarely on the plaintiff. In some of these countries, a person's personal dignity is so crucial to his/her standing in society that it is placed above the importance of freedom of the press, while in others, respect for public officials is the most important because they are working for the better good of the country.

The Americans, unlike most of the countries here, also apply a different standard of proof for public officials/public figures. For these people to successfully have a libel case in court, they must prove all of the usual elements in a libel case plus "actual malice," which refers to the fact that the defendant knows the statement in question is false or has a reckless disregard for the truth. This is not an easy threshold to cross, therefore, in the United States, unlike the UK and France, who have become havens for libel plaintiffs, it is difficult for public officials and public figures to prevail in a libel case.

Chapter 8

Copyright Issues

Copyright is part of the intellectual property law family that also claims trademarks and patent law. To put it succinctly, a copyright is a set of exclusive rights granted by a state to the creator of original work or their assignee for a limited period of time in exchange for public disclosure of the work. Copyright includes the right to copy, distribute and adapt the work. Copyright owners have the exclusive statutory right to exercise control over copying and other exploitation of the works for a certain amount of time, and after that period expires, the work will enter the public domain (Goldstein, 2001).

Copyright is a large part of media law, and concerns everyone who has ever had an original and interesting idea and wants to transform that idea into a concrete form to share with the world. It has a large impact on the circulation of creative works and how authors and creative people can make a living off their intellectual works. As information technology keeps advancing, copyright laws all over the world are faced with the challenge of keeping up with the times. In the last 15 years or so, it has been the advent of the Internet and the problems associated with it that has contributed to new issues in the copyright law realm, forcing countries all over the world to scramble to adapt to this new medium that has become a viable threat to writers, musicians, and moviemakers everywhere. In the following section, the authors discuss the origins of copyright law, the justifications for copyright law, and compare and discuss the copyright laws in the countries examined in this book.

ORIGINS OF COPYRIGHT

The origin of copyright law in most countries in Europe is due to the efforts on the part of the church and the government to regulate and control printing during a period when the printing press was invented and just started to become popular in the 15th and 16th century (Goldstein, 2001). Before the invention of the printing press, a writing could only be physically multiplied by the highly laborious and error-prone process of manual copying. Printing allowed for multiple exact copies of a work, thus information and new ideas began to spread much quicker than before. But the downside of this new technology for the governments and the churches at the time was that out of all these ideas that were starting to circulate, there inevitably would be dissenting voices or criticisms. As a result, governments established controls over printers across Europe, requiring them to have official licenses to trade and produce books. These licenses typically give printers the exclusive right to print particular works for a fixed period of time and enabled the printer to prevent others from printing or importing the same work during that period. This was the very start of copyright (MacQueen et al., 2007).

Sometime around 1710, the Parliament of Great Britain passed the very first copyright statute, the Statute of Anne. As the world's first copyright statute, it granted publishers legal protection for 14 years with the commencement of the statute. It also gave 21 years of protection to any book already published in print before the statute was enacted. At the end of the first 14 year-period, if the copyright holders were still alive, then they would receive another 14 years of protection under the law. It also required the booksellers to register the books, which enabled users to locate the owners of copyrighted works. Under this statute, it was a requirement for copies of published books to be deposited in university libraries, which ensured that there was public access to copyrighted works (Bainbridge, 2006).

Around the same time the British developed their first copyright law and the French also developed their own version of the law; however, French Copyright was not exactly the same as the Statute of Anne. Specifically, while the Statute of Anne focused on copyright, which grants the right to copy to the distributors, French copyright law was based on the concept of the right of the author, which gives the exclusive copyright to profit off one's work to authors (Dietz, 1995). It has been very influential in the development of copyright laws in other civil law jurisdictions, and as Dietz pointed out, it also played a huge part in helping develop international copyright law such as the Berne Convention.

The Statute of Anne and the first version of the French copyright law together represent the first copyright laws of the world. While having different foci, they both had an enormous impact on other copyright laws of the world.

JUSTIFICATION OF COPYRIGHT

So why have this copyright law system? Why should we give the authors or creators of arts this protection? The justifications offered thus far are: those relating to the creator's rights in his creation and society's duty to him because of it, and those concerning the interest of society in promoting its welfare by encouraging creation. There are both moral justifications and economic justifications. The natural rights argument requires that we allow the creator to protect the work from modification or unauthorized exploitation because it is an extension of the persona of its creator. A second argument in favor of the natural right theory is founded on the idea of intellectual labor. This draws on the idea that a person has a natural right over the products of his/her labor and therefore, an author should also have a natural right over the production of their intellectual labor. In other words, one moral justification for copyright is built on the notion that an author is entitled to the fruit of his labor, the property that came from his creative mind, and he should be protected from the appropriation of this property by others who have not made an investment in it (Goldstein, 2001).

Another moral argument in favor of an intellectual property regime is based on what is good for society or the public in general. Specifically, this is the incentive argument that suggests that since the production and public dissemination of cultural objects such as books, music, art, and films is an important and valuable activity, it should be encouraged by making it more appealing for creators to produce these materials. It also makes the assumption that without copyright protection, the production and dissemination of those creative works would not take place at a desirable level. The reasoning behind this is that works are often very costly to produce, and once published they can be easily copied. Consequently, in the absence of copyright protection, a competitor could reproduce a work without having to recoup the expense of its initial production. This could discourage people from putting in the efforts to create excellent work that might benefit society (Goldstein, 2001).

The economic argument for having copyright is that authors and creators should receive rewards for their efforts. Protection of original work is granted because it is fair to reward an author for his or her efforts in creating a work and giving it to the public. Accordingly, copyright may be seen as a legal expression of gratitude to an author for doing more than what society expects or feels they are obliged to do. In this way, copyright can be seen as a reward to the author from society (Bainbridge, 2006).

In the following section, the copyright laws of the countries examined in the book is discussed and analyzed. Specifically, the length of copyright protection in each country is compared, whether moral rights are built into the copyright is examined, and whether some of the defenses are for copyright infringement is analyzed. Copyright in the United States is discussed first, then the copyright laws in the other countries is discussed.

COPYRIGHT IN THE UNITED STATES

It is significant that the Constitution of the United States actually serves as the basis for copyright. Copyright law in the United States is part of federal law and is authorized by the U.S. Constitution. The power to enact copyright law is granted in Article I, Section 8, Clause 8, also known as the Copyright Clause, which states:

> The Congress shall have power... to promote the progress of science and useful arts, by securing for limited times to authors and inventors the exclusive right to their respective writings and discoveries.[117]

This clause forms the basis for U.S. copyright law ("science", "authors", "writings") and includes the limited terms (or durations) allowed for copyrights and patents ("limited times"), as well as the

[117] See The Constitution of the United States, Article I, Section 8.

items they may protect ("exclusive right to their respective writings and discoveries").

The U.S. Congress stuck to their promise of enacting copyright legislation with the Copyright Act of 1790. This Act provided an author the exclusive right to publish and sell maps, charts, and books for a term of 14 years, with the right of renewal for one additional 14 year-term if the author is still alive when the first term is up. The Act did not regulate other types of writing, such as musical compositions or newspapers, and the Act made it a point to note that it did not prohibit copying the works of foreign authors.

Copyright law has been modified many times since that first piece of copyright legislation to adapt to the new technologies such as music recording and other art forms and to consistently extend the duration of protection. In fact, the copyright term in the US has been extended at least four times since the Copyright Act of 1790.[118] For the most part, U.S. courts have interpreted the copyright clause of the Constitution to indicate that the ultimate purpose of copyright is to encourage the production of creative works for the public benefit, and therefore, the interests of the public are considered more important than the interests of the author when the two interests clash. In short, as is the case with other intellectual property doctrines, copyright law attempts to reach a best possible balance between the potential conflicting public interests of: 1) encouraging creativity by giving exclusive property rights for original work, and 2) giving the public the freest possible access to works of authorship and the ideas they encompass (Ginsburg, 2003).

For decades, the United States was a "copyright island" which developed its own copyright rules in isolation from anywhere else in the world (Nimmer, 2003). The American copyright law mainly served the American purposes, and it did not concern itself with the copyright law developments of other countries or how the increasing global interactions among the nations might have a bigger and bigger effect on the American copyright laws, as Nimmer noted (2003). However, this all changed in 1976, when the US Congress finally decided that the globalization effect on copyright was too big to ignore and amended parts of the Copyright Act to reflect international standards so that the

---

[118] The Acts that provided the extensions include the 1831 Act, 1909 Act, the 1976 Act, and the 1998 Act.

American copyright law would be more in line with other countries' (Ginsburg, 2003).

In 1988, after refusing to become a member for 102 years, the United States finally became a Berne Convention signatory, and the treaty entered into force in the U.S. March of 1989 (Nimmer, 2003). After signing this treaty, the U.S. made some changes to the Copyright Act to conform to international standards, such as recognizing a very limited amount of moral rights. The U.S. is also a member of the Agreement on Trade-Related Aspects of Intellectual Property Rights (TRIPS), which requires compliance with Berne provisions and is enforceable under the World Trade Organization (WTO) dispute resolution process. In other words, in the last three decades, after decades of isolation in regards to copyright, the United States has become much more willing to alter its copyright law to meet the international standards.

Under the United States copyright law, there are five basic rights protected by copyright. Specifically, the owner of copyright has the exclusive right to do the following:

1. To *reproduce* the work in copies or phonorecords.
2. To prepare *derivative works* based upon the work.
3. To *distribute* copies or phonorecords of the work to the public by sale or other transfer of ownership, or by rental, lease, or lending.
4. To *publicly perform* the work, in the case of literary, musical, dramatic, and choreographic works, pantomimes, and motion pictures and other audiovisual works, and sound recordings by means of digital audio transmission.
5. To *publicly display* the work, in the case of literary, musical, dramatic, and choreographic works, pantomimes, and pictorial, graphic, or sculptural works, including the individual images of a motion picture or other audiovisual work.[119]

Originally designed to protect books, copyright law in the United States has been updated over the last few decades to include more creative works under its umbrella of protection. As of now, the following works are recognized by the copyright law, and it should be

---

[119] See 1976 Copyright Act Section 106. (17 U.S.C. § 106.)

noted that most of the other countries examined have more or less the same list:

- Literary
- Musical
- Dramatic
- Pantomimes and choreographic works
- Pictorial, graphic, and sculptural works
- Audiovisual works and sound recordings
- Derivative works, which refers to another product that is derived from the original work, such as the movie version of a book
- Compilations
- Architectural Works.[120]

Under the United States copyright law, copyright protection starts from the time the work is created. The copyright in the work of authorship immediately becomes the property of the author who created the work. Only the author or those deriving their rights through the author can rightfully claim copyright. In the case of "work for hire, " which refers to work that was created in the scope of employment, the employers who ordered the work will have the copyright, not the employees who created the work.[121]

Several categories of materials are not eligible for federal copyright protection. This includes:

1. Works that have not been fixed in a tangible form of expression, such as a dance that hasn't been recorded.
2. Titles, names, short phrases, and slogans; familiar symbols or designs; mere variations of typographic ornamentation, lettering, or coloring; mere listings of ingredients or contents.
3. Ideas, procedures, methods, systems, processes, concepts, principles, discoveries, or devices, as distinguished from a description, explanation, or illustration.

---

[120] See note 107.

[121] See 17 U.S.C. § 101

4. Works consisting entirely of information that is common property and containing no original authorship, such as calendars or periodic tables.[122]

Among those, the ideas and expression dichotomy is perhaps one of the most important limitations for copyright in the United States and the distinction between an "idea" and an "expression" is a fundamental part of U.S. law. While copyright law protects the expression of an idea, it does not protect the idea itself (Ginsberg, 2005). This means that in order to receive copyright protection, having an idea itself is not going to be enough. One has to express that idea in a unique enough fashion in order to get the copyright protection, and others are free to express the same idea as the author did, or use the same facts, as long as they do not copy the author's original way of expressing these ideas or facts. For example, one can have a theory about the motives behind the assassination of John F. Kennedy, but until he/she expresses that idea and turns that theory into art form, it is just an idea and therefore not protected under the law. This rule encourages people to share their unique ideas through art, which is perfectly in line with the clause from the constitution that encourages the creation of arts.

As previously stated, the length of protection under US copyright has been extended significantly over the years. From the original term of 14 years in the1790 Act, to the most recent amendment, the Sonny Bono Copyright Extension Act, in which works are granted copyright protection for a term of 70 years after the death of the author.[123] If the work was a work for hire, then copyright persists for 120 years after creation or 95 years after publication, whichever is shorter. This latest extension in 1998 made the US one of the countries with the lengthiest copyright protection, tying it with a few European countries such as France and Germany.[124]

The digital Millennium Copyright Act (DMCA) is the most recent copyright law in the United States. It implements two 1996 treaties from the World Intellectual Property Organization (WIPO) and was created to handle the copyright issues on the Internet (Nimmer, 2003).

---

[122] See 17 U.S.C. § 106.

[123] SeeCopyright Term Extension Act (CTEA) of 1998.

[124] France and Germany both have the same length of copyright protections.

The key provisions criminalize production and dissemination of technology, devices, or services intended to circumvent measures that control access to copyrighted works. It also heightens the penalties for copyright infringement on the Internet. Essentially, it extended the reach of copyright, while limiting the liability of the providers of on-line services for copyright infringement by their users.[125]

There are limitations to the copyright protections. Under the Copyright Act in the United States, when accused of violating copyright, there are several defenses available for the defendants in a copyright infringement lawsuit, including:

1. Subject matter limitations and the aforementioned "idea/expression dichotomy." Copyright applies to certain subject matters, therefore, works that are not original works of authorship fixed in any tangible medium of expression are not subject to copyright protection. As stated, copyright protection does not extend to ideas, procedures, processes, and systems. Facts cannot be copyrighted.[126]
2. The "fair use" exception. The fair use doctrine allows the reproduction and use of work for limited purposes, which includes criticism, comment, news reporting, teaching, scholarship, and research.[127] Fair use can perhaps be best described as the privilege to use the copyrighted materials in a reasonable manner without the owner's consent. This exception is broadly interpreted. Usually, In deciding whether a copier's actions were fair, judges will consider the following factors:
   a) The purpose and character of the copying. For example, copying for educational purposes. To justify the use as fair, one must demonstrate how it either advances knowledge or the progress of the arts through the addition of something new. A key consideration is the extent to which the use is interpreted as transformative, as opposed to just simple copying.

---

[125] See Digital Millennium Copyright Act (DMCA).

[126] See 17 U.S.C. § 102(b).

[127] See 17 U.S.C. § 107.

b) The nature of the original. For instance, originals made for commercial reasons are less protected from copying.

c) The amount and substantiality of the portion copied. Naturally, the less used, the more likely the fair use defense will apply, and

d) The effect that such copying may have on the market for the original. For instance, copying may be permitted if it is unlikely to cause economic harm to the original author.[128]

3. The first sale doctrine limits the rights of copyright holders to control how copies of their works should be distributed and displayed. When a person buys a copy of a book, he/she is entitled to sell the book or display however he/she likes.[129]
4. The "good faith" defense protects educational institutions, libraries, and public broadcasters, by permitting the court to limit statutory damages to only $200 if they reasonably believed their infringement was fair use.[130]
5. The DMCA exempts online service providers from secondary liability for their users' copy infringements. However, they are expected to remove materials from users' web sites that appear to constitute copyright infringement.[131]

Conversely, when an act of copyright infringement occurs, the original authors can seek injunctions or monetary damages. Copyright Act § 502 authorizes courts to grant both preliminary and permanent injunctions against copyright infringement and against violations of the author's rights of attribution and integrity in works of visual art.[132] Section § 504 of the 1976 Act, on the other hand, gives the copyright owner a choice of recovering their actual damages and any additional profits of the defendant or statutory damages.[133]

---

[128] All four factors are listed under 17 U.S.C. § 107.
[129] See 17 U.S.C. § 109.
[130] See 17 U.S.C. § 504(c)(2).
[131] See Digital Millennium Copyright Act (DMCA).
[132] 17 U.S.C. § 502.
[133] 17 U.S.C. § 504.

COPYRIGHT IN EUROPE

The first copyright law in the United Kingdom, the Statute of Anne, was the copyright law that the first copyright statute in the United States was modeled after. Since then, just as in the United States, the development of copyright law in the UK has faced periodic updates to include more and more types of creative works under its protection. In the last 200 years, copyright was also consistently amended to extend its terms of–protection as information technology keeps advancing (Deazley, 2006). All of the other European countries, just as the UK, have the same history of periodic updates in the copyright laws.

However, not all of the countries discussed in the book had the same objectives when they created their copyright laws. In the United Kingdom, the Statute of Anne was created to benefit the reading public, the continued production of useful literature, and the advancement and spread of education (Deazley, 2006). The objective of the statute was to encourage intelligent men to compose and write useful books, and the statute guaranteed the finite right to print and reprint those works. It established a pragmatic bargain involving authors, booksellers, and the public, as Deazley pointed out (2006).

The French Copyright, on the other hand, was conceived to protect the right of the author, as Errera (1985) noted. This has two distinct components: the economic rights in the work and the moral rights of the author. It subscribes to the importance of the principles of natural justice. Under this philosophy, copyright is deemed a natural right, part of the natural law, a true extension of personality, consisting of economic and moral rights, such as the right to forbid uses of a work which would discredit the authors directly or through their creative work. Under this view, French copyright law aims to protect the two important interests held by the author: the financial and exploitative interests on the one hand, and his intellectual and moral interests on the other. Thus, only the author should be the one to decide the way his/her work is published and prevent any harm or injury to his/her works (Piotraut, 2006). This concept had a lasting impact on the development of copyright law in other countries such as Germany, Italy, and

Sweden, where moral rights are included in their copyright statutes.[134] The British, after years of resistance to include moral rights in their copyright statutes, finally recognized authors/creators' moral rights in the Copyright, Designs and Patents Act 1988. Under the Berne Convention, it is a requirement for the member countries to recognize moral rights for the authors/creators.[135] The moral rights in these countries are more or less the same, with minor differences here and there. Generally, the moral rights in copyright laws in these countries have some or all of the following provisions:

1. The right of publication: The author is the sole judge as to when the work may be first made available to the public.
2. The right of attribution: The author has the right to insist that his name and his authorship are clearly stated.
3. The right to the respect of the work's integrity: The author can prevent any modification to the work.
4. Right of withdrawal: The right to withdraw the transfers of his/her right. However, the authors who do so will have to compensate the person who has paid for the right.
5. Right to protection of honor and reputation.[136]

The moral rights within copyright law are usually non-transferrable. When the authors pass away, these moral rights are usually passed onto their spouse and children.[137]

It should be noted that the United States does not usually recognize moral rights for the authors/creators. That has changed, however, in a very limited fashion, when the United States passed the Visual Artists Rights Act of 1990 (VARA), its first-ever copyright legislation that encompasses moral rights. Like the UK's recognition of moral rights in recent years, this American legislation, which only applies to visual arts

---

[134] All these countries' copyright laws were influenced by the French copyright law to some extent, with having moral rights for the authors being one of the biggest manifestation of this influence.

[135] See Berne Convention for the Protection of Literary and Artistic Works.

[136] See French Copyright Law, Art. L121-1.

[137] See French Copyright Law and Copyright, Designs and Patents Act 1988, s.95.

and nothing else, was a response to the Berne Convention requirement (Adler, 2007).

Another reflection of this emphasis on moral rights is the fact that many European counties do not have the "work-for-hire" doctrine in their copyright laws (MacQueen et al., 2007) . This suggests that the rejection of this doctrine was based on an author's theory, which states that the person who creates the work/art should have the ultimate right. The concept behind the "work-for-hire" doctrine, which awards copyright to the people who hire the authors to create the works instead of the authors themselves does not fit into this "author is supreme" picture.

In terms of the kinds of works that can be protected under the copyright law in the European countries examined in this book, the lists of protected work in these countries are all pretty similar to each other and to the list in the United States copyright law. Germany's copyright law has a very typical list of protected works that include literary work, music, works of fine art, computer programs, photographic works, and architecture.[138]

In terms of the length of protection for copyrighted works in these European countries, they all afford the authors/creators the same amount of protection under their copyright laws. Specifically, although there were minor sub-rules in some of the copyright laws discussed here, France, Germany, Italy, Sweden, and the United Kingdom all have the same length of protection for most copyrighted works, which is the lifespan of the author plus 70 years.[139] This is in line with the protection term in the United States, which had the same life plus 70 years rule. However, it should be noted that all European countries adopted the life of author plus 70 years rule earlier than the United States did, as the latter did not extend the protection period to 70 years until the Sonny Bono Copyright Term Extension Act, which only became law in 1998.[140]

---

[138] See German Copyright Law § 2, Art. 2.

[139] See French Copyright Law, Arts. L123-1, L123-2; Germany's Copyright Law, § 64, Italy's Law No. 633 of April 22, 1941, Art. 25; Sweden's Act 1960-729, Art. 43;Copyright, Designs and Patents Act 1988, s.12, to have a detailed look at the terms of copyright in these countries.

[140] See 17 U.S.C. § 302.

In terms of the limitations of copyright and the permissible defenses for copyright infringement charges, most European countries discussed here had laid out exemptions under their copyright laws. In the UK, under the Copyright, Designs, and Patents Act 1988 (CDPA, "fair dealing" is a defense for charges of copyright infringement and is limited to the following scenarios: non-commercial research and private study, criticism, review, and news reporting, recording for the purposes of time-shifting, playing sound recordings for the purpose of a non-commercial club or society.[141] In addition, copying for educational use is allowed as long as it is performed by "the person giving or receiving instruction," and works may be performed in educational establishments without infringing copyright, provided that no public members are present at the time of the performance.[142] Furthermore, librarians are allowed to make and supply single copies of an article or a reasonable portion of a literary, artistic or musical work to individuals who request them for the "purposes of private study or research."[143] Overall, judging from the list of copyright limitations provided by the Copyright, Designs, and Patents Act 1988, it seems that as long as the person using the works is using them for private and educational purposes and not profiting from the usage, then the usage would not be considered as an act of copyright infringement under the current rule in the UK. It should be pointed out that the "fair dealing" limitations in the Copyright, Designs, and Patents Act 1988 are very similar to the "fair use" limitations within the copyright law in the United States. It should also be pointed out, however, that unlike the "fair use" limitations in the United States copyright statute, which can be more broadly interpreted, the list of "fair dealing" copyright exemptions in the United Kingdom is limited, and any act that does not belong to the list will not be allowed.[144]

Other countries in Europe also provide limitations for copyright in their statutes. In Germany, the Copyright Law provides a long list of actions that are protected under the law instead of causing the people who commit these acts to be penalized for copyright infringement.[145] In

---

[141]See Copyright, Designs and Patents Act 1988, ss. 29, 30, 67, 70,178.

[142]See Copyright, Designs and Patents Act 1988, ss. 32, 34.

[143]See Copyright, Designs and Patents Act 1988, ss. 38-40.

[144] See Copyright, Designs and Patents Act 1988, ss.29

[145] See German Copyright Law, § VI, Arts. 45-63.

France, there is a list of restricted exceptions to French copyright law permitting uses of copyrighted works for private personal uses, private performances, analyses, and criticisms.[146] In Sweden, the Copyright Act of Sweden also contains a few limitations on copyright that are similar to the copyright exceptions in other countries, such as private personal uses and uses for educational purposes.[147]

In Italy, Chapter V of the copyright statute provides a list of seven "free uses" that are permitted by the law. Some examples of those free use exceptions include: 1) Articles of current interest of an economic, political or religious character, published in magazines or newspapers, may be "freely reproduced in other magazines or newspapers, or may be broadcasted;" 2) The reproduction of single works or of portions of works for the personal use of the reader, when made by hand or by a means of reproduction unsuitable for marketing or disseminating the work in public, is allowed; 3) Loaning books from libraries for personal study and research; and 4) Criticism discussion, or for educational purposes; and 5) Perhaps the most interesting exemption, which is musical groups from the military do not need to worry about copyright when they perform, as long as the performance is not done for profit.[148]

As for a remedy for the authors/creators in a case of copyright infringement, all copyright statutes in the European countries examined in this book contain provisions that lay down penalties for the infringement. For most countries, there are both civil law remedies, which are usually damages and injunctions, and criminal law remedies, which are prison terms or fines or both; however, in France, the criminal remedies are rather harsh, with fines up to 300,000 Euro and a term of up to three years in prison.[149]

Overall, the European countries examined in this book have very similar copyright law statutes. Unlike the United States copyright law,

---

[146] See French Copyright Law, Art. L122-5.

[147] See Sweden's Copyright Act 1960-729.

[148] See Italy's Law No. 633 of April 22, 194, Arts. 65-71.

[149] See French Copyright Law, Arts. L123-1, L123-2; Germany's Copyright Law, § 64, Italy's Law No. 633 of April 22, 1941, Art. 25; Sweden's Act 1960-729, Art.43; Copyright, Designs and Patents Act 1988, s.12 for the details of the penalties provided for copyright infringement.

[149] 17 U.S.C. § 302.

all five European countries have authors' moral rights, which concern the right of attribution and the right to the integrity of work, built into their copyright laws. All five of them have the same term for the general protection of copyright, which is the lifespan of the author plus 70 years. Similar to the United States copyright law "fair use" doctrine, all of the copyright statutes containing limitations to copyright which permit uses of creative works without having to get the consent from the authors/creators. These exceptions usually permit private, personal, and educational uses of the work, news, and criticisms, and the users cannot benefit financially from these unauthorized uses. As for remedies for copyright infringement, with the exception of France, all of the countries have both civil remedies, which include injunctions to stop the infringers from using the copyrighted works and monetary damages, and criminal remedies for copyright, which are usually imprisonment and fines or both. In France, breaching an author's proprietary right is considered a criminal offense and the punishment is quite severe including a steep fine and prison time.

COPYRIGHT IN ASIA

The copyright laws in Asian nations examined in this book took various different paths to achieve a modern copyright regulation system. When examining the copyright statutes and their history in these countries, one common theme among them is that foreign countries either heavily influenced the content of the laws or they were pressured by western countries to set up a new up-to-date legal system to deal with the issues that originated from copyright. That does not mean, however, that copyright law in Asian countries is entirely influenced by the western countries. In fact, in countries such as South Korea and Japan, their own cultural backgrounds and traditions also played a large role in how copyright has been implemented. Sometimes, the two forces, the western influence and the centuries-old cultural traditions, have a bit of a conflict with each other, which makes the implementation of copyright laws difficult. In the following section, some of the more unique aspects of copyright law developments in Asia are discussed. The actual copyright statutes in those countries is also compared and analyzed.

South Korea is an interesting example of modern ideas working with old ideas. As Choi pointed out, due to American influence and persuasion, the World Trade Organization's agreement on Trade-Related Aspects of Intellectual Property Rights (TRIPS) has been and continues to be the major source of impact on intellectual property systems in South Korea (2004). However, at the same time copyright law is still influenced by old Korean values and cultural traditions, despite the country's leap into democracy and modernism in the last couple of decades (Choi, 2004).

Some scholars, such as Choi, have argued that the "inherent cultural limit that imposes a significant barrier to effective enforcement of copyright legislation" in Korea can be traced back to its social structure during the Yi Dynasty (2004). For hundreds of years, publication and distribution of print materials was entirely controlled by the government and copyright was not in anybody's consciousness. Even after publication was liberalized, it was still controlled by the higher elite class. During these periods, despite Korea's progressive technological developments, the extremely rigid social hierarchy system made it impossible to have a wide-spread dissemination of information in the country (Youm, 2000). Additionally, the considerable influence of Confucianism, which tends to devalue the materialistic compensation of literary work, further impeded the development of copyright in Korea (Choi, 2004).

The first time the concept of copyright seriously entered the Koreans' consciousness was in 1884, when the leading newspaper Hansung Sunbo introduced and elaborated on the subject; however, copyright was not legally recognized in Korea during the Japanese occupation period. In 1908, the United States and Japan signed a treaty, which included a provision on the protection of industrial property in Korea. Under this treaty, the Japanese statutes on copyright and other related rights was applied in Korea. Copyright, however, was not a major concern during Japanese rule and Korea did not seem ready to embrace copyright just yet (Youm, 2000).

After the Japanese ended its rule of Korea in 1948, copyright was recognized as a right when the Constitution of the First Republic of Korea was enacted, despite the fact that the word "copyright" was not included in this constitution (Choi, 2004). In 1957, the first Korean copyright statute, which closely resembled the 1899 Copyright Act of Japan, was finally established. This statute was designed to protect mostly academic and artistic works (Youm, 2000). The 1957 Act did not require the authors to register their copyrighted work with the government under the "self-operating recognition of the copyrighted work" system. The Act also provided that copyrights would last for 30 years in addition to the life of the author.[150]Foreigners' work was not protected by this statute unless the work was first published in Korea.[151]

Unlike the copyright act of the United States, the Korean Copyright Act recognized the moral rights of authors, which refer to the authors' right for attribution and their right to protect the integrity of their work (Choi, 2004). Moral rights are also recognized by the Berne Convention, which was part of the reason South Korea decided to include moral rights in its copyright law.

The Act was amended for the first time in 1986, giving authors more protection for the purpose of improving and developing the culture in Korea. The United States had a tremendous impact on the passage of the 1986 Copyright Act. After the US received complaints about South Korea's lack of copyright protection for American intellectual properties, it started a Section 301 investigation, which dealt with violations of copyright and other related issues in other countries by subjecting the offending countries to trade sanctions, against South Korea. The two countries faced several negotiations to settle the issue, which ultimately resulted in the aforementioned 1986 statute that afforded foreign authors more protections for their works in South Korea (Choi, 2004).

The following is a list of the changes under this amendment:

1. The duration of the protection for the authors was extended to 50 years.
2. Copyright of the work created under employment belongs to the employers, not the authors. This is the "work-for-hire" doctrine that the Americans have.
3. It recognized foreigners' copyright to works under treaties that Korea has signed with foreign countries. However, this did not give the foreigners complete protections for their works.
4. This amendment recognized that computer programs should be protected under the Copyright Act.

---

[150] See Korean Copyright Act of 1957, 30(1).

[151] See Korean Copyright Act of 1957 Art. 46.

5. "Fair Use" is considered a legitimate defense for alleged copyright infringers.[152]

The Act was further amended in 1997. Some of the changes or additions in this Act include the following: a) The authors can decide whether to publish work under their real name or a pseudonym, b) the authors' moral rights belong exclusively to the authors even after their deaths, and c) the punishment for the infringers, including fine and prison terms, became more severe.[153] The Act was amended again in 2000. This version of the Act provided for a right of electronic transmission in accordance with the WIPO Copyright Treaty.[154]

Through the judicial decisions handed down over the years, the copyright rules in South Korea have become clearer. The Supreme Court of Korea ruled that a modicum of "originality" of the works is required for copyright protection. It also stated that creativity is needed, therefore the work intended to receive copyright protection should cannot be an imitation of someone else's work. Instead, it should contain the expression of the author's individual ideas and feelings (Youm, 2000).

America's strong influence on the shaping of Korean copyright law can be seen in these rulings. First of all, the requirement of originality is very similar to the copyright standard in the US. Also similar to the US copyright law is the stipulations that expressions are copyrightable but ideas are not.

The United States, however, was not the only outside influence on Korean copyright law. Aside from the US influence, the impact of international copyright conventions on Korean copyright law was also very strong. In short, Korea's accession to the international treaties had great significance in that after becoming a member to these international copyright conventions, the Koreans began to recognize the importance of copyright in accordance with international regulations. For example, the Berne Convention, the oldest international copyright convention, had an impact on the copyright law development in Korea, as the concept of "moral rights" was incorporated into South Korea's copyright law provisions after this convention. This influence occurred

---

152 See Copyright Act of 1986.

153 See Copyright Act of 1997.

154 See 2000 Copyright Act.

despite the fact that South Korea was not yet a member of the Berne Convention when moral rights became part of the copyright law (Youm, 2000).

Despite all of the copyright-related statutes in place, South Korea still received a tremendous amount of criticism from the international community due to the absence of commitment to global copyright standards and vigorous enforcement against copyright infringement in the country (Choi, 2004). Part of the reason was because South Korea's current legal system is modeled after the civil law system of continental Europe, which Korea adopted through Japan. Consequently, it lacks the procedural characteristics of litigation practice in common law jurisdiction, such as discovery and the right to compel documents, which makes a litigation of copyright case a bit more difficult to proceed (Youm, 2000).

Another problem for the development of copyright litigation is Korea's cultural traditions, which are heavily based on Confucianism. Under the Korean tradition, printing books was associated with the pursuit of higher education, and making money off writing books was simply not a concept accepted by the educated elite because they felt like ideas and creative thoughts should be in the public domain. Copying a book should be encouraged, not outlawed, because it showed a passion for learning (Youm, 2000).

Another reason for the low level of action toward copyright in Korean courts was that some Koreans resented the fact that the copyright law history in their country was filled with foreign influence, and that Korea was pressured into conforming to the western world (Choi, 2004). It does seem, however, that in recent years, South Koreans have become more receptive to the idea of copyright protection for creative works, as copyright issues on the Internet have become more prevalent.

China is another country in Asia that has a unique history with copyright law. China is a newcomer to the legislative arena of copyright protection mainly because the concept of copyright is a foreign concept to the Chinese way of thinking (Cheng, 1997). While China recognized the right to personal and real property, Chinese culture did not see works of the mind as properties, thus, authors did not have ownership rights to their creations. Furthermore, in ancient China, granting authors ownership rights would not have been conducive to the emperor's goal of making ideas widely accessible to the masses, as Cheng pointed out (1997). All of these factors contributed to the slow development of a copyright regime in China (Yang, 1993).

In the late 1970s, as China was trying to build itself, it recognized the importance international trade had on its developing economy and the Chinese government was eager to strengthen its intellectual property system because its lack of effort to protect copyright had stalled its efforts in promoting international trade. To make the business environment more appealing to foreign investors, China began to remodel its economic and political infrastructures based on internationally accepted principles of the Western world and the Copyright Law of 1991 (Cheng, 1997).

Since then, China's effort toward establishing an effective copyright system has been a constant battle between conflicting interests from abroad and within. While U.S. threats of trade sanctions has led China to pay more attention to its copyright regime, China's lack of incentives to enforce copyright also slowed down its efforts to fight against piracy. The result was the constant cycle of the U.S. threats of trade sanctions followed by sporadic enforcement by the Chinese government (Cheng, 1997).

There are several reasons why China still lacks the genuine motivation to enforce copyright protections. First of all, the Chinese cultural traditions still have an influence and private appropriation of the expression of ideas contradicts the Chinese cultural emphasis on the societal benefits rather than individual interests (Schlesinger, 1995) . Second of all, the idea of bringing the level of intellectual property protection in China to the level advocated by international copyright conventions such as TRIPs simply does not deliver any real economic benefit to China. In this sense, China shares the same economic motivations not to enforce intellectual property rights too vigorously as many other developing countries. As a developing nation struggling to modernize after years of isolation from the international market, China cannot afford to provide the high level of economic protection provided in TRIPs because in the short run, intellectual property rights have inhibited China's ability to obtain and use the technological information necessary for economic growth. The act of pirating could help a country obtain useful products and technology without having to pay for the research and development costs. In the short term, piracy could also provide numerous jobs for Chinese citizens depending on the production of pirated goods (Cheng, 1997).

After China officially became a member of the World Trade Organization (WTO), there has been even more pressure for the country to enhance its efforts to crack down on piracy (Chynoweth, 2003), and recent evidence would suggest that China is trying to step up its effort. In May 2011, a court in China actually fined Baidu, China's most popular search engine, for copyright infringement by providing links that led to pirated copies of five novels (Takada & Lee, 2011).

Other Asian countries have also been influenced by the West when it comes to copyright law, particularly India. This is not surprising because India used to be the United Kingdom's colony and but India's copyright statute borrowed heavily from the British copyright act (Mehta, 1979). Singapore also has a copyright law that is heavily influenced by foreign countries. The modern Copyright Act of Singapore was passed in 1987 and is based on Australian legislation (Wong, 2001). However, the original Copyright Act of 1911 in the United Kingdom, which also shaped India's copyright law, remains relevant when it comes to copyright materials created before the current Act became the law.[155]

In terms of the current copyright laws in the Asian countries examined, there are, foreign influences evident everywhere in these copyright laws, as some of them did not consider copyright an issue to be worried about before the foreign forces occupied their countries.

Among these Asian countries, aside from giving the authors/creators the economic rights to profit from their works, South Korea, Japan, and all three Pan-Chinese regions (China, Hong Kong, and Taiwan) legally recognize moral rights as part of the authors/creators' copyright in their statutes. The provisions in these moral rights clauses are very similar to the moral rights provisions in the western world. The Copyright Act of South Korea had a moral rights section that gave the authors/creators the following rights:

---

[155] See an article titled Guide Me Singapore, An Introduction to Copyright Law in Singapore. Retrieved from http://www.guidemesingapore.com/incorporation/trademarks/singapore-copyright-law-introduction,

1. The author shall have the right to decide whether or not to make his work public;
2. The author shall have the right to indicate his real name or pseudonym;
3. The author shall have the right to preserve the integrity of the content, form and title of his work; and
4. Author's moral rights shall belong exclusively to the author and thus are inalienable.[156]

The Chinese and Japanese versions of the moral rights provisions are very similar to the Korean provisions.[157] Given that the Japanese and South Korean copyright statutes were both influenced by the United States, which does not have moral rights in the majority of its copyright act, the inclusion of moral rights could be explained by the influence of the Berne Convention and the Confucius influence. Having the right to protect one's own intellectual properties and prevent them from being destroyed by others is part of the "personal dignity."

The copyright laws in Singapore and India do not contain moral right clauses. This is probably because their copyright laws were heavily shaped by the copyright of their one-time occupier, the United Kingdom, who-did not have a moral right provision in its copyright law until fairly recently.[158] This is an interesting fact because Singapore also places a heavy emphasis on personal dignity and integrity, and yet, moral rights are not included in the statute.

Regarding the terms of copyright protection, Singapore has the longest protection period among these Asian countries, which is life of the author plus 70 years.[159] India's copyright law has the second longest protection period, with the term of life of the author plus 60 years.[160] Japan, South Korea, China, Hong Kong, and Taiwan all have

---

[156] See Copyright Act of South Korea, Arts. 11-15.

[157] See Copyright Law of the People's Republic of China;Copyright Act (2007-07011, Taiwan);Copyright (Amendment) Ordinances 2007 & 2009;Copyright Law of Japan.

[158] See Copyright Act of Singapore and Indian Copyright Act, 1957.

[159] See Copyright Act of Singapore, s. 28(2),

[160] See India's Copyright Act 1957, s. 22.

the same length of protection period, which is life of the author plus 50 years. [161]

As with all the other copyright laws previously discussed in this book, there are limitations to the copyright protections in every single copyright statute in the Asian countries included here. Similar to other exceptions that can be found in other copyright statutes of the West, those exceptions usually include the purposes of research and study, criticism or review, reporting current events, and non-profit performances. Normally, when judging whether a use is permitted under these exceptions, several other factors are considered such as the nature of the work, the amount and substantiality of the part of the work that was copied in relation to the whole work as well as the effect on the potential market. [162] China's Copyright Law, for example, contains fair use provisions which allow reasonable use of a published work for which no authorization or payment is necessary. Examples include works used for translation, personal enjoyment, and official state purposes.[163] Compared to the United States "fair use" clause in its copyright law, most of the copyright exception lists in the Asian countries discussed here are more concrete and rigid, meaning if a certain kind of use is not listed in the statute, then it is probably not going to be permissible.

When an act of copyright infringement occurs, the Asian copyright laws also provide remedies for the copyright holders, both in civil cases and criminal cases. For criminal cases, the penalties for copyright infringement usually includes prison time and fines. For civil cases, the remedies usually include demanding the immediate suspension of infringement, monetary damages, and injunctions. Japan and South Korea have also included an author or a performer's right to demand the person who has infringed on the author's or performer's moral rights intentionally or by negligence to take measures necessary for the "recovery of his honor or reputation in return for or together with

---

[161] See Copyright Law of People's Republic of China, Copyright Ordinance (Cap.528), Art. 51(2), Law No. 48 of 6 May 1970, Copyright Act of 30 December 1989, Art.36, Copyright Act of Taiwan, Art. 30.

[162] See Copyright Act of Singapore.

[163] See Copyright Law of People's Republic of China.

compensation for damages."[164] Once again, this rule is in line with how much South Korea and Japan value personal dignity and integrity.

It should be noted that China did not have criminal actions for copyright infringement at first. Before criminal code was used to prosecute copyright infringers, enforcement measures set forth in China's Copyright Law and the Implementing Regulations were generally consistent with TRIPs, and the Copyright Law lists actions that led to civil liability and provided remedies such as "public apologies" or monetary compensation by the infringer, immediate cessation of the infringement, and the elimination of the infringing act's effects.Copyright infringement eventually became a criminal offense in 1994, set up to further eradicate illegal reproduction activities and other aggravated acts of copyright. The new law provided criminal penalties of three to seven years in prison for reproducing other people's work without prior authorization (Cheng, 1997).

Overall, the copyright statutes in all three continents-America, Europe, and Asia, are similar to some extent but dissimilar in other important aspects. While the copyright statutes in Asia were all heavily influenced by the West, this does not mean that the Asian nations do not have their own unique ways of handling copyright disputes.

The biggest difference between the copyright law in the United States and most of the other countries examined here is that it essentially does not provide moral rights for the copyright holders. There are two likely reasons for having moral rights in the copyright statutes: The first is that the Berne Convention, which was heavily influenced by the French copyright law, requires their members to contain moral rights clauses in their copyright law. The second reason is that in Asian countries that were rooted in the tradition of Confucianism, which highly values an individual's personal integrity, reputation, and placement in the world, having his/her honor harmed, even in the form of a misuse of a creative work, should warrant a punishment.

Another aspect of the copyright law in the United States that differs from other countries' copyright law is the exceptions provisions. Every single piece of copyright legislation discussed here contains limitations to copyright, but there is typically an exhaustive list of uses that the laws permit, usually including personal, private, educational,

---

[164] See Copyright Law of Japan and Copyright Law of South Korea.

and non-profit uses of the copyrighted works. On the other hand, the American copyright law broadly interpreted the “fair use” clause without a finite list, which makes it a little more uncertain to predict whether a court would interpret a certain use to fall under the permissible category.

With the exception of Singapore, the western countries all provide a longer period of protection for the copyright holders in their statutes, perhaps signaling the fact that the Asian countries, which were slower to embrace the concept of copyright, are still more cautious when it comes to providing protection for artistic expression.

Most of the countries provide remedies for the copyright holders when an act of infringement occurs. For criminal infringement cases, the remedies usually include prison time and fines, while in civil cases, remedies usually include injunctions and monetary damages. South Korea and Japan’s copyright statutes also provide that when an author’s moral rights are violated, he/she has the option of demanding the recovery of his/her honor or reputation in return for or together with compensation for damages. This is also in line with the high value they place on personal integrity.

All things considered, it would seem that out of all the countries examined, the European nations provide the most protection for copyright holders. The Asian nations are newer to copyright regulations and generally have shorter protection periods than the other regions. Americans have no moral rights protection for the copyright holders except for some limited areas of visual arts. The European nations grant the longest term for copyright protection and they also provide moral rights for the copyright holders, which even the British added into the law after long periods of resistance. The moral rights provisions give the authors/creators one more avenue to protect their honor and creative works; therefore, at least based on statutes alone, the European nations provide the most amount of protection for copyright holders.

Chapter 9

Cyber-piracy Issues

Cyber and piracy are perhaps two of the most dreaded words for musicians, moviemakers, and the executives who run record companies and movie studios. The advent of technology and the proliferation of Internet use made it much easier to illegally download a song or a movie, and much harder for the copyright owners to track down the copyright infringers because there are so many. Along with this, the methods deployed to download illegally have gotten more and more sophisticated and clever.

There have been numerous accounts of cyber-piracy in the United States since the advent of Internet. One of the most high-profile cyber piracy cases is probably the leaking of a rough and incompletely edited version of *Wolverine*, which occurred in early April of 2009, about a month ahead of its scheduled May 1st, 2009 release, on the Internet (Nasaw, 2009). The on-line leak of an almost complete movie a month before its release was unprecedented therefore making it one of the biggest Internet piracy cases to date.[165] In response to this, the FBI launched an investigation of the leak, and the movie studio releasing the movie, 20th Century Fox, terminated the service of a Fox website columnist who, around the same time the incomplete version of *Wolverine* was leaked, wrote a review of the movie based on the pirated version (West, 2009).

The United States has certainly done its part in dealing with the issue of copyright infringement and cyber-piracy. After the Internet

---

[165] See another article about the leak of the Wolverine movie titledFBI Called in Over Wolverine Leak.Retrieved from http://news.bbc.co.uk/2/low/entertainment/7978379.stm.

became a major factor, Congress enacted the Digital Millennium Copyright Act (DMCA in 1998 and the Family Entertainment and Copyright Act in 2005 in order to have a better handle on the issue.

The Digital Millennium Copyright Act is most relevant to cyber-piracy. Under the DMCA, which is essentially an update of the existing copyright law, several computer and web-related copyright regulations were introduced, including 1) the heightening of the penalties for copyright infringement on the Internet, 2) making it a crime to circumvent anti-piracy measures built into most commercial softwares, 3) outlawing the manufacture, sale, or distribution of code-cracking devices used to illegally copy softwares, and 4) limiting Internet service providers from copyright infringement liability for simply transmitting information over the Internet. However, service providers are expected to remove materials from users' websites that appear to constitute copyright infringement.[166] It should be noted that Chapter 6 of the Copyright Act of South Korea titled "Limitation on Liability of Online Service Providers" contain almost the exact same language and provisions.[167]

SOPA AND PIPA

In response to the growing concern over the prevalence of cyber-piracy in recent years and the intensifying pressure from the entertainment industry to combat this problem which is costing the industry millions of dollars every year, the United States Congress subsequently proposed two sets of new and aggressive legislations to address the problems. On October 26th, 2011, Texas House Representative Lamar Smith introduced a bill titled Stop Online Piracy Act (SOPA) to the House of Representatives. The goal of this bill is made clear in its full title: "To promote prosperity, creativity, entrepreneurship, and innovation by combating the theft of U.S. property, and for other purposes." PIPA (PROTECT IP Act) is a similar bill that was introduced in 2011 by Senator Patrick Leahy.

The law posits that it "authorizes the Attorney General (AG) to seek a court order against a U.S.-directed foreign Internet site committing or facilitating online piracy to require the owner, operator,

---

166 See Digital Millennium Copyright Act.

167 See Copyright Act of Korea, Chap. 6.

or domain name registrant, or the site or domain name itself to cease and desist further activities constituting specified intellectual property offenses under the federal criminal code including criminal copyright infringement, unauthorized fixation and trafficking of sound recordings or videos of live musical performances, the recording of exhibited motion pictures, or trafficking in counterfeit labels, goods, or services."

It is designed to crack down on copyright infringement by restricting access to sites that host or facilitate the trading of pirated content. Some of the more aggressive provisions in the proposed bill include requesting court orders to bar advertising networks and payment facilities from conducting business with the websites suspected of allowing copyright infringement, and search engines such as Google and Yahoo from linking to the websites, and court orders requiring Internet Service Providers to block access to the websites. Furthermore, this new Internet legislation would expand existing criminal laws to penalize unauthorized streaming of copyrighted content, with the maximum penalty of five years in prison for violators.[168]

SOPA also provides those whose rights have been violated a way to remedy the problem, as it posits that the law "sets forth an additional two-step process that allows an intellectual property right holder harmed by a U.S.-directed site dedicated to infringement, or a site promoted or used for infringement under certain circumstances, to first provide a written notification identifying the site to related payment network providers and Internet advertising services requiring such entities to forward the notification and suspend their services to such an identified site unless the site's owner, operator, or domain name registrant, upon receiving the forwarded notification, provides a counter notification explaining that it is not dedicated to engaging in specified violations."[169]

SOPA's biggest ambition is revealed in its main targets, which are the rogue overseas websites such as torrent hub The Pirate Bay, which are treasure troves for illegal downloading (Pirate Bay is discussed later in this chapter). If you go to the Pirate Bay and type in any current hit movie or TV show such as <u>Mad Men</u>, you will see various links to

---

[168] See H.R.3261.

[169] See note 161.

download full seasons and recent episodes for free. Consequently, intellectual property owners in the United States have been battling this serious problem–while the DMCA addresses the issue and lays out enforcement measures. For example, a website that is potentially a hotbed for violations of intellectual property law is YouTube, where anyone can post a performance of a song or a clip of a television show that is protected by the intellectual property law. Under the DMCA, if a YouTube user uploads a copyrighted song, that song's copyright holder(s) could send a so-called "takedown notice" to YouTube. In turn, YouTube is protected against liability-as long as it removes the content within a reasonable timeframe.

However, it is very difficult for U.S. companies to take action against foreign websites such as the Pirate Bay, whose servers are physically located in Sweden. SOPA's aim is to put a dent into the operations and financial well-being of websites such as the Pirate Bay by requiring U.S. search engines, advertising networks and other providers to withhold their services. What does that mean exactly? It means that search engines such as Google will not show the flagged sites in their search results. Additionally, popular payment processor websites such as eBay and PayPal will not be able to legally transmit funds to them.

It is an understatement to say that SOPA generated a strong response both positive and negative. On the one hand, supporters of the bill stated that this new law would effectively deal with new problems emanating from the rampant cyber-piracy nowadays that DMCA is not equipped to regulate. On the other side, opponents expressed a deep concern that this new legislation would threaten not only freedom of speech but also discourage the fine tradition of innovation. Moreover, this new law would allow the government to block access to entire Internet domains because of infringing content posted on a single blog or webpage. They have also been concerned that SOPA would bypass the "safe harbor" protections, from liability presently afforded to websites by the DMCA. This is due to the fact that SOPA would essentially bypass the DMCA's safe harbor protections by placing the responsibility for detecting and policing infringement on the website itself and allowing judges to block access to websites dedicated to theft of U.S. property. Perhaps more significantly, educators have also been worried about the impact of this new law. Specifically, Library associations have expressed concerns that SOPA's emphasis on tougher copyright enforcement could potentially expose libraries to prosecutions. Other opponents have argued that requiring search *f* to erase domain names violates the First Amendment and in the worst case scenario could even lead to a worldwide epidemic of unprecedented Internet censorship.

The battle between the opponents and the proponents of SOPA came to a breaking point a few months after the bill was proposed. On January 18, 2012, Wikipedia, Reddit, and about 7,000 other smaller websites organized a large-scale service shutdown to raise awareness on the perceived problems SOPA could've engendered if Congress passed it. Other similar protests included boycotts of companies and organizations that supported the legislation and a demonstration/rally held in New York City.

The massive website block-outs and the high-profile rally became front-page news and had a major impact on the fate of SOPA. Immediately after all of the protests, Congress failed to pass the bill and Lamar announced that the House Judiciary Committee would postpone consideration of the legislation until wider consensus on a solution could be reached, and Sen. Reid announced that the PIPA test vote scheduled for January 24, 2012, would also be postponed. As of January 2013, there has not been much movement.

Despite the failed attempt to pass SOPA and PIPA, it is clear that DMCA is not enough to cover all of the copyright issues springing up on the Internet. After successfully cracking down Napster about a decade ago, it is apparent that illegal downloading of music and movies is still a problem in the United States (Gardella & Forzato, 2011). Perhaps, then, it would be helpful to examine what other countries around the world are doing to handle this very current and serious problem.

In the following section, we examine and have a current update on how countries/regions such as France, Sweden, Taiwan, and South Korea and others have done legislatively and/or judicially in the face of rampant cyber-piracy and illegal file-sharing, and whether their new laws will work in the United States.

THREE STRIKES RULES AND OTHER ANTI-PIRACY DEVELOPMENT IN EUROPE

In Europe, there have been several attempts on the part of the governments to address the cyber-piracy problem and to crack down on illegal file-sharing on the Internet. Most notably, the "three-strikes rule" legislation became a new tool to fight cyber-piracy in a couple of nations. Others, such as Italy and Sweden, passed their own rules to restrain cyber-piracy.

In France, in May of 2009, the French National Assembly approved its "Créationet Internet" three-strikes bill (Pfanner, 2009). This measure was strongly supported by the then French President Nicolas Sarkozy and would punish digital pirates by suspending Internet service if they were caught illegally sharing copyrighted materials (Soodin, 2009). It should be noted that the bill was also pushed by Sarkozy's wife, Carla Bruni, a professional singer who wanted to act against what she called "the lawless wild west of the internet," according to Soodin's report.

The bill passed in France's National Assembly by a very narrow margin of 296 to 233 (Fouquet, 2009). The legislation essentially created a new government agency known as HADOPI (the Haute Autorité pour la Diffusion des Oeuvres et la Protection des droitssur Internet), which is tasked with sending notices to illegal file sharers (Saez, 2009). As Saez reported, this new measure doled out punishment in two ways: First, the suspected offenders would receive two warnings about their illegal activities, and on the third suspected offense, their Internet access would be cut off for two months to a year. Additionally, the offenders will still have to pay the Internet Service Providers while they are banned. Violators of the law will also be put on a "three-strikes" blacklist so that they cannot get around the regulation by signing up for services from another Internet Service Provider. Secondly, there will be an injunction to take preventive measures such as the installation of special software that limits access to legitimate content from the Internet (Reardon, 2009). According to a summary of the law issued by the French Senate, this second form of punishment is aimed at companies for which the connection suspension could have drastic effects.

The bill was voted against initially in early 2009 when it first came up before the National Assembly because not enough members of parliament from the ruling UMP party were in attendance for the vote. Also, the major opposition party at the time, the Socialist Party, which vehemently opposed the law, said that it planned to ask the Constitutional Council, France's highest authority, to rule on the legality of the law (Reardon, 2009) . In response to this, a revised bill eventually became the official law in the fall of 2009 after the first draft was declared unconstitutional by the French Constitutional Court (Sandoval, 2009b).

Reactions to the bill were mixed. A major reason for this mixed, or even negative reaction to what has been branded by some people as the "strictest law to crack down cyber piracy" is because the passage of the bill put France on the opposite side of the European Union in terms of dealing with cyber-piracy and French opposition lawmakers protested legal issues that were echoed by European Parliament members (Reardon, 2009) . The European Parliament reiterated that it considered access to the Internet as a fundamental right, making the HADOPI law a direct contradiction with the EU Parliament recommendation.[170]

In response to this bill, European Parliament Member Guy Bono, who belongs to the Socialist Party in France, said he would ask the European Commission to take this matter to the EU Court of Justice to carry out an infringement proceeding against France for lack of respect for European Community rules if the French constitutional judge did not react to this law. Not surprisingly, Bono is one of the authors of Amendment 138, recently adopted by the European Parliament, which prevents sanctions against Internet users without a judicial ruling. Essentially, French opposition and European Parliament said Internet services should only be restricted after a judge's order, while other critics expressed their concern about the effectiveness of the bill. Opponents of the law insist that this measure will not foster creation or bring larger royalties to artists as intended (Sandoval, 2009b) .

The new law, just like any other, is not immune to violators' efforts to find potential loopholes. Already, in the short life of this new law, there are indications that many websites have published ways to circumvent the HADOPI surveillance. In fact, giving credence to the critics' concern, the Internet is filled with tips on avoiding detection by HADOPI, according to French newspaper *Le Monde*, thus potentially weakening the impact of the new law (Sandoval, 2009b).

---

[170] But France ignored this statement and implemented the law anyway.

In the end, the speculation as to how effective this new law will be is still in question. As of July of 2011, the French government has sent out close to 500,000 email warnings to violators since the law was passed, but French courts so far have prosecuted no one for illegal file sharing (Sayer, 2011). This could change soon, though, as French authority is now considering whether to initiate legal proceedings against a dozen or so subscribers who have already been reported a third time. This legal action could lead to a fine of up to €1,500 (US$2,100) and suspension of Internet access for up to a month, according to the report from Sayer (2011).

Another country in Europe that passed a similar law is the United Kingdom. In 2010, the House of Commons voted 189 to 47 to pass the Digital Economy Act, which also attempts to give the government the authority to block access to websites suspected of engaging in pirated materials (Sandoval, 2010) . The Act allows the Secretary of State to block access to a location on the Internet from which a substantial amount of materials has been, is currently or is likely to be made available in infringement of copyright, or a location which "facilitates" such behavior.[171] The "three strikes rule" in the United Kingdom, as in France, is used to describe the sending of multiple warnings to suspected illegal file sharers. Under such laws, after a certain number of warnings, if the accused does not stop, an Internet service provider is required to suspend or terminate service (Sandoval, 2010) .

On the other hand, the German government has rejected the "three strikes" approach to combat Internet piracy (Spahr, 2009). This does not mean that Germany does not want to deal with the problem of cyber-piracy, however. In the summer of 2011, the German government conducted a major raid of several offices, seized computers and documents, arrested several people, and eventually shut down the biggest online piracy website in Germany, Kino.to (Roxborough, 2011).

In Italy, as in Germany, there is no "three-strikes" rule to combat the problem of cyber-piracy; however, the Italian government is making an effort in other ways. In the summer of 2011, the Communications Authority (Agcom) in Italy approved a ruling which gave itself the power to order the removal of materials from websites that violate copyright, but reserved the right to block access from Italy to foreign sites guilty of the same infringement for the courts (Willan,

---

[171] See Digital Economy Act 2010.

2011). Previously, both measures required the intervention of an independent court.

Sweden also did not have a "three-strikes" rule in place. Instead, the Swedish government decided to fight cyber-piracy by arresting the founders of a highly popular piracy website. In 2008, four men, Peter Sunde, Gottfrid SvartholmWarg, Fredrik Neij, and Carl Lundstrom, who were the founders of the extremely popular file-sharing site, the Pirate Bay, were arrested in Stockholm, Sweden. They were accused of helping millions of Internet users illegally download copyrighted movies, music, and computer games (Musil, 2009).

Pirate Bay, which is a Swedish-based BitTorrent indexing site, had intentionally linked pirated copies of films, TV shows, music videos, and other content while often boasting that it ignores Hollywood's constant requests to remove them (Musil, 2009). While Pirate Bay does not host any unauthorized content, the site is accused of facilitating piracy by directing its 22 million users to copyrighted movies and music, according to the report from Musil (2009).

In mid-April 2009, a Swedish court found the four defendants guilty and sentenced all four to one year in jail (Lewan & Palm, 2009). The defendants were also ordered to pay a total of 30 million Swedish kronor ($3.6 million) in damages to copyright holders, among them a number of American media giants, including Warner Bros. Entertainment, MGM Pictures, Columbia Pictures Industries, 20th Century Fox Films, Sony BMG, Universal, and EMI. The largest portion of the compensation was allotted to Twentieth Century Fox, who was awarded $1.3 million, followed by Columbia Pictures, who was awarded $504,000, and Warner Bros., who was awarded $300,000.

The $3.6 million punishment was considered one of the harshest sentences in Swedish history. However, months after the ruling came down, very little had changed. With at least 22 million peers online at any moment, Pirate Bay continues to rule the file-sharing landscape despite the entertainment industry's legal victory in court (Tharp, 2009). The traffic of the website is just as busy as it was before the ruling and remains one of the most popular websites in Sweden and around the world. In fact, not long after the verdict, the website upgraded.

Pirate Bay is indeed a major milestone for cyber-piracy litigation for Sweden. Before that guilty verdict came down, Sweden had a fairly relaxed attitude about Internet file-sharing. This judgment against the founders of a file-sharing website, along with the passage of anti-cyber-piracy law IPRED, seems to suggest that the Swedish government is taking a more aggressive stand towards cyber-piracy. However, after the news got out that behind the scenes, the United States government had pressured the Swedish government to take care of its Internet piracy issues, some argued that Sweden's anti-piracy efforts and the initiation of the Pirate Bay case were both responses to the pressure of the United States government (Petrou, 2010). If this is the only reason the Swedish government decided to make these efforts to combat cyber-piracy, then it remains to be seen how committed to the cause of fighting Internet piracy the Swedish government will be in the future once that pressure from the United States is off the Swedish government.

THREE STRIKES RULES AND OTHER ANTI-PIRACY DEVELOPMENT IN ASIA

South Korea became the first country in the world, beating France, to implement a nation-wide "three-strikes" law to fight cyber-piracy in 2009 (Lemon, 2009). As previously discussed, South Korea was not a country that completely embraced the concept of copyright in the past, so this should be considered a huge leap in copyright development in the country. Specifically, though laws have been enacted in South Korea to protect intellectual property rights and combat piracy, Korea's Confucian value system and emphasis upon education laid the foundation for a cultural resistance to IP protection (Choi, 2009) .

South Korea is one of the most Internet-saturated countries in the world, with more than 34 million Koreans over the age of five, which is about 74.8% of the total population, regularly utilizing the Internet. South Korea also has the fourth largest number of broadband subscribers with over 14.4 million, behind Japan, Germany, and the United States, all of which have a much larger population (Choi, 2009). This fast and widespread penetration of the Internet in Korea, coupled with infinite enthusiasm and a need for media and entertainment, represents a huge potential for Internet piracy in this country. As one of the leaders in the digital world, South Korea probably feels the need to be a leader in the ongoing battle against rampant cyber-piracy, which may have contributed to the passage of this anti-piracy law.

Under the passed anti-piracy law in South Korea, the government shut down Internet message boards that refused to heed warnings on removing copyrighted content.[172] Message boards which allow users to post illegal content could be shut down for up to six months if they fail to take care of the pirating on their websites after two warnings. Users who upload infringing content may also have their Internet accounts cancelled. Even though this South Korean law targets message boards instead of the much more prolific file sharing networks such as Sweden's Piracy Bay website, it is still the first time a government has passed a law to cut off the Internet connection of copyright pirates.

Since the implementation of the law, South Koreans have been keeping their eyes on how the Internet landscape of the country would be altered by the law. Not long after the law was passed, authorities in South Korea conducted one of the biggest piracy crackdowns involving websites that have the potential to contribute or abet the act of cyber-piracy. Specifically, the Ministry of Culture in South Korea had indicated that 19 of the country's top services were targeted which together served up to 4 million users.

Despite the fact that it is still relatively early in the implementation of the "three-strikes" rule, there was a study conducted to find out whether the law had any impact on the country. The study showed that from the time the law was passed in the fall of 2009 to mid-2010, there had been about 15,000 warnings sent out to Internet users who were suspected of being engaged in pirating on the web. However, interestingly enough, 'Suspension of User Account, 'which was the 3rd strike that would lead to the Internet cut-off, had not been used at all when the study was conducted. This led to the discussion as to whether this stringent law was really necessary to deal with this issue, or whether the mere existence of the law was enough to serve as deterrence for cyber-piracy.

Things have changed in South Korea since the completion of that study, however. In recent months, the South Korean government seems to have stepped up their efforts in the implementation of the law. Over the last two years, there have been over 60,000 actions taken by the

---

[172] See another useful article on Intellectual Property Magazine on Line about South Korea's passage of the three-strikes law. Retrieved from http://www.ipworld.com/ipwo/doc/view.htm?id=217097&searchCode=H.

government in relation to this law, and at least 32 South Koreans have lost their Internet access in violation of the law.[173] These new statistics indicated that during the first year the law was implemented, the South Korean government started out gingerly and did not make any major moves, perhaps wanting to give its people some time to get used to the law. However, in the second year, more warnings were handed out, and around 30 people had their Internet connections cut off. While this is not a big number, it is an increase.

Despite the fact that the country was adverse to copyright protections in the past, South Korea has since recognized the effects of piracy on its own economy, and its need to offer copyright protection (Lindvall, 2011). Although Korea's copyright policy still lags behind global standards, the "three-strikes" law is definitely doing its part to make up for it.

Given that South Korea was the first country to implement the "three-strikes" law, and new numbers have suggested that the Korean government is now more aggressive in its implementation of the law, it would be prudent to keep a watchful eye on the continuing development of the fight against cyber-piracy in South Korea in the next few years to see whether this law is an effective tool to deter piracy and illegal file-sharing on the Internet. It's still early, but there is indication that the Korean music industry is benefiting from this law already (Lindvall, 2011) .

The island of Taiwan was also one of the first regions to implement the "three-strikes" rule. In fact, before France approved their version of the "three-strikes" law, Taiwan, raced ahead and passed a similar law. In late April 2009, Taiwan passed revisions to its copyright laws, which sent a strong message to illegal file-sharers on line (Worth, 2009). The amendment makes it a crime to use P2P technology to facilitate the distribution of copyrighted works online, which was not good news for the Taiwanese BitTorrent sites previously operating in a legal gray area.[174]

---

[173] These numbers are provided by Freedom for IP. Retrieved from http://freedomforip.org/2010/10/25/three-strikes-in-south-korea-stats.

[174] See the article "Taiwan Bans Torrent Sites, Brings in 3 Strikes for File-Sharers" on the website, TorrentFreak. Retrieved from http://torrentfreak.com/taiwan-bans-torrent-sites-brings-in-3-strikes-for-file-sharers-090427.

As pointed out by people who are experts in this area, there is an upside and a downside to this new law for Internet Service Providers in Taiwan. The upside is that they are exempt from taking responsibility for the copyright infringing actions of their customers, which is similar to the DMCA's 'safe harbor' provision. The down side is that they have to introduce a 'three strikes' regime for subscribers accused of infringement by copyright holders, which is the same measure France is trying to implement. After the third strike, the ISP can take a range of measures against the user, including Internet disconnection (Worth, 2009).

One thing worth noting is that the 'three strikes' rule in Taiwan does not protect file-sharers from the copyright holders taking legal actions against them (Worth, 2009). Consequently, violators could face Internet disconnection and a claim for damages. Perhaps most importantly, the change in the law is aimed primarily at heavy downloaders, not casual file-sharers. Additionally, ISPs will not be allowed to hand over the personal details of alleged file-sharers to copyright holders. One exception to this rule is that should the individual submit a counter claim to restore previously removed content, his or her details can be made available to the rights holder.

In Singapore, the government has not adopted a "three-strikes" law as of yet, since it believes that existing laws in the country are already in place for appropriate action to be taken against illegal content-sharing offenders, and therefore there is no need to enact a new law to combat piracy on the Internet (Kwang, 2009).

According to the Intellectual Property Office of Singapore (IPOS), the country currently has no plans to introduce a three strikes law. Some have even suggested that the best way to fight piracy is for the police force in Singapore, operating within the IP Rights branch, to take the lead because this division has a lot of power–under the Criminal Procedure Code. This could compel ISPs to disclose the identities of frequent down-loaders of pirated materials, which would allow the police to conduct raids and get the necessary evidence to prosecute these offenders (Kwang, 2009). The rationale seems to be that once there is a high-profile raid and/or arrest, it should serve as a deterrent to illegal file-sharing and downloading.

Another reason that Singapore has not enacted a stringent anti-Internet piracy law such as the "three strikes" law was because some people in Singapore believe that education, not the tough measures employed under the three strikes law, should be utilized to take care of the cyber-piracy problem (Kwang, 2009). It would seem that these people regard education as a more effective tool than strict laws to fight pirating on the Internet.

In China, the Internet piracy problem has become such a big concern that the Chinese government also took steps to handle the issue. In the past, China has been notorious for its wide-spread piracy of intellectual properties. As with South Korea, copyright was a foreign concept to the Chinese in the past, and it was not until the West pressured China to regulate it in the late 1980s and early 1990s for economic reasons that the idea of copyright began to enter the Chinese' consciousness. Perhaps due to a lack history of copyright in China, it became the world's major intellectual property infringement culprit and accounted for nearly two-thirds of counterfeit goods, including DVDs, music CDs, prescription drugs, and others, on the estimated $512 billion worldwide counterfeit market (Priest, 2006). Not surprisingly, China has been heavily criticized for its rampant piracy and the government's lax copyright protection standards by the international community. However, in the last year or so, China has made efforts to deal with cyber-piracy that could either be a new trend for the country, or just a phase designed to appease the international community.

Specifically, the target of the Chinese government's crackdown on Internet piracy was the biggest Internet player in China. Perhaps to make a statement, the Chinese Ministry of Culture took on the immensely popular online Chinese search engine, Baidu, for facilitating illegal music and book downloads in April 2011 (Lee, 2011).

Earlier in 2011, Baidu got into trouble for allowing its users to illegally download books from its online library, and the search engine removed 2.8 million unauthorized and unlicensed books from its library (McDonald, 2011). In April, the Chinese government announced that it would punish 14 websites that have provided illegal music downloads, including Baidu, and also stated that these websites continued to provide illegal downloads despite repeated warnings not to.

The Chinese government's big move seemed to have a positive effect on the improvement of the cyber-piracy issue in the country. In July of 2011, Baidu agreed to pay record labels to offer songs on its website in a landmark deal between Baidu and three of the world's largest record labels, Sony, Universal Music and Warner Music, thus ending a six-year legal battle between all of the parties involved (Neate, 2011).

THE UNITED STATES AND THE THREE STRIKES LAW

Cyber-piracy is a big issue the world's intellectual property rights holders and nations all around the world are facing today. Naturally, every country has its own way of dealing with the issue. Some countries, such as China and Sweden, may have been pressured by outside forces to crack down on their popular search engines/file-sharing websites. Others have taken the more drastic step of implementing the "three-strikes rule." Overall, only four countries/regions have adopted the anti-piracy measure of a "three-strike" rule so far including South Korea, France, the United Kingdom, and Taiwan. This tough law, which could take away people's access to the Internet if they are found illegally file-sharing/downloading, has met with a mixture of criticisms and praises from the intellectual property advocates.

So can the United States take a stronger stand against cyber piracy? Is it possible for the US to pass a "three-strikes" law as in France and South Korea? This seems unlikely as of now for the United States to adopt such a harsh and drastic measure to fight cyber piracy. After the debacle and controversy the introduction of SOPA and PIPA created, which has put the fate of these two bills in limbo, the possibility passing a similar draconian law is even more remote now.

First of all, Internet Service Providers are not on board with the "three-strike law." According to a US industry representative, although AT&T did agree to send notices to consumers suspected of illegally distributing copyrighted content, the majority of the US Internet service providers do not support the measures in France and South Korea, but rather prefer voluntary, bilateral negotiations with rights owners (Sandoval, 2009a) .

Second of all, the main objection of the law, which was the curtailment of people's freedom, surely will be brought up if the President of the United States and the US Congress seriously consider passing a similar law. The value of liberty is not something the American people will be willing to give up easily, especially considering the law is pushed by giant media companies.

All of these speculations could all be rendered moot if the "three strikes law" actually works in the countries that have adopted them and if illegal downloading becomes more rampant than it is today in the US. Then, the combination of wanting to appear to be dealing with the problem, peer pressure, and the clout of media conglomerates have on the government might force the United States to join the "three-strikes" club, regardless of how much resistance there will be. The economic pressures to do so might simply prove too great for the government of the United States to not implement such a rule. But until then, the Americans are more likely to stick with the existent copyright laws to handle the problem of cyber-piracy in the foreseeable future.

Chapter 10

Comparisons of the Media Laws and Implications

As evidenced in the previous chapters, no two countries examined in this book took the same routes to establish their regulations and philosophies regarding freedom of the press and other aspects of media law. There are some similarities in some respects among the nations, since countries do interact and influence one another one way or the other; however, even when these similarities are present, each countries laws and concepts are not applied exactly the same. In the following section, the authors compare and analyze the concepts and laws regarding freedom of the press in each of the countries examined in this book to answer all of the research questions. The constitutions of these countries and their inclusions or exclusions of the protection of freedom of the press are compared and analyzed. Following the analyses of the constitutions, laws affecting freedom of the press including freedom of information laws, reporters' privileges, and libel laws are also discussed. Next, copyright laws and cyber-piracy law are also compared and analyzed to a lesser extent. In the following section, the authors attempt to offer an explanation as to why the laws are the way they are, discuss whether political, cultural and economic factors have helped to shape and develop these laws, and whether one factor was more influential than another. In addition, when appropriate, the authors also offer their opinions on whether one law is better than the other.

COMPARISONS OF THE CONSTITUTIONS

Almost all of the countries discussed in this book are committed to press freedom in some way. Some explicitly mention "press" in their constitutions, while others seem to include press protection under the "freedom of speech" or "freedom of expression" clauses. However, how they go about achieving the goal of having a free press and justifying having press freedom varies from country to country. The western countries' concept of freedom of the press originated from the same idea, while the Asian countries examined in this book, who generally embraced that concept later than their western counterparts, had different ideas as to how a free press should function in their societies.

Based on the examination of the history and development of the concept of freedom of the press and whether the constitutions offer to protect this right, it is clear that the original concept of a free press came from the West and there are similarities in the interpretations of the concept among the United States and the rest of the western countries examined in this book. Generally speaking, the Western models of press freedom were based on the natural law tradition within liberalism. From that natural law tradition, Western culture developed a belief in the importance of individual self-expression, and in the legitimacy of criticizing existing authorities to keep them in check. Furthermore, modern democracy is based on the idea that all men are created equal, hence capable of participating in the political decision making process. Those beliefs and ideas lead to the general justifications for having a free press: the quest for individual self-fulfillment, the concept of the marketplace of ideas and that there needs to be a competition among ideas so that the best ideas will emerge and benefit society and the individual, the search for the ultimate truth, and the ability to participate in a democracy.

The United States is a very good example of a country that fully embraced all of the ideas mentioned above. Judges and philosophers in the country at the time of the creation of the Constitution of the United States believed that having a free press was essential because it would help an individual achieve self-fulfillment, self-government, self-valve and the search for truth. In other words, freedom of the press is a concept that would not only help a person grow intellectually, but would also assist society in achieving a true democracy. The United

Kingdom, whose concept of press freedom influenced the Americans in a major way, also has the same beliefs. Specifically, the British believe that an individual is capable of using reason and distinguishing right from wrong and good from bad. But, in order to be able to exercise this right, the individual must have unlimited access to other people's ideas in order for the best ideas to emerge. The liberal belief that "there should be a marketplace of ideas" and "the best ideas would win out in the end" essentially formed the basis for the concept of freedom of the press in the UK. Additionally, the concept of press freedom was also developed in the context of economic liberalization and the emergence of a free market in the country. With the emergence of free trade, the British regarded a free flow of information as indispensable in a truly free market (Supperstone, 1985) . Based on these beliefs, in the scheme of Siebert's four theories of the press, both countries are considered to be subscribing to the "libertarian theory." However, in the 20th century, American W.E. Hocking wrote in the Hutchins Commission on Freedom of the Press that the press must assume social responsibility and that it was very important for the press to follow an ethical code of conduct. In other words, the press has an obligation to society and should take it upon itself to make sure that they are making the country a better, more informed place. In the wake of the publication of the Commission on Freedom of the Press, the United States have become more of a social-responsibility-theory-following country. Arguably, to a lesser extent, the United Kingdom now also subscribes to the social responsibility theory.

On the other hand, France, whose concept of freedom of the press also originated from the Enlightenment, natural rights, and individualism, seems to have regarded the concept as more of a means towards a political end, namely democracy, and not so much for personal growth. Specifically, the French envision the press as both the instrument and expression of democracy. The press provided the means for all to participate in political debate and safeguarded political pluralism. While the belief in natural rights would suggest that at the beginning of the press freedom debate in France the country was leaning towards the libertarian theory, under Siebert's four theories of the press scheme France is also a subscriber of the social responsibility theory.

Sweden has the same attitude in regards to the primary purpose of a free press. Justification for strong protection of the press is that, historically, the purpose of a free press in Sweden has been regarded as primarily political. Accordingly, the Freedom of the Press Act in Sweden emphasizes that in deciding whether certain types of expression constitute abuses of press freedom, the important factor to take into consideration is that freedom of the press constitutes the basis of a free government. However, this is not to say that the Act only protects political speech. The Act broadly defines the purpose of press freedom as the securing of free interchange of opinions and enlightenment of the public, thus protecting expressions about religions, science, and culture (Strömberg, 1985) . In terms of Siebert's four theories of the press spectrum, Sweden is a consistent subscriber to the libertarian theory and firmly believes that the press should be free of government control. Perhaps that is why Sweden is consistently ranked at the top of Freedom House's Press Freedom Index.

Germany is also more politics-oriented with the free press concept. The Germans regarded freedom of the press as the basis of a free, democratic order. The Constitutional Court in Germany stated that since a free press helps the public make important political decisions by informing them about the current events, the press is a medium in the process of forming public opinion and something a democratic society absolutely needs (Kohl, 1985) . Germany is also consistently ranked quite high on Freedom House's Press Freedom index; however, like many other western countries that previously subscribed to the libertarian theory, scholars have argued that the country is now leaning toward social responsibility theory. The press is expected to follow a certain code of ethics and do their best to inform the public.

In Asia, the conceptual foundation for a free press was not as strong as in the western countries. Constitutional clauses protecting freedom of the press in the Asian countries discussed here were mostly added or included because of the Western influence, as most of them have been occupied by a western country at one point or another. Therefore, in a way, one can argue that the concept of freedom of the press also originated from the idea of "natural right" and individualism. However, closer examinations reveal that these Asian countries have vastly different ideas about what a free press should represent compared to their western counterparts. In particular, there are two reasons why there is a gap between how the Westerners and Asians interpret the free press clause. One is political, and the other is cultural. Politically, most of the Asian countries discussed here were developing their countries economically and politically when they first included freedom of the press/expression clauses in their constitutions, they strongly believed that the press in their countries should not play the "adversarial" and "watchdog" role as it does in the West and disrupt or undermine the governments' efforts by criticizing them. Instead, the press should help the government educate and rally the public and assist with nation-building. It should be noted that even though the Asian nations discussed here are now fairly developed, this belief is still prevalent in some countries, such as Singapore. Culturally, some of the Asian nations/regions discussed here were deeply influenced by Asian values and Confucius' teachings and still are. Confucianism teaches the importance of respecting the authority and keeping the peace and harmony in society, which does not match the concept of an "adversarial" press.

Japan and South Korea are prime examples of those who believe in these philosophies. These countries were both occupied by foreign forces and their freedom of the press protections were added in their respective constitutions because of American influence. However, their attitudes towards the concept of a free press are different from the Americans. For Japan, Confucianism heavily influenced the Japanese. The Japanese subscribe to the belief that people should seek to create social harmony by envisioning a strict hierarchical society based upon key family relationships that defined everyone's role. For that to succeed, a sense of respect for authority is needed because fundamental to this system of hierarchy is the idea that people should know their place. This Japanese reliance on order is in stark contrast to the American faith in freedom and equality, even though the Americans imported the idea of a free press in the first place. Instead of championing the need of having to question authority, Japan's faith in its society's hierarchy is unquestioned. The philosophy shaped the concept of freedom of the press for the Japanese. Such a cultural tradition contradicts the Western concept of media as a

watchdog and the ultimate goal of libertarian philosophies. In Japan, the media has a close relationship with the government and the big industries through the press club system, or "information cartels," which comprise press clubs, industry associations, and media conglomerates. (Yin, 2008). An analysis of the Japanese press system makes it clear that the ideas available at the "marketplace of ideas" are somewhat limited. Some have argued that free competition, which is the core of the libertarian theory is stifled under the infamous press club system. This system bars foreign and non-mainstream reporters from attending exclusive press briefings and getting official press releases. Nevertheless, Japan is still enjoying a rather free press and the country is consistently ranked as having the freest press in East Asia. With the emphasis on helping the country without much interference from the government (although some scholars have argued that the government did not need to intervene because the press club system already functions as a watchdog of the press), under Siebert's four press theory model, Japan is believed to be following the social responsibility theory.

South Korea is similar to Japan in this regard. Also influenced by Confucianism, South Korea prefers the concept of freedom of the press to be based on the media's cooperative relationship with the government, where the press supports the government, instead of the adversarial one espoused by the West. Additionally, given that the country does not have a historical tradition of democratic principles, the very idea of press freedom is more of an imposed foreign concept, and therefore not fully embraced by the locals. Press freedom in South Korea improved noticeably during the tenure of Kim Dae Jung, when the press became more aggressive in covering the government and more vocal in criticizing government policies. Press freedom is still fragile in South Korea and its press system is in a transitional stage; however, generally speaking, South Korea is considered to be subscribing to the social responsibility theory today.

Singapore also has a philosophy regarding freedom of the press that is more similar to South Korea and Japan rather than the West. In Singapore the authorities, believe that mass media should reinforce instead of undermine the cultural values and social attitudes of Singapore. More significantly, integrity of the country is key and of utmost importance; therefore, press freedom must not interfere with the over-riding needs of preserving the integrity of Singapore. Some journalists even flat-out rejected the western notion that all newspapers should be watchdogs for the government. They believed that media should focus on helping a society get organized in a time of great change instead of subscribing to the notion of press freedom and letting the press undercut the government's effort to build a nation.

There is also a more political explanation as to why freedom of the press in Singapore has always been weak. During the foreign rule period in Singapore, the current ruling party PAP felt that the newspapers at the time did not support the independence movement. Instead, the papers tirelessly attacked the party, which severely soured PAP on the notion of press freedom. Its turbulent past with the British and Malaysian's also explains the reasons behind some of the harsher punishments imposed on the press.

Nowadays, the Singaporean government still keeps a watchful eye on the press for any stories that deal with race relations, religion, or problems in neighboring countries. Stories like those are banned in the Singaporean press because of the mixed racial and religious makeup of its population and its often sensitive relationships with its neighbors. Violence and chaos caused by racial and religious differences in neighboring countries make the Singaporean government very nervous that reports on those stories will have a negative impact on their country and cause social unrest. Former Prime Minister Lee Kuan Yew even said that any journalist who did not support Singapore-Malaysia relations would be sent to jail.

Overall, Singapore has one of the lowest Press Freedom rankings for a democratic country. For the most part, the government still dictates which stories are "appropriate" for public consumption, and the journalists are reluctant to criticize the government and its officials. Given all of this, it is not difficult to see that Singapore still subscribes to the authoritarian theory.

India also has constitutional protection for freedom of the press-not explicit protection, but implied. Nevertheless, India has had very weak protection for freedom of the press since the British left the country. Although the press system has developed significantly since its early days, it has failed to come up with a cohesive and defining philosophy and principles that are vital to maintaining its own goals and traditions. In the absence of this, the Indian press system was left vulnerable to governmental intrusion and unable to maintain its freedom and responsibility. The lack of an overarching national mass communication philosophy and policies, has created very little public support for a strong mass media system in India. With that said, things seemed to have changed a bit in recent years. Some have noticed that the Indian "brand" of journalism "focuses on the needs of the poor, the deprived, and the marginalized and emphasizes their effective participation in developmental planning." It encourages the participation of the people and advocates for their interests instead of the views of the policy makers and the planners. Journalists in the country believe that the media should discuss issues that are important for a civil society because only the mass media can reach the vast rural population and give them a voice in issues that are affecting their lives. The mass media can also play a crucial role in social progress, as any transitional society will encounter "new attitudes, a new mindset, and a new value system." (Yin, 2008.) As such, India would seem to be a follower of the social responsibility theory when it comes to its press.

In China, freedom of the press is guaranteed under the constitution, but the country also has a press freedom philosophy that is politically influenced and different from the West's. In particular, the protection of the state is the most important goal for the Chinese government and the press is viewed as a tool to achieve this goal. This is still the prevailing philosophy towards the press. Another reason for tightly controlling the press had to do with the belief among the elite and government leaders that the ordinary citizens were generally unworthy to have a forum for expression. In the past, the masses were never perceived as being capable of direct participation in the country's rule; instead, they had to be guided. This philosophy is different today.

Today China has around 2,000 newspapers, more than 9,000 magazines, 1,000 radio stations, and 200 TV stations broadcasting 2,900 channels. The choices and competition on the media market today stand in sharp contrast to the one voice on the media scene in the past when every city had only one Party paper (Yin, 2008.) Choices, instead of one voice, symbolize the major changes Chinese media consumers have experienced. The majority of the news media in China today are still owned by the state. However, foreign investment has entered the Chinese media sector, with interest in China among international media groups surging in 2005 when the Chinese government issued regulations allowing foreign investment in joint-venture television, radio, and film production companies. News Corporations, Viacom and Sony Pictures were among the big names involved in joint ventures with Chinese media companies (Feuilherade, 2005).

China still follows the Soviet-Communist theory, but in recent years, there are signs that the Chinese government is attempting to give the press more freedom to do their jobs. For example, stories about government corruptions are now occasionally allowed, and in early 2013, the government permitted the news media to report on the worsening pollution problem the country is experiencing. Moreover, there was a case in Shanghai where a reporter, based on a city law mandating the disclosure of public information, sued the city planning department for repeatedly declining interviews (Zhou, 2006). This was the first case in China where a reporter sued a government department for violating press freedom. The reporter complained that city government departments often denied his interview requests, thus clearly in violation of the city ordinance, which required city departments to disclose information concerning the economy, city management, and public services (Yin 2008.)

A lot of these new changes had to do with the Internet. With the advent of the Internet, it is now even more challenging for the Chinese government to control the media, as some information that the Chinese government would like to suppress can easily get out to the public. With its power of reaching millions of people at the same time, the Internet has directly effected legislative changes in the country by exposing corruptions and other government wrongdoings. This brought about public outrage on an unprecedented scale and caught the attention of legislators and the government.

As previously stated, some of the countries discussed in this book have formal constitutions, while others do not. The United Kingdom is the only country examined here that does not have a formal written constitution but considers the principle of freedom of speech and of the press as part of the country's tradition. This type of informal protection for the press means that the British courts lack the power to truly invalidate statutes that violate the principle of free expression/press. However, when the courts consider a statute to violate this important right, they can render the law less harmful by interpreting it in such a way that could make it possible (Supperstone, 1985) . On the other hand, despite the lack of constitutional protection, there is a high degree of press freedom afforded to journalists in the country, according to freedom of the press surveys. Therefore, it is safe to say that just because there is official constitutional protection for freedom of the press in a country does not mean that the journalists in that country enjoy more freedom to do their jobs than journalists in a country that does not offer constitutional protection for freedom of the press.

Conversely, there are countries with formal constitutions, such as the United States, Sweden, and Japan that specifically grant freedom of the press. This does not mean the languages they use regarding press freedom or the philosophies they subscribe to are the same. Overall, it seems that the countries who adapted a constitution with specific protection for freedom of the press early on, usually used broader and more general albeit shorter languages in their press freedom provisions like the United States. In comparison, countries that have freedom of the press provisions written into their constitution in the twentieth century generally used more elaborate and specific language. Some scholars have argued that this difference reflects stages of sociopolitical development. The constitutions written in the 20th century, such as Japan and South Korea's, reflect the post-industrial, bureaucratic, and highly elaborate form of government, while the constitutions written in earlier times, such as the United States', showed a more simple structure (Lahav, 1985). This generalization does not mean that there are no significant differences among the constitutions within each group.

The number one difference among countries that have an explicit constitutional protection for freedom of the press is whether the language in this clause is an absolute protection, or are there other languages and provisions in the statues that could limit this freedom? In the United States Constitution, the First Amendment provision used absolute and negative language, specifically stating that Congress "shall make no law" to abridge freedom of the press. The freedom of the press clause in the French constitution, on the other hand, uses positive language, "everyone can publish," but then the right was qualified because the law also states that a person can also be held liable for his/her words. Some scholars have argued this difference exists as a result of the two countries' dissimilar legal systems. After going through the Revolution, the French embraced the idea of majority rule and developed faith in the actions of the legislature, which represents the people. On the other hand, they had a mistrust of judges and judicial discretion, which during earlier times, were known for their unpredictable rules and capricious oppression (Lahav, 1985). They felt much more confident about handing the job of keeping an eye on as important of a right as free expression/press to the legislatures, who they believed could do a better job telling right from wrong for society. In other words, they consider any laws and restrictions adopted by the legislatures, to be better equipped to handle any legal questions that stemmed from freedom of the press issues.

In contrast to the French, the American legal system, which was rooted in common law, does not share the French's mistrust of judicial power. More importantly, the American political philosophy places great emphasis on a system of checks and balances in which each power---executive, legislative, and judicial---could neutralize the other. Hence, they feel confident about the absolute language of the First Amendment (Lahav, 1985).

Examining all the constitutional clauses regarding freedom of the press from the countries discussed in this book, it can be found that most countries chose to adapt the French model (positive/qualified) instead of the American model (negative/absolute.) In fact, the United States is the only country to use absolute language. This means that most countries do not want freedom of the press to be completely unrestricted and prefer to have it controlled by law. For example, Article 21 of the South Korean Constitution stated that neither "speech nor press shall violate the honor or rights of other persons or undermine public morals or social ethics."[175] As mentioned before, constitutions enacted in the 20th century such as Germany's and India's, took a more modern approach to the protection of freedom of the press by specifying categories in which restriction is permissible. They usually contain an endorsement of the press freedom, followed by a list of legal limitations. Article 5 of Germany's Basic Law is a very good example. In contrast, constitutions enacted earlier, such as the French and Swedish, simply contain the language that stated the right of press freedom is subject to law.

This not only shows that the United States has great confidence in the balance of its three branches, but it also demonstrates that the United States views freedom of the press as a person's sacred right that cannot be easily restricted. In this respect, the First Amendment to the Constitution of the United States does seem to provide the press more freedom, with its emphatic "Congress shall not no law" language, than other constitutional protections of press freedom in other countries.

---

[175]See Constitution the Republic of Korea, Art. 21.

COMPARISONS OF FREEDOM OF INFORMATION LAWS AND THE RIGHTS TO PROTECT CONFIDENTIAL SOURCES

A very important aspect of a journalist's job is to have access to official documents in order to disseminate important information to the public. Without this access, journalists would not be able to present the full picture of a story, thus hampering their abilities to do their job properly. In the last couple of decades, countries all around the world have become more willing to recognize the importance of being open and in response, have set up appropriate laws to grant access to the public.

Most of the countries/regions examined in this book have enacted laws granting the public access to official documents, with Singapore being a major exception. Not surprisingly, two of the most vocal supporters of freedom of the press and freedom in general were the first countries to adopt such a law. Sweden, who has always been a pioneer on the topic of freedom of the press and an open society, was the first country to adopt a freedom of information law to grant the public access to official documents in 1949. With the enactment of the Freedom of Information Act" in 1966, the United States was the next country to officially recognize such a right.

A more surprising finding is the fact that the United Kingdom and Germany, two countries that have high rankings on the Freedom House Press Freedom index, did not have comprehensive freedom of information laws officially in place until after 2000. Japan and South Korea have such laws a few years before the United Kingdom and Germany did. Perhaps this could be explained in terms of the political situations these nations were facing in the years prior. The United Kingdom had an extremely tense and volatile relationship with Northern Ireland, while the two parts of Germany did not reunite until 1989. Due to the political turmoil in these countries, the British and (West) German governments were more reluctant to give the public too much access to official documents out of fear that their enemies would get their hands on state secrets.

An interesting finding regarding freedom of information laws was that China also enacted a type of such law. In 2007, "Regulations of the People's Republic of China on Open Government Information" came into force, which grants the public some access to official documents. Some have speculated that the main motivations for creating this law are largely to improve domestically, with goals of having a broader sharing of government information in the service of economic development, making people's lives better, enhancing trust between the public and the government, curbing government corruption and promoting better governance at all levels.[176]

All of the freedom of information laws examined here have exemptions, which refer to documents that the governments are allowed to withhold from the public. These exemptions are all very similar across the board, with the most important exemptions being documents that could qualify as possibly inhibiting "national security." This is in line with the attitude the volatile political climate in the last few years has brought, which is preserving national security trumps the people's right to know and the press' right to impart information to the public. In fact, national security has been invoked frequently as a reason to curb freedom of the press. Countries such as the United Kingdom and India still have an "Official Secrets Act" that punishes anyone who might have exposed sensitive information that could potentially embarrass the government or endanger the country.

In terms of "reporter's privilege" or "shield laws," which gives journalists the right not to testify in front of a jury to reveal their confidential sources the United States does not currently have a federal law for the protection of confidential sources. One attempt to create such a right was shut down by the Supreme Court in *Branzburg v. Hayes*. This means that if a journalist in the United States is ordered to testify in front of a grand jury, he/or she will not be able to opt out, they must testify. If he/she refuses to comply, then just like former *New York Times* reporter, Judith Miller, jail time might await. This is especially true if the reporter has vital but confidential information about a criminal case. In such a case, the courts usually compel the reporters to testify. This is because "the right to a fair trial" is also an important right in the Constitution of the United States, and that the "right to a free press" should not trump that right. This "everyone should have his/her day in court" notion is very sacred to the Americans and the journalists' desire to keep their confidential sources secret is not enough to defeat that notion. It should be pointed out that the courts weigh several factors, such as whether there are alternative means that are less intrusive, before deciding whether to compel a

---

[176] See Regulations of the People's Republic of China on Open Government Information.

testimony from the journalists. The majority of the states in the United States have some type of shield law in place to protect journalists from having to reveal their sources. In addition, several proposals for a federal shield law has been circulating in Congress for many years now, but it does not seem very likely that this law will be passed anytime soon.

The protection of journalistic sources is very important for press freedom in Europe. It is defined by Article 10 of the European Convention on Human Rights and shaped by the constant caselaw of the European Court of Human Rights (ECHR). This is why all of the European nations examined in this book have some type of nation-wide legal protection for journalists who do not wish to reveal their confidential sources in courts. Among them, Germany actually has constitutional protection for the right not to reveal confidential sources, while the Swedish law for reporter's privilege states that the journalists who reveal their confidential sources could be penalized. Naturally, there are exceptions to the protection, as when the courts decide it is in the best interest of the country and society for the journalists to reveal their sources.

In Asia, reporter's privilege is not widely recognized. In fact, out of all the Asian countries and regions examined in this book, only Japan has legal protection for journalists not to reveal their confidential sources. For others, this does not seem to be a topic of discussion that came up very often. Given that the concept of freedom of the press entered Asia late and that Asians generally view the press as a tool to help society as a whole instead of being a watchdog for authorities, the fact that these countries do not want to give the press special rights is somewhat expected.

COMPARISONS OF LIBEL LAW

One area of media law that has been used to restrain freedom of the press is defamation law, which includes slander and libel. Since this book mainly focuses on the press, the topic of libel, which deals with punishing someone for his/her written words, is more suitable.

As stated, libel can be used to restrict press freedom. If government officials or celebrities do not like the criticisms lodged against them by the press and they feel as though their reputations have been sullied by the media, they have the option of pursuing a libel lawsuit. In certain countries, such as Singapore, the legal system favors the plaintiffs in a libel suit so strongly and the punishment is so severe, that it can be argued that the libel law functions as de facto censorship.

The United States libel law puts the burden of proof on the plaintiffs. For a private citizen plaintiff, he/she only has to prove the defendant's negligence, meaning the journalist was not careful enough when he/she wrote the story. However, the burden of proof becomes considerably heavier when the plaintiffs are public officials and public figures. In that case, the plaintiffs would have to prove "actual malice," which means the journalists know the stories or facts mentioned in the reports about the plaintiffs are untrue but decide to publish them anyway. This is a very high burden of proof that was decided by the Supreme Court and why it is extremely difficult for a public figure plaintiff to succeed in a libel suit in the United States. (How do you prove that the journalists know the information is false in the first place?) The rationale for this rule goes back to the concept of the press being an "adversary" to the authorities. If the press is to perform its duty as a watchdog for the government properly and effectively, there should not be a constant threat of being sued for publishing stories that are not to the government's liking. If the journalists have to constantly defend themselves against such suits, then the health of freedom of the press will naturally diminish. Therefore, unless the journalists' actions are seriously egregious, the plaintiffs would have the heavy burden of proof. This demonstrates how Americans value the sanctity of freedom of the press.

Most of the other countries discussed here do not share the same view. That is to say, none of the other countries examined in this book have the same standards and tests for libel litigations, nor the same heavy burden of proof placed on the plaintiffs. In fact, most of the countries discussed here, whether Asian or European, with the possible exception of Sweden and Germany, all strongly favor the plaintiffs in libel suits. For example, in France, Singapore, and South Korea, who place a heavy emphasis on personal reputations, the burden is squarely on the plaintiff. In the Asian countries, under the influence of Confucianism, a person's personal dignity is so crucial to his/her standing in society that it is placed above the importance of freedom of the press; while in the European countries, a public official is considered to be someone who deserves to be respected because he/she is working for the better good of the country.

One very recent example that can illustrate the libel law system which places the burden of proof in a libel case on the defendant is the Lance Armstrong v. The Times of London case. As previously discussed, Armstrong sued the newspaper in 2004 after it published a story claiming that the cyclist had been using performance enhancing drugs to help him win 7 Tour de France titles. After two years of protracted legal battles, the newspaper ended up paying Armstrong a lot of money because it could not unequivocally prove that Armstrong did take drugs. Seven years later, Armstrong had been proven to indeed cheat his way to all of those titles and actually publicly admitted to doing so. Subsequently, the Times of London now wants to explore the possibility of suing Armstrong to recoup the money they paid him; however, a legal expert in the UK agreed that it would be a long shot, since the paper did not actually present evidence of the cheating at the time the article was published. Given the drastically different libel law system in the United States, it would be virtually impossible for Armstrong to get the same legal victory if he were to sue a newspaper for publishing a similar story in the US. In the US, Armstrong would have to prove that the paper knew that the story was not true but intentionally published it anyway.

Another aspect of libel law that is different from country to country is whether "right of reply" is an option for the plaintiffs. "Right of reply" here refers to the right of plaintiffs in a libel suit to demand the media outlets who publish the original defamatory stories to publish their responses to those stories. The United States does not offer " right of reply" to the libel plaintiffs because the Supreme Court rejected this right. For the Americans, this right is a major invasion of the press' editorial autonomy. This once again demonstrates the American's high regard for press freedom. Conversely, almost all of the other countries examined here grant plaintiffs this right. Given that most of them favor plaintiffs in the libel suits, this is not surprising.

COMPARISONS OF COPYRIGHT LAWS

Copyright law is a major part of media law. These laws are constantly being updated and amended to catch up with the time and the advancement of information technology. After examining all of the copyright statutes in all three continents-America, Europe, and Asia, it should be said that they are all similar to some extent but dissimilar in other important aspects. The differences can once again be explained in terms of the cultural differences among the nations.

As established, the biggest difference between the copyright law in the United States and most of the other countries examined here is that it does not provide moral rights for the copyright holders. There are two likely reasons for having moral rights in the copyright statutes: The first is that the Berne Convention, which was heavily influenced by the French copyright laws, requires their members to contain moral rights clauses in their copyright law. The second reason is that in Asian countries that were rooted in the tradition of Confucianism, which highly values an individual's personal integrity, reputation, and placement in the world, having his/her honor harmed, even in the form of a misuse of a creative work, would warrant a serious punishment.

Another aspect of the copyright law in the United States that is different from other countries' copyright law is the exceptions provisions. Every single piece of copyright legislation discussed here contains limitations to copyright, but there is typically an exhaustive list of uses that the laws permit, usually including personal, private, educational, and non-profit uses of the copyrighted works. The American copyright law, on the other hand, has a broadly interpreted "fair use" clause, which makes it more difficult to predict whether a court would interpret a certain use permissible.

COMPARISONS OF CYBER-PIRACY LAWS

Cyber-piracy is a big issue the world's intellectual property rights holders and nations all around the world are facing today. Naturally, every country has its own way of dealing with the issue. Some countries, such as China and Sweden, were pressured for economic reasons by outside forces to crack down on their popular search engines/file-sharing websites. Others have taken the more drastic step of implementing the "three-strikes rule, " which cuts off a violator's Internet connections. Overall, only four countries/regions have adopted the anti-piracy measure of a "three-strike" rule so far, including South Korea, France, the United Kingdom, and Taiwan. This tough law, which could take away people's access to the Internet if they are found to be illegally file-sharing/downloading, met with a mixture of criticisms and praises from the intellectual property advocates.

The United States failed to pass a more comprehensive anti-piracy law, SOPA, in 2012 and right now does not have a three-strikes law to combat this problem, relying instead on the existent copyright law. Given how drastic the "three-strike" law is and how it takes away people's personal freedom, it would be reasonable to assume that the country will not adopt this law anytime soon.

FINDINGS AND IMPLICATIONS

In the following paragraph, the authors try to provide an answer to Question 1: What are the concepts of freedom of the press in these 11 countries? How is press freedom protected under the constitutions in those countries? In short, what is the relationship between the constitutions and the press freedom in those countries?

To summarize and answer Research Question 1, with the exception of the United Kingdom, all of the countries discussed here provide freedom of the press, or at least freedom of expression, in their constitutions. Some use absolute language for the press freedom clause, while most the countries examined provide a qualified constitutional protections for freedom of the press, meaning other sections of their constitution include limitations to this protection. Additionally, the concepts of freedom of the press varies from country to country and continent to continent and the analysis of all the opinions regarding the role and function of the press in a society among the countries/regions examined in this book suggests that despite having similar languages in their constitutions to protect press freedom, Asia and the West have vastly different views on this concept. For the western countries, a free press is a necessary tool to have various ideas compete and the best ones to emerge, which would benefit the development of a true democracy, and for the Americans, personal growth as well. Additionally, they view the press as an adversary to the government and a watchdog for the authorities so that those in power could be kept in check. On the other hand, most Asian countries, view the press as a tool to help their countries develop instead of acting as a watchdog for the government. Due to a deeply rooted cultural influence, these Asian countries also have a high respect for authority, thus further lessening the press' desire to question and criticize the government. In terms of the relationship between the constitutions and freedom of the press in these countries, it is clear that the Western countries take the press freedom clauses in their constitutions far more seriously and often use them as a strong foundation for how they handle press freedom issues. On the other hand, the Asian countries, who also have these clauses in their constitutions, seem to treat these clauses more as a symbol than a sacred right, resulting in a highly restricted press.

For Question 2, "what is the history of press freedom development in these countries?" The answer was provided in Chapter 3.

To answer the first part of Question 3.1, which is whether the First Amendment to the Constitution of the United States actually offers more protection for freedom of the press, our analysis shows "yes on paper." The press freedom clause in the First Amendment uses absolute and emphatic language to protect this freedom, which none of the other constitutions discussed here use. The others usually have other clauses in their statute to restrict this freedom. Of course, this does not mean the United States enjoys the most press freedom in practice. As previously pointed out, a country's constitution is not the only law that can control and restrict freedom of the press. For example, the lack of federal law protection for confidential sources prevents the United States from achieving the utmost press freedom. Sweden, for example, consistently ranked as No. 1 or near No. 1 at the Freedom House Freedom of the Press index.

To answer the second part of Question 3.1, "Do the countries that have explicit constitutional protections for freedom of the press in reality really have a freer media environment than those that don't?" the research shows an emphatic no. The United Kingdom does not have a written constitution but does enjoy a great amount of press freedom, while China, who does have explicit protection for press freedom in its constitution, has one of the lowest press freedom rankings in the world. This is because in a complex society, everything from political system, economic system, to religion or educational structure, interacts with the media, which would ultimately determine how a country's freedom of the press shapes up. Judging from the short press freedom histories of the countries discussed, it is increasingly clear that economic considerations have become a huge factor in the development of press freedom. The press, as an increasingly money-losing industry, has to watch out for the bottom-liners and make a profit for their financial backers. This dependency on the financial support from those higher up often result in self-censorship in order not to offend those supporters, thus limiting the journalists' freedom to report on whatever they want. In fact, in a democratic society, the main restraint on press freedom often comes from economic pressure, especially with declining revenues coming in for the press. Heavy media concentrations all over the world, including France and Italy, also pose a threat to press freedom because of the lack of diversity in the news content this heavy concentration could lead to.

To conclude, the answer to the last part of Question 3.1, "Do American journalists enjoy more freedom in terms of having access to official documents and protecting their confidential sources, " should be "no," on both counts, but for different reasons. For access to official documents, American journalists have the right to view these documents under the Freedom of Information Act". With Singapore" as a major exception, most of the countries examined here have their versions of freedom of information laws; therefore, after comparing all these similar laws, one can conclude that while Americans were legally given access to official documents earlier than most countries, they were not given more freedom than any other country in this area. As for shield laws, or protection of confidential sources, the Americans, who have some state shield law protections but no federal protections, do not compare with the European countries discussed here, as all of them have nation-wide legal protections for confidential sources. However, American journalists do have more protection in this area than almost all of the Asian countries, which recognized freedom of the press later than the West and are generally more leery about giving journalists special treatment.

To conclude and answer Question 3.2, "Does the United States libel law give the defendants in a libel suit an advantage over the plaintiffs compared with libel laws in other countries? Generally, in a libel case, who has the burden of proof and why is that the case?" The findings show that in the United States, the defendants, especially in cases where the plaintiffs are public figures, do have an advantage over the plaintiffs because of the belief that the press should be free to criticize those in power without having to worry about facing lawsuits. In other countries discussed in this book, however, the burden of proof in libel cases are usually placed on the plaintiffs. That is because these countries place a higher premium on individual's reputation and human dignity. Based on this assessment, one can certainly argue that for the press, the United States libel law is the better law, as it is extremely difficult for a public figure to successfully sue a news organization for libel in the United States. The burden of proof for the public figure to overcome is simply too high. The situation is completely reversed in the United Kingdom, where the public figures have a much better chance of winning a libel case. Due to this fact, a lot of foreign public figures went to London to bring libel suits on whomever published unflattering articles about them, even if both the plaintiff and the defendant had very little connection to the UK. This bizarre popularity has earned London the nickname, "libel tourism capital of the world."

Based on the findings, the answer to Question 3.3 "Does the United States give the authors/creators stronger or weaker copyright protection compared with other nations?" seems to be "weaker" when compared with the copyright laws of the European countries. In fact, the authors would argue that the European nations provide the most protection for copyright holders. The Asian nations, who in the past were reluctant to grant copyright to authors because of their cultural traditions, dictated that copying work is encouraged since it shows a passion for learning. The Americans have no moral rights protection for the copyright holders except for some limited areas of visual arts. The European nations grant the longest term for copyright protection, which is life of the author plus 70 years, and they also provide moral rights for the copyright holders. The moral rights provisions, if nothing else, give the authors/creators one more avenue to protect their honor and creative works. Therefore, the European nations provide the most amount of protection for copyright holders. For copyright holders, this means the Europeans have the best copyright law system.

The answer to Question 3.4 "Do recent cases in Europe and Asia indicate that the United States is lagging behind in providing copyright protection in cyberspace" is yes. Unlike other nations that have adopted a stringent "three-strikes" law to fight cyber-piracy, the United States has not done so, and it does not seem as if it will in the foreseeable future. The same fate seems to befall the proposed anti-cyber-piracy bills SOPA and PIPA. The intrusion on civil liberty the "three-strikes" law, SOPA and PIPA demand might simply prove too much for the Americans to accept. For the countries that adopted the "three-strike" law, including South Korea, France, the UK, and Taiwan, it is still too early to tell whether the law will actually be effective in curtailing cyber-piracy.

Chapter 11 Conclusion:

Tasks and Challenges for Further Research

The goal of this book is to compare the laws regarding freedom of the press, libel, intellectual property, and cyber-piracy across three continents-Americas, Europe, and Asia, and attempt to find out whether the three continents approach these areas of law in a similar way. If they have different approaches, it is the authors' aim to figure out whether these differences could be explained through political, cultural, or economic factors.

Before examining the laws, this book attempts to discover how these countries view the role the press plays. Specifically, what is the concept of freedom of the press in these countries? What does that mean to them? In answering this question, our findings show that there is a great divide between the East and West in terms of how the press is perceived. In the West, where the original concept of a free press came from, the models of press freedom were based on the natural law tradition within liberalism. From that natural law tradition, Western culture developed a belief in the importance of individual self-expression and the importance of criticizing authority to keep them in check. Furthermore, modern democracy is based on the idea that all men are created equal, hence capable of participating in the political decision making process. These cultural influences and political motivations shaped how the United States and the rest of the West structured their constitutions to protect freedom of the press and how they developed media-related laws later.

In the East, for both strong cultural, political, and economic reasons, the concept of freedom of the press took on a completely different meaning. Culturally, a lot of these Asian countries were heavily influenced by the teachings of Confucianism, which espoused the ideas of keeping a sense of peacefulness among the society and the deep respect for authority. Politically, a lot of these countries went through long periods of colonial rule and tried to establish themselves as legitimate authorities. Economically, in relation to the political factor, these countries were also trying to build their nations and transform into strong economic powers. All of these factors combined led to a completely different concept of press freedom than the West. For the Asians, it is believed that the press should be respectful of authority because of the Confucianism teachings, but they should also assist and support the governments to build their nations politically and economically instead of playing the role of a "watchdog" and undermining the authorities by criticizing them.

All of these factors contributed to how they interpreted the freedom of the press/expression/speech clauses in their constitutions. The first area of law we looked at is the constitutions of every country examined in this book. Namely, the goal was to find out whether the constitutions of these countries guarantee the protection of freedom of the press. Our findings show that nearly every country discussed here, with the exception of the United Kingdom who does not have a formal constitution, contains at least a "freedom of speech" clause in their constitutions, which in Asia was the product of a heavy Western influence, since the concept of press freedom entered the region late. However, just because all of the clauses look similar does not mean that they were/are interpreted in a similar fashion. These cultural and political factors played an essential role in how these clauses were applied in reality.

Cultural influences also deeply affected the libel law systems in the countries examined. In the United States, libel law is heavily tilted towards the defendant media's favor, meaning the plaintiffs bear a very heavy burden of proof in a libel suit, especially when they are public officials and public figures, and the "offending" reports are of public interest. This law speaks volumes about how committed the Americans are to press freedom. In other Western countries, the burden of proof in a libel suit is usually placed on the shoulder of the media defendants. The authors argued that this is because a lot of them put emphasis on the "honor" and "integrity" of the individual, especially when that individual is a public official who is serving the country. This sentiment is even more pronounced in Asia, where cultural influences dictate that an individual's dignity and his/her place in society is paramount. Therefore, the plaintiffs in a libel suit would have a huge advantage.

The development of another area of media law that was also affected culturally is the copyright law. As established, the biggest difference between the copyright law in the United States and most of the other countries examined here is that it does not provide moral rights for the copyright holders. There are probably two reasons for having moral rights in the copyright statutes: The first is that Berne Convention, which was heavily influenced by French copyright laws, requires their members to contain moral rights clauses in their copyright law. The second reason is that in Asian countries that are rooted in the tradition of Confucianism, which highly values an individual's personal integrity, reputation, and placement in the world, having his/her honor harmed, even in the form of a misuse of a creative work, should warrant a serious punishment. This great emphasis on personal dignity also manifests in the rule of "right of reply," which allows the "defamed" to respond and defend themselves.

Overall, after examining all the relevant media laws, the authors found that there is ample evidence that cultural, political, and economic factors helped prominently shape the media laws across all three continents. The authors would argue that in the past, cultural and political factors were especially instrumental in the media law development.

However, evidence gathered by the authors has led them to predict that political and economic factors would play much bigger roles in how media laws will advance in the future.

Economically, the increasing frequency of media ownership concentration is an issue in many countries now, such as Italy and France. This heavy concentration means that there will be less and less diversity and more self-censorship in the media, thus seriously jeopardizing freedom of the press conditions. Nations all around the world would have to look at this undesirable situation and enact laws that could put a stop to this. Another economic factor is the effect of globalization. With the increase in globalization and interactions among countries, the economic pressures they put on one another often result in the creation of new laws, such as China's development of a copyright law. Sweden's handling of the Pirate Bay case was also heavily influenced by outside economic pressure.

Politically speaking, its influence also stays very strong. Specifically, questions such as "What are the government's political objectives towards the media?" and "Which political goals are more prominent at the moment?" are still relevant. For example, the concern over terrorism worldwide has led to the increase in restrictions on press freedom in the name of "national security" in the last decade or so. In order to effectively combat the continuing existence of terrorism worldwide, governments have argued restricting the publication of certain information even if doing so would limit press freedom.

In general, it seems that there are several areas that separate the western and Asian philosophy towards the press:

1. Individual Freedom v. Social Responsibility: In the East, the emphasis is on being responsible and loyal rather than on being free. Western libertarian philosophers' focus of attention falls on the welfare of the individual, so it is only logical that these philosophers advocate that these individuals be equal and free to pursue what they want. Confucian thought lays emphasis on the group; hence, there is a concern of being responsible and loyal to the group; however, the west has been advocating for the press to be more mindful of their social responsibilities as of late.
2. To be free v. to know right from wrong: Western libertarians advocate for a free marketplace of ideas, where the public should be left free to explore and discover the truth on their own. Truth would emerge victorious over falsehood if there are several ideas competing for acceptance. On the other hand, in Asian societies truth is deemed to be self-evident. Under such philosophy, the focus is on teaching people what is right and what is wrong instead of the freedom to explore what is right and wrong. The real challenge is the task of convincing the people, or in an ideal Confucian way, for people to convince themselves, to always make right choices.
3. Civil Liberties v. Social Order and Stability: The concept of human rights was developed during the Enlightenment. The Bill of Rights as amendments to the U.S. Constitution marked a milestone in mankind's fight for civil liberties. Western

democratic societies firmly believe that it is critical to keep a watchful eye on the government to prevent it from encroaching upon those rights. In contrast, a salient feature of Confucian thinking in government is the primacy of political order (Tu, 1997). Accordingly, in Confucian societies, governments expect respect and obedience to keep social order. Social stability often takes precedence over civil liberties and is regarded as vital to the strength of a country and the welfare of its people.

4. Adversarial Watchdog v. Tool for National-Building: News media in the West takes pride in being a watchdog for the government. On the other hand, in Confucian societies, the government is supposed to take care of the people, and the people are expected to respect the government. The media's role in these societies is to help the nation-building process, not to criticize everything the government does.

TASKS AND CHALLENGES FOR FURTHER RESEARCH

This book is a comparative law research. Some difficulties came with gaining access to comparable data. Additionally, researchers in this area of study may make mistakes and encounter problems, such as the cultural differences between legal systems, difficulties in achieving comparability in the comparison, the desire to see a common legal pattern in legal systems, and the tendency to impose one's own legal conceptions and expectations on the systems being compared.

Other potential challenges facing scholars of comparative media law study include inadequate availability of statutory and secondary materials, the quick expiration of information due to the rapid and constant change in communication, and the possibility that information, even if available and correct, may not be easily summarized, compressed, or reduced to elements that are comparable.

One of the biggest challenges for this research is the translations and interpretations of the law documents in various languages. Considering the number of languages involved in a comparative law study and the unlikelihood that the scholars participating in the studies understand each language, it is only natural that scholars in this area of research rely on secondary literature written by foreign law specialists to complete the studies. This is what happened with this project.

In addition to the above mentioned tasks and challenges for further comparative research on media laws, there are also new tasks and challenges for further research on media laws in general. As indicated in the beginning of this book, these challenges include, for example, many of the current media laws are seriously outdated (*Media Laws Threaten Freedom*, 2013; Bodey, 2015), and many newly emerged "new media" or "digital media" lack the necessary relative laws or regulations, thus putting them in a "lawless" or "unregulated" chaotic situation (Packard, 2012 & 2013; Creech, 2013; Stewart, 2013; Lipschultz, 2014; Pearson & Polden, 2015). Furthermore, media laws are always associated to media ethics and policy-making, which are the two very importantly related subjects and areas that also deserve equally adequate and timely studies (Lewis & Crick, 2014; Moore & Murray, 2011; Villaraos, 2014).

Nevertheless, despite all these challenges, the authors strongly feel that, with the prominent role the media plays in affecting our everyday life, this is an area that needs to be constantly studied and updated. In the future study of the subjects discussed in this book, perhaps other scholars could consult specialists from every country examined. This would be helpful when discussing cultures and traditions radically different from the authors' own. More participants would also make it easier to gather information and compare their perspectives, thus presenting a fuller picture.

Tables

Table 1. Comparisons of Constitutional Protection for Freedom of the Press

Asia		
Country/region	Explicit constitutional protection for freedom of the press?	Is the right absolute or does the Constitution provide that the governments can make laws to restrict it?
Japan	Yes	Can be restricted
South Korea	Yes	Can be restricted
Singapore	No (Recognized by Courts)	Can be restricted
India	No. (But was implied)	Can be restricted
China	Yes	Can be restricted
Taiwan	No (Speech and publication)	Can be restricted
Hong Kong	Yes	Can be restricted
Europe		
Sweden	Yes	Can be restricted
Germany	Yes	Can be restricted
Italy	Yes	Can be restricted
France	Yes	Can be restricted
United Kingdom	No (no formal written constitution)	N/A
Americas		
United States	Yes	Absolute on its face

Table 2. Comparisons of Freedom of Information Laws and Reporter's Privilege

Asia			
Country	The name of the freedom of information law	The year the law wa passed	Is there a federal shield law?
Japan	Law Concerning Access to Information Held by Administrative Organs	1999	Yes, but very limited
South Korea	Act on Disclosure of Information by Public Agencies	1996	No
Singapore	No such law exists	N/A	No
India	Right to Information Act	2005	No
China	Regulations of the People' on Open Government Information	2007	No
Taiwan	Freedom of Government Information Law	2005	No
Hong Kong	Code on Access to Information	1998	No
Europe			
Sweden	Freedom of the Press	1949	Yes
Germany	Act to Regulate Access to Federal Government Information	2005	Yes
Italy	No. 241 of 7 August 1990	1990	Yes
France	Law on Access to Administrative Documents	1978	Yes
United Kingdom	Freedom of Information Act	2000	Yes, but can be easily taken away
Americas			
United States	Freedom of Information Act	1966	No

Table 3. Copyright Comparison

Asia		
Country/Region	Copyright terms based on authors' deaths	Does the copyright law provide moral rights?
Japan	Life + 50 years	Yes
South Korea	Life + 50 years	Yes
Singapore	Life + 70 years	No
India	Life + 60 years	No
China	Life + 50 years	Yes
Taiwan	Life + 50 years	Yes
Hong Kong	Life + 50 years	Yes
Europe		
Sweden	Life + 70 years	Yes
Germany	Life + 70 years	Yes
Italy	Life + 70 years	Yes
France	Life + 70 years	Yes
United Kingdom	Life + 70 years	Yes
Americas		
United States	Life + 70 years	Yes

Table 4. Freedom of Information Law Comparison Chart

Asia		
Country/region	Is there a Freedom of Information Law?	What is the law that provides this right to the press?
Japan	Yes	Law Concerning Access to information Held by Administrative Organs
South Korea	Yes	Act on Disclosure of Information by public Agencies
Singapore	No	N/A
India	Yes	The Indian Right to Information Act
China	Yes	Regulations of the People' on Open Government Information
Taiwan	Yes	Freedom of Government Information Law
Hong Kong	Yes	Code on Access to Information
Europe		
Sweden	Yes	Freedom of the Press Act
Germany	Yes	German Freedom of Information Act
Italy	Yes	Chapter V of Law No. 241 of 7 August 1990
France	Yes	The Law of 1978
United Kingdom	Yes	Freedom of Information Act
Americas		
United States	Yes	Freedom of Information Act (FOIA)

Table 5. "Shield Law" Comparison Chart

Asia		
Country/region	Is there a law that protect journalists from having to reveal their sources?	What is the law that provides such protection?
Japan	Yes	The Japanese Constitution
South Korea	No	N/A
Singapore	No	N/A
India	Yes (but limited)	The Indian Constitution The Newspaper Rule
China	No	N/A
Taiwan	No	N/A
Hong Kong	No	N/A
Europe		
Sweden	Yes	Freedom of the Press Act Law on Freedom of Expression
Germany	Yes	German Constitution
Italy	Yes	Press Law of 1963
France	Yes	1881 Press Law
United Kingdom	Yes	Sec. 10 of Contempt of Court Act of 1981
Americas		
United States	No federal shield law, but 40 states + DC have state shield laws	No federal shield law

Table 6. Freedom House Freedom of the Press Ranking in 2015

Asia		
Country/region	What is the press freedom ranking?	Is it considered free, partly free, or not free?
Japan	41	Free
South Korea	67	Partly Free
Singapore	148	Not Free
India	80	Partly Free
China	186	Not Free
Taiwan	48	Free
Hong Kong	83	Partly Free
Europe		
Sweden	1	Free
Germany	22	Free
Italy	64	Partly Free
France	35	Free
United Kingdom	38	Free
Americas		
United States	31	Free

References

Adler, A. M. (2007). Against moral rights. *California Law Review,* Vol. 97, 263-299.

Alexander, L.B & Bush, E.M (1997). Shield laws on trial: State court interpretation of the journalist's statutory privilege. *Journal of Legislation,* Vol. 23, 215-230.

Amar, V. (Ed.) (2009). *The First Amendment: Freedom of speech.* Amherst, NY: Prometheus Books.

Amenomori, I (1998). Chapter 11: Japan. In A. Latif (Ed.), *Walking the tightrope: Press freedom and professional standards in Asia* (pp. 108-118). Singapore, AMIC.

Anderson, D. A (1974). Libel and self-censorship. *Texas Law Review,* Vol.53, 422-481.

Anderson, D. A (1991). Is libel law worth reforming? *University of Pennsylvania Law Review,* Vol. 140, 487-554.

Anderson, D. A (2002). Freedom of the press. *University of Texas Law Review,* 80 (3), 429-530.

Anderson, D. A (2009). The origins of the press clause. In V. D. Amar (Ed.), *The First Amendment freedom of speech: Its constitutional history and the contemporary debate* (pp. 65-81). Amherst, NY: Prometheus Books.

Ang, P.H. & Yeo, T.M (1998). *Mass media laws and regulations in Singapore.* Singapore: Asian Media Information and Communication Centre.

Asante, C. E. (1997). *Press freedom and development: A research guide and selected Bibliography.* Westport, CT: Greenwood Press.

Atwill, N (2010) France: New law on protection of journalistic sources. *Library of Congress Official Website.* Retrieved from http://www.loc.gov/lawweb/servlet/lloc_news?disp3_l205401787_text.

Bainbridge, D. I. (2006). *Intellectual property.* London, UK: Longman.

Banisar, D (2006). *Freedom of information around the world 2006.* London, UK: Privacy *International.*

Banisar, D (2007). *Silencing sources: An international survey of protections and threats to journalists' sources.* London, UK: Privacy International.

Barnett, A. D (1979). The communication system in China: Some generalizations, hypothesis, and questions. In G. C. Chu & F. L.K. Hsu (Eds.), *Moving a mountain: Cultural change in China* (pp. 386-395). Honolulu, HI: University of Hawaii Press.

Barr, R (2011). UK government tries to overhaul notorious libel laws. *The Huffington Post.* Retrieved from http://www.huffingtonpost.com/2011/03/15/uk-government-tries-to-ov_n_835980.html, retrieved on April 1st, 2011.

Behmer, M (2009). Measuring media freedom: Approaches on international comparison. In A.

Belmas,G. & Overbeck, W. (2015). *Major Principles of Media Law* (1st ed.). Belmont, CA, USA: Wadsworth Publishing.

Bennett, I (2011). Media censorship in China. *Council on Foreign Affairs.* Retrieved fromhttp://www.cfr.org/china/media-censorship-china/p11515.

Bennhold, K (2008, May 12th). A feud over press freedom boils over France. *The New York Times.* Retrieved from http://www.nytimes.com/2008/05/12/world/europe/12iht-afp.4.12817824.html.

Bezanson, R (2003). *How free can the press be*? Urbana, IL: University of Illinois Press.

Bodey, M.(2015, July 29). *Hywood: media law hopelessly outdated.* Retrieved from The Australian: http://www.theaustralian.com.au/business/media/fairfax-chief-greg-hywood-media-laws-hopelessly-outdated/story-e6frg996-1227460870213.

Bonsaver, G (2007). *Censorship and literature in Fascist Italy.* Toronto, Canada: University of Toronto Press.

Brauck, M, Rosenbach, M. &Verbeet, M. (2007, November 1st.). Big brother eyes German journalists. *Spiegel Online.* Retrieved from http://www.spiegel.de/international/germany/0,1518,druck-514872,00.html.

Chen, S. Y. (1998).State, media and democracy in Taiwan. *Media Culture & Society*, Vol. 20, 11-29.

Cheng, J. (1997). China's copyright system: Rising to the spirit of TRIPS requires an internal focus and WTO membership. *Fordham International Law Journal,* Vol. 1(5), 1939-2013.

Cheung, A. S. (2003). *Self-censorship and the struggle for press freedom in Hong Kong*. Hong Kong: Kluwer.

Choi, C-K. (2005). *Law and justice in Korea: South and North.* Seoul, Korea: Seoul National University Press.

Choi, E. (2009). With great power comes great responsibility: Korea's role in the war against online piracy. *San Diego International Law Journal*, Vol.10, 555-590.

Choi, Y. (2004). Development of copyright protection in Korea: Its history, inherent limits, and suggested solutions. *Brooklyn Journal of International Law*, Vol. 28, 643-674.

Choudhry, S. (1999). Globalization in search of justification: Toward a theory of comparative constitutional interpretation. *Indiana Law Journal*, Vol. 74 (3), 819-948.

Christians, C. &Traber, M. (1997). *Communication ethics and universal values*. Thousand Oaks, CA: Sage Publications.

Chynoweth, G. (2003). Reality bites: How the biting reality of piracy in China is working to strengthen its copyright laws. *Duke Law &Technology Review*, 0003. Retrieved from http://www.law.duke.edu/journals/dltr/articles /2003dltr0003.html

Coliver, S. (1993). Press law and practice: a comparative study of press freedom in European and other democracies. London, UK: Article 19 for the United Nations Educational, Scientific, and Cultural Organization.

Cook, P. S. (Ed.) (1990). *Liberty of expression.* Washington DC: Wilson Center Press

Cornwell, N. C. (2000). *Freedom of the press: Rights and liberties under the law*. Santa Barbra, CA: ABC-CLIOS, Inc.

Cozens, C. (2004). Top cyclist to sue Sunday Times over doping claims, *The Sunday Times*. Retrieved from http://www.guardian.co.uk/ media/2004/jun/15/pressandpublishing.cycling?INTCMP=SRCH.

Crick, P., & Pember, D. (2014). *Media Law and Ethics in the 21st Century: Protecting Free Expression and Curbing Abuses.* New York, NY, USA: Palgrave Macmillan.

Curran, J. & Seaton, J. (2009). Power without responsibility: The press, broadcasting, and new media in Britain. New York: Routledge.

Curry, J. L. & Dassin, J.R. (Eds.) (1982). *Presscontrol around the world.* New York: Praeger.

Czepek A. (2009). Pluralismand participation as desired results of press freedom: measuring media system performance. In A. Czepek, M. Hellwig, & Eva Nowak (Eds.), *Press freedom and pluralism in Europe: concepts and conditions* (pp. 37-74). Chicago: The University of Chicago Press.

Czepek, A. Hellwig, M. & Nowak, E. (2009). Introduction: structural inhibition of media freedom and plurality across Europe. In A. Czepek, M. Hellwig, & Eva Nowak (Eds.), *Press freedomand pluralism in Europe: concepts and conditions* (pp. 9-22). Chicago: The University of Chicago Press.

Czepek, A., Hellwig, M. & Nowak, E. (Eds.) (2009). *Press Freedom and Pluralismin Europe: Concepts and Conditions*. Chicago: The University of Chicago Press.

Czepek, M. Hellwig, & E. Nowak (Eds.) *Press Freedom and Pluralism in Europe: Concepts and Conditions* (pp. 23-36). Chicago: The University of Chicago Press.

Dahrendorf, R. (1979). *Society and democracy in Germany*. New York: Norton.

Deazley, R. (2006). *Rethinking copyright: History, theory, language*. Northampton, MA: Edward Elgar Publishing, Inc.de Lange, W. (1998). *A history of Japanese journalism: Japan's press club as the last obstacle to a mature press*. Surrey, UK: Japan Library.

Dietz, A. (1995). The moral right of the author: Moral rights and the civil law countries. *Columbia Journal of Law & the Arts*, Vol.19, 199-213.

Doronila, A. (2000). Press freedomin Asia: An uneven terrain. In L. Williams & R. Rich (Eds.), *Losing control: Freedom of the press in Asia* (pp. xi-xvi). Canberra, AUS: Asia Pacific Press at the Australian National University.

du Mars, R. (2000). South Korea: Fear is a hard habit to break. In L. Williams & R. Rich, (Eds.), *Losing control: Freedom of the press in Asia* (pp. 190-207). Canberra, AUS: Asia Pacific Press at the Australian National University.

Einaudi, M. (1948) The Constitution of Italy. *The American Political Science Review*, Vol. 42 (4), 661-676.

Eisendrath, C.R. (1982). Chapter 3: Press freedom in France: Private ownership and state controls. In J. Curry & J. R. Dassin (Eds.), *Press controls around the world* (pp. 62-84). New York: Praeger.

Ellis, E. (2002, September 6th). Singapore authorities use libel law to silence critics. *The Australia*. Retrieved from http://www.singapore-window.org/sw02/020926au.htm.

Emerson, T. I. (1970). *The system of freedom of expression*. New York: Vintage Books.

Errera, R. (1985). Press law in France. In P. Lahav (Ed.), *Press Law in Modern Democracies: A comparative study* (pp. 229-265). New York: Longman.

Eto, J. (1982). Chapter 10: The censorship operation in occupied Japan. In J. L. Curry & J. R. Dassin (Eds.), *Press control around the world* (pp. 235-253). New York: Praeger.

Fargo, A. (2006). Analyzing federal shield law proposals: What congress can learn from the States, *Communication Law & Policy*, Vol. 11, 35-82.

Faris, S. (2011, January 20th). Berlusconi sex scandal: Ruby tells her story. *Time*. Retrieved from http://www.time.com/time/world/article/0,8599,2043352,00.html.

Feuilherade, P. (2005). China "ripe" for media explosion. BBC News. March. 13, 2005.Retrieved from http://news.hbc.co.uk/2/hi/technology/4341413.stm.

Flower, B. (2010). *The French Constitution: With remarks on some of its principal articles*. Charleston, SC: NabuPress.

Foerstel, H. N. (1998). *Banned in the media: A reference guide to censorship in the press, motion pictures, broadcasting, and the Internet*. Westport, CT: Greenwood Press.

Fouquet, H. (2009). Sarkozy's web piracy law passes; raises European ire. *Bloomberg*. Retrieved from http://www.bloomberg.com/apps/news?pid=20601085&sid=abgwVQh9yNLw&refer=europe.

Freeman, L. A. (2000). *Closing the shop: Information cartels and Japan's mass media*. Princeton, NJ: Princeton University Press.

Fürstenau, M. (2011, January, 19th).German press freedom in constant struggle against political influence. *Deutsche Welle*. Retrieved from http://www.dw-world.de/dw/article/0,,14774883,00.html.

Gardella, R. & Forzato, J. (2011, May 28th). US goes on offense against digital piracy. *Open Channel*. Retrieved from http://openchannel.msnbc.msn.com/_news/2011/05/28/6732624-us-goes-on-offense-against-digital-piracy.

Gardner, E. (2011, February 22nd). Why celebrities will soon be jetting to France over tabloid gossip. *The Hollywood Reporter*. Retrieved from http://www.hollywoodreporter.com/blogs/thr-esq/why-celebrities-will-soon-be-160070.

Ginsberg, J. (2005). The right to claim authorship in U.S. copyright and trademarks law. *Houston Law Review*, Vol. 41, 263-308.

Goldstein, P. (2001). *International copyright: Principles, law, and practice*. New York: Oxford University Press

Greenslade, R. (2010, November 16th). Mission finds serious press freedom concerns in Berlusconi's Italy*The Guardian*. Retrieved fromhttp://www.guardian.co.uk/media/greenslade/2010/nov/16/press-freedom-italy.

Gunaratne, S. A. (2002). Freedom of the press: A world system perspective, *International Communication Gazette*, Vol. 64 (4), 343-369.

Gunther, R. & Mughan, A. (Eds.) (2000). *Democracy and the Media: A Comparative Perspective*. New York: Cambridge University Press.

Hallin, D. & Mancini, P. (2004). *Comparing media systems: Three models of media and politics*. New York: Cambridge University Press.

Hamilton, W. (2000). Japan: The warmth of the herd. In L. Williams & R. Rich (Eds.), *Losing control: Freedom of the press in Asia* (pp. 93-114). Canberra, AUS: Asia Pacific Press at the Australian National University.

Hayes, J. (2004). The right to reply: A conflict of fundamental rights. *Columbia Journal of Law and Social Problems*, Vol. 37, 551-584.

Hendler, C. (2010). A Swedish shield, unraised. *Columbia Journalism Review*. Retrieved from http://www.cjr.org/campaign_desk/a_swedish_shield_unraised.php.

Hoong, C. L. (1998). Chapter 15 Singapore. In A. Latif (Ed.), *Walking the tightrope: Press freedom and professional standards in Asia* (pp. 142-155), Singapore: AMIC.

Horibe, M. (1985). Press Law in Japan. In P. Lahav (Ed.), *Press law in modern democracies: A comparative study* (pp. 315-338). New York: Longman.

Horsley, J. P. (2007, May 9th). China adopts first nationwide open government information Regulations. *Freedominfo.org*. Retrieved from http://www.freedominfo.org/2007/05/china-adopts-first-nationwide-open-government-information-regulations

Houn, F. (1961). *To change a nation*. New York: Free Press.

Humphreys, P. (1996). *Mass media and media policy in Western Europe*. New York: Manchester University Press.

Humphreys, P. (2009). Media freedom and pluralism in the United Kingdom. In A. Czepek, M. Hellwig& E. Nowak (Eds.), *Press freedom and pluralism in Europe: Concepts and conditions* (pp.197-211). Chicago: The University of Chicago Press.

Jackson, D. (2008, April 15th). McCain and Obama back shielding reporters. *USA Today*, p. A3.

Johnson, P. (2003, September 14th). Amanpour: CNN practiced self-censorship. *USA Today*, p. D1.

Jonasson, D. (2010, August 7th). Swedish protection does not apply to Wikileaks. *The Stockholm News*. Retrieved from http://www.stockholmnews.com/more.aspx?NID=5771.

Kalhan, A. (2006). Colonial continuities: Human rights, terrorism, and security laws in India. *Columbia Journal of Asian Law*, Vol. 20, 93-234.

Karlecker, K. D. (Ed.) (2009). *Freedom of the press 2009: Further declines in global media independence*. Retrieved from http://www.freedomhouse.org/uploads/pfs/372.pdf.

Karlecker, K. D. (Ed.) (2010). *Freedom of the press 2010: Broad setbacks to global media freedom*. Retrieved from http://www.freedomhouse.org/uploads/pfs/371.pdf.

Karlecker, K. D. & Cook, S.G. (Eds.) (2008). *Freedom of the press 2008: A global survey of media independence*. New York: Freedom House.

Kennedy, D. (2011, February 16th). Knox's parents are just the latest to run afoul of Italy's libel laws. *AOLNews*. Retrieved from http://www.aolnews.com/2011/02/16/amanda-knoxs-parents-are-just-the-latest-to-run-afoul-of-italy.

Kent, N. (2008). *A Concise history of Sweden*. New York: Cambridge University Press.

Kohl, H. (1985). Press law in the Federal Republic of Germany. In P. Lahav (Ed.), *Press law in modern democracies: A comparative study* (pp. 185-228). New York: Longman.

Kohli, V. (2006). *The Indian media business*. Thousand Oaks, CA: Response Books.

Koltay, A. (2015). The concept of media freedom today: new media, new editors and the traditional approach of the law. *Journal of Media law*, 7(1), 36-64.

Kuhn, R. (1995). *The media in France*. New York: Routledge.

Kwang, K. (2009, November 16th). Three-strikes piracy deterrent not for Singapore.*ZD NetAsia*. Retrieved from http://www.zdnetasia.com/three-strikes-piracy-deterrent-not-for-s-pore-62059358.htm.

LaFraniere, S. & Wong, E. (2011, March 7th). Even with protests averted, China turns to intimidation of foreign journalists. *The New York Time*, p. A4.

Lahav, P. (1985). Conclusion: An outline for a general theory of press law in democracy.

In P. Lahav (Ed.), *Press law in modern democracies: A comparative study* (pp. 339-360). New York: Longman.

Lam, W. W. (2000). China: State power versus the Internet. In L. Williams & R. Rich (Eds.), *Losing control: Freedom of the press in Asia* (pp. 37-57). Canberra, AUS: Asia Pacific Press at the Australian National University.

Latif, A. (Ed.) (1998). *Walking the tight rope: Press freedom and professional standards in Asia*. Singapore : Asian Media Information and Communication Center.

Lauren P.G. (2003). *The evolution of international human rights: Visions seen*. Philadelphia: University of Pennsylvania PressLee, C-C (Ed.) (1994). *China'smedia, media's China*. Boulder, CO.: Westview Press.

Lee, H-S. (2011, May 3rd). S. Korea press ranking falls. *The Korea Times*. Retrieved from http://www.koreatimes.co.kr/www/news/nation/2011/05/117_86370.html.

Lee, M. (2011, April, 25th). China to punish Baidu for illegal music search service. Reuters. Retrieved from http://www.reuters.com/article/2011/04/25/baiduidUSL3E7FP0WD20110425.

Lee, T-H. (2010, September 9th). Censorship on pro-NK websites tight. *The Korea Times*. Retrieved from http://www.koreatimes.co.kr/www/news/nation/2010/09/113_72788.html.

Lemon, S. (2009, August 24th). No 'three strikes' law planned for Singapore, agency says. *IDG News Service*. Retrieved from http://pcworld.about.net/od/pcw/No-three-Strikes-Law-Planned.htm.

Levy, S. (2011, April 15th). Inside Google's China misfortune. *CNN Money*. Retrieved from http://tech.fortune.cnn.com/2011/04/15/googles-ordeal-in-china.

Lewan, M. & Palm, E. (2009, April 17th). Pirate Bay defendants found guilty. *CNET*. Retrieved from http://news.cnet.com/8301-1023_3-10221666-93.html.

Lewis, A. (2007). *Freedom for the thought that we hate: a biography of the First Amendment*. New York: Basic Books.

Liebman, B. (2006). Innovation through intimidation: An empirical account of Defamation litigation in China. *Harvard International Law Journal*, Vol. 47 (1) 33-78.

Lim, H.S. (1974). A study on legal values in Korea: An analysis of attitude toward Law. *Social Science Journal*, Vol. 2, 59-79.

Lindvall, H. (2011, April 20th). K-pop: How South Korea turned round its music scene. *The Guardian*. Retrieved from http://www.guardian.co.uk/media/organgrinder/2011/apr/20/k-pop-south-korea-music-market.

Lipschultz, J.H.(2014). *Social Media Communication: Concepts, Practices, Data, Law and Ethics* (1st ed.). New York, NY, USA: Routledge.

Lively, D. (1992). *Essential Principles of Communications Law*. New York: Praeger.

Livingstone, S. (2003). On the challenges of cross-national comparative media Research. *European Journal of Communication*, Vol.18(4), 477-500.

Lowther, W. Shih, H-C, & Chao, V. Y. (2011,May 4th). Freedom Houselowers Taiwan's press ranking. *The Taipei Times*. Retrieved from http://www.taipeitimes.com/News/front/archives/2011/05/04/2003502357,

Lu, K. (1982). The Chinese press as I see it. In J. L. Curry & J. R. Dassin (Eds.), *Press Controls Around the World* (pp.128-145). New York: Praeger.

MacQueen, H. L, Waelde, C. & Laurie, G. T. (2007). *Contemporary intellectual property: Law and policy*. New York: Oxford University Press.

Macur, J. (2012, October 15th). Details of Doping Scheme Paint Armstrong as Leader, the New York Times, p. A1.
Markham, J. W. (1967). *Voices of the red giants: Communications in Russia and China*. Ames, IA : Iowa State University Press.
Marletti, C & Roncarolo, F. (2000). Media influence in the Italian transition from a consensual to a majoritarian democracy. In R. Gunther & A. Mughan (Eds.), *Democracy and the media: A comparative perspective* (pp. 195-240). New York: Cambridge Press.
Mayer, C (2011, July 25th). Tabloids bites man. *Time*, 178. Retrieved from http://www.time.com/time/world/article/0,8599,2082991,00.html.
McDonald, J (2010, March 30th).China's Baidu removes millions of pirated works. *The Huffington Post*. Retrieved from http://www.huffingtonpost.com/2011/03/30/chinas-baidu-piracy_n_842385.html.
McManus, E. (2009, March 27th).Will British libel law kill net free speech? *Open Democracy*. Retrieved from http://www.opendemocracy.net/article/email/will-net-free-speech-survive-british-libel-litigation.
Media laws threaten freedom. (2003, February 27). Australian (National, Australia), p. 13. Retrieved from http://ic.galegroup.com/ic/ovic/NewsDetailsPage/NewsDetailWindow?failOverType=&query=&prodId=&dispalyGroupName=Name=News&dviSelectedPage=&limiter=&limiter=&currPage=&disableHighlighting=&displayGroups=&sortBy=&sortBy=&zid=&searchwithinresults=&p=OVIC&action=e&catId=&activityType=&scanId=&documented=GALE%7ca32035702&source=Bookmark&u=sunybuff main&jsid=eb27d0aed0d204dcfbabb2ce54fe1466
Mehra, S. K. (2007). Post a message and go to jail: Criminalizing Internet libel in Japan and the United States. *University of Colorado Law Review*, Vol.78 (3), 767-816.
Mehta, D.S. (1979). *Mass communication and journalism in India*. New Delhi, India: Allied Publishers Private Limited.
Michalowski, S. & Woods, L. (1999). *German constitutional law: the protection of civil liberties*. Brookfield, VT: Ashgate.
Middleton, K.R.,& Lee, W.E.(2013). *The Law of Public Communication* (9th ed.). New York, NY, USA: Routledge.

Moore, R. M. (1999). *Mass communication law and ethics*. Mahwah, NJ: L. Erlbaum Associates.

Moore, R.L., & Murray., M.D.(2011). *Routledge Communication Series: Media Law and Ethics* (4th ed.). New York, NY, USA: Routledge.

Musil, S. (2009, February 15th).The Pirate Bay trial to begin in Sweden. *CNET*. Retrieved from http://news.cnet.com/8301-1023_3-10164777-93.html?tag=mncol;txt.

Nasaw, D. (2009, April 2nd). Upcoming X-Men movie leaked online ahead of release. *The Guardian*. Retrieved from http://www.guardian.co.uk/world/2009/apr/02/wolverine-xmen-leak-online-piracy?keepThis=true&TB_iframe=true&height=650&width=850.

Natta. D.V., Liptak, A. & Levy, C.J. (2005, October 16th). The Miller case: A notebook, A cause, a jail cell and a deal. *The New York Times*. Retrieved from http://www.nytimes.com/2005/10/16/national/16leak.html.

Neate, R. (2011, July 19th). China's top search engine agrees deal to pay record labels for music. *The Guardian*. Retrieved from http://www.guardian.co.uk/business/2011/jul/19/music-industry-downloads-china-baidu.

Negrine, R. M. (1994). *Politics and the mass media in Britain*. New York: Routledge.

Nerone, J. (Ed.) (1995). Last rights: Revisiting four theories of the press. Urbana, IL: University of Illinois Press.

New York Times Staff. (2010, March 22nd). Internet censorship in China. *The New York Times*. Retrieved from http://topics.nytimes.com/topics/news/international/countriesandterritories/china/internet_censorship/index.html.

New York Times Staff. (2010, May 18th). US promotes press freedom, *The New York Times*, p. A10.

Nimmer, D. (2003). *Copyright: Sacred text, technology, and the DMCA*. New York: Kluwer Law International.

O'Carroll, L. (2013, January 22nd). How UK libel laws undermined Sunday Times in Lance Armstrong case, the Sunday Times. Retrieved from http://www.guardian.co.uk/media/2013/jan/22/uk-libel-laws-sunday-times-lance-armstrong.

Ogus, A. (1999). Competition between national legal systems: A contribution of economic analysis to comparative law. *International and Comparative Law Quarterly*, Vol. 48, 405-418.

Ourvan, J. A. (2002). Damage control: Why Japanese courts should adopt a regime of larger libel awards. *New York Law School Journal of International and Comparative Law*, Vol. 21, 307-321.

Packard, A. (2012). *Digital Media Law* (2nd ed.).Somerset, NJ, USA: Wiley-Blackwell.

Padovani, C. (2009). Pluralism of information in the television sector in Italy: History And contemporary conditions. In A. Czepek, M. Hellwig& E. Nowak (Eds.), *Press freedom and pluralism in Europe: Concepts and conditions* (pp.289-304). Chicago: The University of Chicago Press.

Park, H-S. (2004). Korean norm and reality, and the press reform in Korea. *Journal of Media Law, Ethics and Policy Research*, Vol.3 (2), 143-171.

Pang, K-F. (1998). Chapter 17: Taiwan. In A. Latif (Ed.), *Walking the tightrope: Press freedom and professional standards in Asia* (pp. 173-182). Singapore: AMIC.

Park, S.H. (2002). Film censorship and political legitimation in South Korea, 1987-1992. *Cinema Journal*, Vol. 42 (1), 120-138.

Petrou, A. (2010, December 29th). USA forced Sweden's hand on piracy and Pirate Bay crackdown. *TechEYE.net*. Retrieved from http://www.techeye.net/internet/usa-forced-swedens-hand-on-piracy-and-pirate-bay-crackdown.

Pfanner, E. (2009, May 13th). France approves crackdown on piracy. *The New York Times*. Retrieved from http://www.nytimes.com/2009/05/13/technology/internet/13net.html?_r=1&ref=technology.

Pfanner, E. (2010, September 19th). EU Laws shielding journalists' sources limited. *The New York Times*, p. B8.

Piotraut,J. (2006). An author's rights-based copyright law: The fairness and morality of French and American Law compared. *Cardozo Arts & Entertainment Law Journal*, Vol. 24, 549-616.

Price, M. E., Rozumilowicz, B. &Verhulst, S.G. (Eds.) (2002). *Media Reform: Democratizing the media, democratizing the state*. New York: Routledge.

Priest, E. (2006). The future of music and film piracy in China. *Berkeley Technology Law Journal*, Vol. 21, 795-871.

Rawnsley, G. D. (2007). The media and democracy in China and Taiwan. *Taiwan Journal of Democracy*, Vol. 3 (1), 63-78.

Reardon, M. (2009, May 12th). France ignores EU and passes antipiracy law. *CNET*. Retrieved from http://news.cnet.com/8301-1023_3-10238912-93.html.

Reitz, J. C. (1998). How to do comparative law. *The American Journal of Comparative Law*, Vol. 46 (4), 617-636.

Reporters Without Borders Staff. (2007). French website blocked for warning of risks of investing in China. *Reporters Without Borders*. Retrieved from http://en.rsf.org/china-french-website-blocked-for-warning-30-03-2007,21492.html.

Reporters Without Borders (2010). Press freedom index 2010. *Reporters Without Borders*. Retrieved from http://en.rsf.org/press-freedom- index-2010,1034.html.

Reporters Without Borders Staff. (2011a) Censorship reaches new heights. *Reporters Without Borders*. Retrieved from http://en.rsf.org/china-censorship-reaches-new-heights-23-02-2011,39617.html.

Reporters Without Borders Staff. (2011b) Court cites need to protect confidentiality of journalists' sources. *Reporters Without Borders*. Retrieved from http://en.rsf.org/france-court-cites-need-to-protect-11-05-2011, 40269.html.

Reporters Without Borders Staff. (2011c). Propaganda department in attack on "false news." *Reporters Without Borders*. Retrieved from http://en.rsf.org/chine-propaganda-department-in-attack-on-31-01-2011,39421.html.

Rodan, G. (2000). Singapore: Information lockdown, business as usual. In L. Williams &R. Rich (Eds.), *Losing control: Freedom of the press in Asia* (pp. 169-189). Canberra, AUS: Asia Pacific Press at the Australian National University,

Roxborough, S. (2011, July 12th).German piracy site Kino to re-launch as KinoX.to. *The Hollywood Reporter*. Retrieved from http://www.hollywoodreporter.com/news/german-piracy-site-kinoto-relaunches-210099.

Sa, E-S. (2009). Development of press freedom in South Korea since Japanese colonial Rule. *Asian Culture and History*, Vol.1 (2), 3-17.

Saez, C. (2009, May 13th). French parliament passes final Internet piracy law; reaction expected. *Intellectual Property Watch*. Retrieved from http://www.ip-watch.org/weblog/2009/05/13/french-parliament-seals-restrictive-internet-anti-piracy-law-reaction-expected.

Sandoval, G. (2009a, March 24th). AT&T First to Test RIAA Antipiracy Plan. *CNET*. Retrieved from http://news.cnet.com/8301-1023_3-10203799-93.html.

Sandoval, G. (2009b, October 22nd). French adopts three-strikes law for piracy. *CNET*. Retrieved from http://news.cnet.com/8301-31001_3-10381365-261.html.

Sandoval, G. (2010, April 8th). U.K. embraces 'three strikes' for illegal file sharing. *CNET*. Retrieved from http://news.cnet.com/8301-31001_3-20002018-261.html.

Sayer, P. (2011, July 13th.)French three strikes law: 470,878 warnings, no lawsuits yet. *IDG News Service*. Retrieved from http://www.networkworld.com/news/2011/071311-french-three-strikes-law-470878.html.

Schlesinger, M. N. (1995). Sleeping giant awakens: The development of intellectual property law in China. *Journal of Chinese Law*, Vol. 9, 93-140.

Schlesinger, P. (1982). Princes' Gate, 1980: The media politics of siege management in Britain. In J. L. Curry & J. R. Dassin (Eds.), *Press control around the world* (pp. 62-84). New York: Praeger.

Schwanitz, T. (2007, June 20th). In first year, Germany's federal agencies struggle to adapt to FOIA: But requesters off to slow start as well. *Freedominfo.org*. Retrieved from http://www.freedominfo.org/2007/06/in-first-year-germanys-federal-agencies-struggle-to-adapt-to-foia.

Sedler, R. A. (2011). Self-censorship and the First Amendment. *Notre Dame Journal of Law, Ethics & Public Policy*, Vol. 25 (1), 13-45.

Siebert, F., Peterson, T. & Schramm, W. (1956). *Four theories of the press*. Urbana, IL:
University of Illinois Press.

Siebert, F. S., Peterson, T., & Schramm, W. (1963). *The authoritarian, libertarian, social responsibility, and Soviet Communist concepts of what the press should be and do*. Champaign, IL: University of Illinois Press.

Singh, I. B. (1980). The Indian mass media system: Before, during and after the National Emergency. *Canadian Journal of Communication*, Vol. 7 (2), 38-49.

Singhal, A. & Rogers, E.M. (1989). *India's Information Revolution.* New Delhi, India: Newbury Park, Sage Publications.

Smith, E. M. (1993). Reporting the truth and setting the record straight: An analysis of U.S. and Japan libel laws. *Michigan Journal of International Law*, Vol. 14, 871-904.

Smith, P. (1998). *Japan: A reinterpretation.* New York: Vintage Books USA

Soifer, A. (1985). Freedom of the press in the United States. In P. Lahav (Ed.), *Press Law in modern democracies: a comparative study* (pp. 79-136). New York: Longman.

Soodin, V. (2009, May 13th). France passes tough web laws. *The Sun.* Retrieved from http://www.thesun.co.uk/sol/homepage/news/article2427306.ece.

Spahr, W. (2009, February 10th).Germany rejects three-strikes piracy plan. *Billboard.biz.* Retrieved from http://www.billboard.biz/bbbiz/content_display/industry/news/e3i73b3660e2c6025e6507555e3cfec977d.

Srinivasan, R. (1998). Chapter 9: India. In A. Latif (Ed.), *Walking the tightrope: Press freedom and professional standards in Asia* (pp. 94-101). Singapore: AMIC.

Stark, H. (2010). German spy agency watched journalists. Spiegel Online International. Retrievedfromhttp://www.spiegel.de/international/0,1518,416238,00.html.

Stein, M. L. (1966). Freedom of the press; a continuing struggle. New York: Messner.

Stevenson, R. (1994). Global communication in the twenty-first Century. New York: Pearson.

Strömberg, H. (1985). Press law in Sweden. In P. Lahav (Ed.), *Press law in modern democracies: A comparative study* (pp. 229-265). New York: Longman.

Su, S. (1994).Chinese Communist ideology and media control. In C-C Lee (Ed.) *China's media,media's China* (pp. 75-88). Boulder, CO: Westview Press.

Sullivan, B. (2012). *FOIA and the First Amendment: Representative Democracy and the People's Elusive Right to Know*, Maryland Law Review, 72 (1).

Sun, X. (2001). *An orchestra of voices: making the argument for greater speech and press freedom in the People's Republic of China.* Westport, CT.: Praeger.

Supperstone, M. (1985). Press law in the United Kingdom. In P. Lahav (Ed.), *Press law in modern democracies: A comparative study* (pp. 9-78). New York: Longman.

Sussman, L. R. (2000). Censor dot gov: the Internet and press freedom 2000. *Journal of Government Information* Vol. 27 (5), 537-545.

Takada, K. &Lee, M. (2011, May 12th). China's Baidu fined for copyright infringement: Report. *Reuters*. Retrieved from http://www.reuters.com/article/2011/05/12/us-baidu-idUSTRE74B0EW20110512.

Takeichi, H. (1997). Japanese-style communication in a new global age. In C. Christians &M. Traber (Eds.), *Communication ethics and universal values* (pp. 244-258). Thousand Oaks, CA: Sage.

Tan, K. (2005). *An introduction to Singapore's constitution.* Singapore: Talisman.

Tao, Z. (2006). Media control and self-censorship in Hong Kong. *Trend Magazine*. Retrieved from http://www.zonaeuropa.com/20061125_1.htm.

Teo, Y. L. (2005). *Media law in Singapore.* Singapore: Sweet & Maxwell Asia.

Tey, T-H. (2008). Confining the freedom of the press in Singapore: A "pragmatic" press for "nation-building?" *Human Rights Quarterly*, Vol. 30 (4), 876-905.

Tharp, P. (2009, May 13th). Swedish phish: Web pirates won't pay booty. *New York Post*. Retrieved from http://www.nypost.com/p/news/business/item_eEKedkGxPacPcEWrsoRMKL;jsessionid=5CA09201A4875B085BC0A7A44D9A4AF2.

Tong, J. (2009). Press self-censorship in China: A case study in the transformation of discourse. *Discourse & Society,* Vol. 20, 593-612.

Trilling, G. A. (2010). Press freedom critical analysis, the examination of East Asia: China, Singapore and North Korea. *The Elon Journal of Undergraduate Research in Communications*, Vol. 1 (1), 104-111.

Trionfi, B. (2011). Three journalists in Italy handed prison sentences on defamation charges. *International Press Institute*. Retrieved from http://www.freemedia.at/singleview/5561.

Tu, W. M. (1997) "Chinese philosophy: A synoptic view." In A companion to world philosophies. Eliot Deutsch & Ron Bontekoe (Eds.). Malden, MA: Blackwell Publishers.

Turpin, C. & Tomkins, A. (2007). *British government and the constitution: Text and materials*. New York: Cambridge University Press.

United Nations (2001). NGO Committee hears arguments for, against Freedom House, Press Release NGO/432, May 25th. Retrieved from http://www.un.org/News/Press/docs/2001/ngo432.doc.htm.

Van Belle, D. A. (2000). *Press freedom and global politics*. Westport, CT: Praeger.

Verhulst, S. G. & Price, M.E. (2008). Comparative media law research and its impact on Policy. *International Journal of Communication,* Vol. 2, 406-420.

Villaraos, A.M. (2014). A comparative analysis of the reformation of American and agentinian media laws and the public policies behind such changes.. *ILSA Journal of International & Comparative law.*, 20(3), 439-457.

Watkins, J. J. (1994) *The mass media and the law*. Lebanon, Indiana: Prentice Hill.

Weisenhaus, D. (2007). *Hong Kong media law: A guide for journalists and media professionals*. Hong Kong: Hong Kong University Press.

Willan, P. (2011, July 6th). Italy pressed ahead with piracy clampdown. *IT World Canada*. Retrieved from http://www.itworldcanada.com/news/italy-presses-ahead-with-piracy-clampdown/143462.

Williamson, E. (2007, December 17th). Congress votes to broaden openness law. *The Washington Post*. Retrieved from http://www.washingtonpost.com/wp-dyn/content/article/2007/12/18/AR2007121800918.html.

Williams, L. (2000). Censors: At work, censors out of work. In L. Williams & R. Rich (Eds.) *Losing control: Freedom of the press in Asia* (pp. 1-15). Canberra, AUS: Asia Pacific Press at the Australian National University.

Williams, L. & Rich, R. (Eds.) (2000). Losing control: Freedom of the press in Asia. Canberra, AUS: Asia Pacific Press at the Australian National University.

Winfield, B. H., Mizuno T. & Beaudoin, C. E. (2000). Confucianism collectivism and constitutions: Press systems in China and Japan. *Communication Law and Policy*, Vol. 5 (3), 323-347.

Wong, E. (2013, January 15th).China Lets Media Report on Air Pollution Crisis, *The New York Times*, p.A6.

Wong, K. (2001). *Media and culture in Singapore: A theory of controlled commodification*. Cresskill, N.J.: Hampton Press.

Worth, T. (2009, April 27th). Taiwan passes three-strikes piracy law. *Billbord.biz*. Retrieved from http://www.billboard.biz/bbbiz/content_display/industry/news/e3ib20649ac4d6059c216967baf5dfee28b.

Yang, Y (1993). The 1990 Copyright Law of the People's Republic of China. *University of California at Los Angeles Pacific Basin Law Journal*, Vol. 11, 260-284.

Yang, M & Engbarth, D (2000). Taiwan: All politics, no privacy. In L. Williams & R. Rich (Eds.), *Losing control: Freedom of the press in Asia* (pp. 208-218). Canberra: AUS: Asia Pacific Press at the Australian National University.

Yin, J (2008). Beyond the Four Theories of the Press: A New Model for the Asian & the World Press. *Journalism & Communication Monographs*, Vol. 10 (3).

Youm, K-H (1990). Libel laws and freedom of the press: South Korea and Japan reexamined. *Boston University International Law Journal*, Vol. 8, 53-83.

Youm, K-H (1993). Right of reply under Korean press law: A statutory and judicial perspective. *The American Journal of Comparative Law*, Vol. 41(1), 49-71.

Youm, K-H (1998). Chapter 16: South Korea. In A. Latif (Ed.), *Walking the tightrope: Press freedom and professional standards in Asia* (pp. 156-172). Singapore: AMIC.

Youm, K-H (2000). Copyright law in the Republic of Korea. *UCLA Pacific Basin Law Journal*, Vol. 17, 276-300.

Youm, K-H. (2002). Freedom of expression and the law: Rights and responsibilities in South Korea. *Stanford Journal of International Law*, Vol. 38, 123-151.

Youm, K-H. (2004). Defamation law and the Internet in South Korea. *Media & Arts Law Review*, Vol. 9, 141-153.

Yeung, C. (2000). Hong Kong: A handover of freedom? In L. Williams & R. Rich (Eds.), *Losing control: Freedom of the press in Asia* (pp. 58- 73). Canberra, AUS: Asia Pacific Press at the Australian National University,

Yu, X. (1994). Professionalization without guarantees: Changes of the Chinese press in post-1989 years. *International Communication Gazette*, Vol. 53, 23-41.

Zhou, K. (2006). Shanghai reporter sues municipal planning bureau for withholding information. China Youth Daily June 1, 2006. Retrieved from http://zqb.cyol.com/content/2006-06/02/content-1404266.htm.

Index

N

O

P

CPSIA information can be obtained
at www.ICGtesting.com
Printed in the USA
BVOW08*0553021217
501668BV00003B/44/P

9 781593 328054